The New Americans
Recent Immigration and American Society

Edited by
Carola Suárez-Orozco and Marcelo Suárez-Orozco

A Series from LFB Scholarly

Cambodian Refugees' Pathways to Success:
Developing a Bi-Cultural Identity

Julie G. Canniff

LFB Scholarly Publishing LLC
New York 2001

Copyright © 2001 by LFB Scholarly Publishing LLC

Library of Congress Cataloging-in-Publication Data

Canniff, Julie G.
  Cambodian refugees' pathways to success : developing a bi-cultural identity / Julie G. Canniff.
       p. cm. -- (The new Americans : recent immigration and American society)
  Includes bibliographical references and index.
  ISBN 1-931202-15-X (alk. paper)
  1. Cambodian Americans--Ethnic identity. 2. Cambodian Americans--Social conditions. 3. Cambodian Americans--Economic conditions. 4. Refugees--United States--Social conditions. 5. Biculturalism--United States. 6. Success--United States. 7. Buddhism--Social aspects--United States. 8. Family--United States--Case studies. 9. Asian American families--Case studies. I. Title. II. New Americans (LFB Scholarly Publishing LLC)
  E184.K45 .C36 2001
   305.895'93073--dc21
                                                    2001003676

ISBN 1-931202-15-X

Printed on acid-free 250-year-life paper.

Manufactured in the United States of America.

Table of Contents

v

Acknowledgements

In many ways I began this research in the fall of 1992 in a seminar on World Religion and Pluralism in America taught by Dr. Diana Eck at Harvard University. That semester Dr. Eck challenged the members of the seminar to document the impact of world religions in American cities, speculating that the religions of Islam, Buddhism, Hindusim, Jainism, Sihkism, and the Afro-Atlantic traditions were changing the context of the cities in which they were found as well as being changed by the inexorable power of American culture. It was then I began my association with the Cambodian community in Forest City, an association which has continued to the present day.

As an ethnographer, I am mindful that there is an element of exploitation in using the stories of my informants to build an academic career. However, my relationship with these three families has long ago moved from that of researcher to subject and is now built on a base of reciprocity and mutual interdependence. It is with profound humility that I offer this interpretation of their words and experiences and with the deepest gratitude that I acknowledge the contributions of Pirun, MP, Avy, Alyana, Long, Rath, Kusal, Touch, Srey, Chinda, and April to my study.

Other debts of gratitude go to my research colleagues at Harvard Graduate School of Education: Teresa Huerta, Jill Jefferis, and Julie Mendoza. These are women of great compassion, insight, and commitment who read endless drafts of my research, challenged my interpretations and demanded clarity and focus in my writing. Their perspectives of the Latino immigrant experience proved invaluable checks on the validity of my findings.

Dr. Donald Oliver, Dr. Marcelo Suárez-Orozco, and Dr. Nancy Richardson provided me with brilliant insights at critical points during the writing: Donald for his unflinching loyalty to the richness of genuine culture and the vital center of village life, Marcelo for his vast experience with ethnographic methods and the ever unfolding story of immigration at the end of the twentieth century, and Nancy for her commitment to the place of spiritual values in our daily lives as well as her ability to teach white people about the part they play in perpetuating the legacy of structural racism in American society.

I owe a great debt to Craig Lapine who has been unusually skillful at reading my original text and transforming it into this book. I have come to value his perceptive questions and rigorous attention to the details of editing, indexing, and especially coherence.

Finally, I acknowledge my husband Karl Smith who encouraged me along this path, patiently accepting that I would complete what I had started. He is my anchor in the world beyond academia where being successful is defined more by companionship, conversation, and attention to the art of living and loving well.

Introduction

Spring is a holy season for people all over the planet. For people in northern latitudes it represents the return of the light and life from the austere, cold death of the winter. For people in equatorial latitudes, it represents the end of the monsoons which flood the rich alluvial shore land. It is the time to begin again the cycle of planting and fertility. It is no wonder that human beings have created potent rituals of celebration the intent of which are to renew vows of generosity, compassion, and diligence to be followed in the year ahead.

The month of April is when Cambodian Buddhists celebrate the New Year, reenacting a time when this ancient culture flourished in the center of Angkor Thom where *Kambuja* princes lived surrounded by Hindu gods. Cambodian dance and music are integral to the New Year's celebration. To the celebrants they represent the phenomenology of the Cambodian universe and blend the cultural epistemologies of Hinduism and Buddhism. At the New Year the pageants of the royal court are reenacted once again and the dancers become the embodiment of metaphysical Devas, souls who have evolved beyond this earthly existence. In rituals as old as the culture, the monks chant the wisdom of Lord Buddha and reestablish the universal balance as another year begins.

In Cambodian enclaves all over the United States, Khmer families celebrate this festival even as they adapt its forms to their new context.

The Khmer of Forest City began arriving in 1979, and within two years this tiny community had returned to this ancient cycle of rebirth and renewal. They have adjusted the typically five-day celebration to encompass a long three-day weekend. The festivities begin Friday evening with a performance of classical music and dance at which families come together to eat and enjoy the spectacle. Saturday is a day of prayer and feasting led by a senior monk and his three novices. Saturday night young people gather to dance to the sounds of Cambodian and American rock music. Sunday is a day for family gatherings.

On April 12, 1996, the Cambodian New Year in Forest City took on special significance. The Forest City Performing Arts Council brought Master Sam Ang Sam and his wife Chan Moly Sam to teach classical music and dance to a new generation of young Cambodian men and women. Sam Ang Sam is among the most highly esteemed masters of Cambodian musical traditions in the world. In 1994 he was awarded a MacArthur Fellowship in recognition of his contributions to the preservation of Khmer culture. Chan Moly Sam is a former soloist in the royal court ballet of Phnom Penh. A specialist in both the classical and folk styles, she is among a handful of dancers who are currently passing along the rich Cambodian dance tradition to young Cambodians in the diaspora.

On that April day it is with a sense of irony that I enter the hall. The space for this debut performance is the Italian Heritage Center—a long, low building adjacent to a long established Italian neighborhood. The performing area is lavishly decorated. A monumental painting of Angkor Wat hangs at the back of the improvised stage, and the perimeter of the stage is designated by a series of white Christmas lights. At one corner is the American flag, at another the national flag of Cambodia, which repeats the image of Angkor Wat in the center of its red field. In the back corner, white sheets conceal a dressing area for the performers.

I am immediately aware of the festival atmosphere. Two tables at the back of the room are covered with steaming hot food—spring rolls, jasmine rice, baked chicken marinating in a spicy curry, and vegetables in a fiery sauce of coconut milk, lemon grass, and hot Thai peppers. Diners move slowly through the line, balancing their plates of food with the inevitable cans of Pepsi, Coke, orange drink, or Sprite. Children chase each other between rows of chairs as their mothers sit in groups and exchange gossip while their fathers lounge against the wall or amble outside to smoke a cigarette.

Up on the corner of the stage, five men are seated, dressed in sparkling white jackets and black pants. The jackets, which have high Nehru-style collars, are tightly fitted and resplendent with gold buttons. Each man is playing an instrument—a xylophone, drums, a gourd-shaped stringed instrument, a crocodile zither, a flute. Sam Ang Sam plays the flute, stopping to sing a song whose melody is strange to my Western ear. He is accompanied by another singer who is blind but sings as he plays the stringed instrument.

At 8:30 the apprentice dancers enter from behind the improvised curtain. For this debut performance, only six young women have completed the extremely rigorous training of the Apsara dancer. Four of them are high school students; two are recent high school graduates. One dancer is Vietnamese-Cambodian; the others are Khmer. The dancers are dressed in red and gold silk costumes; the tight short-sleeved bodice is made of red silk with rows of gold braid encircling the neck and center front. The elaborate pants are also made of stiff red silk edged with wide gold embroidery. The fabric is folded around the waist from back to front, then drawn between the legs and looped over a gold mesh belt at the center of the back. On their heads the girls balance an elaborate gold mesh crown that is shaped like a miniature stupa with wing-like panels which come down to cover their ears.

The company glides onto the stage in exaggerated slow motion, their bodies in perfect mimicry of the images of ancient Hindu dancers. Their faces and their hands provide the only expression as they dance *Robaim Buong Suong*. Each girl carries a bowl of flower petals which represent wishes for happiness and prosperity in the New Year. The audience sits and stands transfixed as the girls move and pose in patterns that carry deep religious and cultural meanings.

According to Chan Moly Sam, the court dances originated in the Hindu influenced courts of the 13th century. The dancers were exclusively female since female gods dominate all of Cambodian art derived from Classical India. The postures were copied from sculptures of the Hindu Apsaras based on the carvings and art at Angkor Wat. The intent was to maintain constant and deep contact with the ground, accentuating the curves of the feet, spine, arms, fingers, knees, and head. The curve represents the *karmic* circle of life and the feminine force.

The other mantra of court dance is "control, balance, and flexibility." The control is illustrated by the highly contained postures of the body and the highly patterned facial expressions. For instance, one does not show one's teeth; the mouth is closed and serene. It is the eyes and the position of the head that demonstrate emotion. And the greatest expressiveness comes through the hands which illustrate sadness, joy, fear, or despair. The body is very arched and centered on the ground; feet are bare. All movement is forward and back, up and down, with an emphasis on the silhouette.

At the end of the dance, the six young dancers kneel and face the audience, showering them with flower petals. The musicians chant the words of blessing and prosperity for the new year. The spell is broken, and the children begin to chase each other around again as their parents turn to talk or stand to leave. Most of the children in the audience are American citizens by birth. Instead of growing up immersed in the spiritual, geographic, and historical realities that gave rise to this dance, the ceremony at the Italian Heritage Center may be a rare experience of their rich Cambodian heritage. Its enactment is as essential to the resilience of Cambodian identity as speaking Khmer, graduating from college, or raising one's family.

Holding a modified a celebration in a facility dedicated to another, longer-established ethnic minority may be emblematic of the bicultural strategies that Cambodians in America have had to adopt. To some this may appear no different from the biculturalism innumerable waves of immigrants have practiced. It is important to note, however, that Cambodians have *always* been bicultural. From the first, the Khmer managed to incorporate the caste system inherent to Brahmanism with the compassion and sacrifice of Buddhism. My argument here is that understanding the specific nature of Cambodian biculturalism is essential for understanding how Khmer families are adopting to American culture and, more importantly, how they interpret and understand their own success in their new homeland.

Living a successful life now as Americans almost inevitably means that culturally relevant strategies may (or may not) be transformed as they integrate elements of the American success story. Expressive strategies for the Khmer are captured in metaphors such as "operating within the frame of the culture," following the rule of "not too strict, not too loose," or "eating time by remaining in the present moment." Pragmatic strategies are also culturally coherent insofar as they sustain a step-by-step approach to achievement. Inherent in both expressive and pragmatic strategies are the repeated Theravada Buddhist metaphors of balance, control, and flexibility. As a rule the Khmer prefer to seek the middle way between a stressful, individually competitive lifestyle, and one where the family and the community are at the center of one's life. Control is connected to the belief that extremes of wealth and poverty, power and oppression, pull the individual off his or her center. And flexibility requires that the Khmer be willing to flow with whatever life brings; planning for the future is undertaken step-by-step with the expectation that one's destiny unfolds over time. And because every action taken in one's life has a consequence for *future* lives, the Khmer tend to place those actions which they believe guarantee "a good next life" ahead of short-term, self-centered ambition. It is this worldview, one that is deeply grounded in Cambodia's bicultural history and cosmology, that I intend to foreground as I look at Cambodian refugees' pathways to success.

Portes (1993, 1995) and Gibson (1987, 1995) have written extensively about a phenomenon which they call "segmented assimilation" or "additive acculturation without assimilation." Their work is predominantly with immigrant communities in California and their analysis mirrors the findings from most of the micro-level studies on immigrants in the last ten years. The premise is that the immigrant who remains grounded in his culture and its values is consistently the most successful in economic, social, and educational settings.

Portes describes the process of acculturation for most immigrants to be one of segmented assimilation. He notes that there is no longer (if there ever was) a single, generic "mainstream" whose mores and prejudices dictate a common path of integration.[1] Immigrants, he states, actually have two directions they can go—one is to acculturate to white middle class values and structures, the other is to acculturate into the social underclass characterized by permanent poverty and marginalization. Portes points out that the first option is constrained by institutionalized racism which bars most non-whites from fully assimilating into the white mainstream. This is further exacerbated by what Portes describes as the "hourglass economy" which means that

> children of immigrants must cross a narrow bottleneck to
> occupations requiring advanced training if their careers are to
> keep pace with U.S. acquired aspirations. This "race" against

> a narrowing middle demands that immigrant parents
> accumulate sufficient resources to allow their children to
> effect the passage and to simultaneously prove to them the
> viability of upward, mobility aspirations.[2]

Those who don't make it through the bottleneck are left to struggle at the bottom of the hourglass among America's impoverished, adversarial subcultures. Min Zhou's (1997) research on immigrant children draws our attention to the crucial role the family plays in the assimilation process.

> When immigrant children are under pressure to assimilate but
> are unsure which direction of assimilation is more desirable,
> the family or the ethnic community can make a difference if it
> is able to mobilize resources to prevent downward
> assimilation.[3]

A third option for the immigrant which Portes and Zhou discuss and which is more fully elaborated by Gibson (1987) is the choice to remain within the ethnic enclave taking advantage of ethnic networks and sustaining ethnic values and solidarity. Gibson's research reveals that the more the immigrant is allowed to "add" effective elements of the new culture to supplement the ethnic culture, the more self-reliant and successful are the children. As she followed a community of Punjabi Sikhs over a number of years, Gibson found a consistent correlation between the success of the children and their level of ethnic resilience. Parents motivated the children to do well in school, to respect the teacher and the rules of the school, but to be proud of their ethnic heritage and recognize that the family reputation rested on their shoulders. The parents who were able to integrate strategies that allowed their children to do well on American measures of success without subverting cultural expectations helped their children to become balanced, bicultural individuals.

In order to understand the power that ethnic resilience plays in supporting successful outcomes for refugee students, one must understand the deeply embedded historical, contextual, and metaphysical models of success that make up a cultural identity. Therefore, my purpose in undertaking this ethnographic study is to make explicit the spiritual beliefs and values that inspire the individuals in three Cambodian families to be successful. The adults and adolescents consistently describe the ways in which they draw on Buddhist norms as the inspiration for their thoughts and actions, particularly as they define what it means to be a successful or a good person. I believe, therefore, that acceptance of and knowledge about religious philosophies deserve a more prominent place in socio-cultural analyses of refugee adaptation and acculturation.

My objective is to understand what "being successful" means for Cambodian refugee families in a small East Coast city and how they connect meanings of success to their Buddhist and Cambodian traditions, the family, and other social institutions. This book builds on earlier pilot studies of mine which analyzed this question from the perspective of seven Cambodian families. The adults in those families claimed that being successful required balancing traditional Buddhist values and beliefs with more goal-oriented "American" behavior. Their perceptions of Americans, mediated by secondary institutions (schools, media, business), led them to equate "American Way" success with an individual, means-end pursuit of education, wealth, and material possessions. In contrast, Cambodian visions of success typically include the belief that schooling, for example, is an important means to get ahead in society, but the truly successful Cambodian is characterized by generosity to others and by adherence to Cambodian norms.

While my findings from the pilot studies provide a rudimentary understanding of what it means to be successful for the adults in my interviews, the findings do not fully describe the complex process by which grandparents and parents transmit what it means to be successful to their children. The findings also do not include how the children themselves conceptualize success or how they interpret and respond to their parents' expectations.

Therefore, this research focuses on three families who have lived in "Forest City" for fifteen years. Two of the three families include three generations and a widespread kinship network representing a total of thirty-eight people. I have developed in-depth case studies that document the ways in which the adults and their children perceive success through their own traditions and through their interpretation of American models of success.

Chapters 1 and 2 are a review of the literature that has informed this research. Chapter 1 focuses on literature that compares and contrasts the success of Southeast Asian ethnic groups primarily according to economic and educational indicators. My discussion looks at the myth of the model minority commonly ascribed to Asian immigrants and analyzes the performances of the distinctly different Southeast Asian ethnic groups within this framework. The work of Trueba, Cheng, and Ima (1993), Rumbaut and Cornelius (1995), Rumbaut and Ima, (1987, 1988, 1989) and Kiang, (1990) forms the core of this discussion.

Chapter 2 is a discussion of cultural epistemology through an examination of the literature in psychological and philosophical anthropology. My analysis unpacks the concept of ethnic resilience that is central to Portes and Gibson's theories, by introducing a brief historical review of interpretive theory. Starting with cultural pattern theory pioneered by Ruth Benedict (1934) and examining the work of anthropologists and sociologists (Geertz, Shweder, Berger & Luckmann) along with psychologists (Quinn and Holland, D'Andrade, Clarke and Holloway), I argue that in order to understand the complexity of bicultural identity, it is important to understand the deeply embedded historical, contextual, and metaphysical models of success that are transmitted from one generation to another.

Chapters 3 and 4 are an extensive discussion of cultural epistemology which is built from the geography and history of Cambodia and the philosophical tenets of Buddhism. The description at the beginning of this introduction is clear evidence that history, context, and religion continue to be powerful indicators of cultural values insofar as they are continually reenacted for each new generation of Cambodian children. Certain of these cultural constructions remain resistant to revision even in the face of beliefs or behavior that are appropriated from a dominant, more "powerful" culture.

Chapter 5 is a discussion of the research design and data analysis methods used for these three case studies. The chapter opens with a brief summary of two pilot studies that I conducted in this community between 1993 and 1996. This chapter is devoted to an extensive description of the research design including sampling criteria, data collection strategies, contextual and categorical methods of analysis, and a commentary on validity and generalizability.

Chapter 6 is a description of the research setting. My theoretical position is based on the salience of context for understanding cultural meanings of beliefs and behavior. Therefore, in order to understand the experience of Cambodian refugees in this setting, I believe it is important for the reader to know something about the history and demographic composition of Forest City. Forest City has a rich immigrant and religious history that continues with the resettlement of more than 3,000 refugees from around the world.

I fill out the discussion of context with a portrait of the Cambodian community from the point at which a group of elders began to establish essential community institutions, specifically a Buddhist Center. The description also includes a brief commentary on the relationship of the Cambodians in Forest City to the educational and health care systems.

Chapter 7 comprises the three case studies and is the heart of my story. I have divided each family's case into two parts. The first part consists of an in-depth biography of the members of each family and includes a physical description of the individual and their homes, their birth stories, accounts of parents and family members, migration history, schooling, work experience, personal and career aspirations, and perceptions of cultural identity.

The second part includes narrative summaries for each individual which interpret the findings from interviews, observations, and documents that answer my research questions:

1. What does being successful mean to Cambodian refugee parents and children in this group?

2. In what ways do these parents connect their perceptions of success to cultural models represented by Theravada Buddhist beliefs, Cambodian institutions, and/or American institutions?

3. In what ways do these children connect their perceptions of success to cultural models represented by their parents, Theravada Buddhist beliefs, and/or American institutions?

The findings are organized into categories that were influenced by the research questions. These categories are 1) success for the individual, 2) success within the context of the family, and 3) success as a Cambodian or an American.

Chapter 8 is a discussion of the themes that were revealed in the narratives from the six adults and nine adolescents. Each family shared its perspective on what it means to be successful by talking about goals, expectations, role models, and the family. Finally, the discussion focuses on the process of becoming bicultural and reveals different pathways to success as adopted by the adults and the adolescents.

Chapter 9 relates these findings to the theories regarding criteria and potential for success posed by Rumbaut and Ima, Portes and Zhou, Sin, Welaratna, and Ebihara, and Kiang, and offers implications for this research.

The book closes with an epilogue. Written three years after this study, I describe the paths and some of the journeys each of these families have taken. Some of the journeys have become more outwardly focused, some have stabilized, and others have diverged from what I might have predicted. My ability to add to this story comes from my ongoing relationship with each of the families, and as a result, the data are more complex and infinitely messier. Nonetheless, the connection that I draw between ethnic resilience and a concept of success that balances Cambodian culture with American culture is confirmed.

Who am I and where do I stand in relationship to this research?

To begin with, I approach this research as an ethnographer. Pioneered by anthropologists in the 1930s such as Franz Boas, Ruth Benedict, Margaret Mead, and Bronislaw Malinowski, ethnography is the scientific description and classification of the various cultural and racial groups of mankind. The scientific method requires researchers to separate and define a culture's structures, customs, and beliefs. Studying each of the parts and speculating on what they mean to the whole, one hopes to arrive at the truth of the culture. The ethnographer, therefore, must position herself as an external observer, close enough to interpret the meanings behind roles and rituals, but distant enough to provide an account uncontaminated by her personal subjectivity. Her interpretation is accepted as truth because of its claim to objectivity. The scientific validity of the study is guaranteed if the ethnographer keeps the focus exclusively on the informant, deflecting any references to her own personal identity or assumptions (Patai, 1991).

Feminist ethnographers over the past three decades reject the notion that ethnographic research could ever be objective. They point out that so-called scientific data are the result of a subjective relationship between the researcher and her informants. The material the researcher gathers and interprets is profoundly influenced by the many "selves" she brings into the research relationship, by the questions she chooses to ask, by how she selects the words of her informants, and finally by the way in which she represents her informants and interprets their meanings (Reinharz, 1992; Reinharz, 1997).

Post-structural ethnographers emphasize the role of interpretation pointing out that the truth lies somewhere among the stories narrators tell, researchers write, and the audience reads (Althiede & Johnson, 1994; Erickson, 1987; Geertz, 1983; Isaacs, 1975; Maanen, 1988; Oakley, 1981). Clandinin and Connelly claim that scientific inquiry is, in fact, a story about experience in a particular setting—the experiences of the participants, the experiences of the researchers, and the experience of their collective story. The final text is a story about how participants evolved and changed and the role that the researcher played as change-agent and narrator (Clandinin & Connelly, 1994).

I also approach this research as a narrator, and the story I tell resembles a journey which has an archetypal theme. The mythic journey follows a pattern in which an individual separates from a place, an identity, or a belief system, goes through a transition or initiation, and finally comes full circle returning as a new person. It occurs to me that this style of narrative is a perfect fit for a culture whose oral tradition for thousands of years has been based on Hindu myth and legend. The most powerful archetypal journey in the Cambodian universe is the story of Buddha, and his spiritual quest precisely follows the pattern of separation, transition, and return. Moreover, the mythic journey also mirrors the diaspora of the Cambodian refugees who have separated from their homeland, undergone painful and profound transitions in their new host countries, and are slowly returning to their traditional customs as they establish temples and take up the life cycle ceremonies in their communities once again. Therefore, my own journey of separation, transition, and return is central to my research relationship and mirrors in subtle ways the journeys of the adults and adolescents with whom I have spent the last ten years. I cannot tell their story without accounting for my own.

As I write this story, I am a 55-year-old Caucasian woman. I grew up in New Mexico, as did my mother and grandmother. We were always surrounded by culture and cultures, and I regret to say that I learned very little of their epistemology during that time. What I did learn was that culture—as defined by Navajo, Mexican, Africans—was an *obstacle to be overcome* if the person wanted access to the American standard of living, the American dream.

In 1985 I began working as a consultant to the fourteen year-round communities on Maine's offshore islands. Ostensibly, my responsibilities were to support the teachers, students, and parents who were involved in the island public schools—over half of which were one-room, K-8 schools. I soon learned that the most successful schools were those where the island culture was an explicit and valued part of the school curriculum. I discovered that the identity of "islanders" was deeply internalized as a way of seeing the world, the structure of families and relationships, and the relationship to the environment; it mattered whether your ancestors came from Matinicus or Isle au Haut. However, when the island students began attending high school on the mainland, they discovered that "islander" carried a stigma, one that labeled them inferior or "hicks." Some acculturated to the mainland and moved on; others found a way to return to the island to work and raise their children and continue the cycle for another generation. My experiences in these communities and questions about the phenomenon of deep culture led me to graduate school and have remained at the center of my research interests.

I applied to graduate school twenty-four years after completing my bachelor's in history in order to pursue a master's in Theological Studies at the Harvard Divinity School. My course of study focused on the epistemological and phenomenological theories of feminist liberation theology and the analytical techniques of hermeneutics. Having always been a student of history, I was compelled by the stories of women (and men) from non-Western, non-industrial, or pre-modern cultures that had been ignored in the creation of contemporary historical texts. I also began to notice that each cultural text incorporated within itself a coherent and inherently elegant reality. That discovery has led me deeper into the philosophy of knowledge and the social construction of reality.

Given this personal history, I bring a variety of "selves" into the field. I hold a perception of culture as the vital center, the life force, which holds us in relationship with worlds seen and unseen. Without knowing the ground on which we stand, without knowing our native stories and beliefs, we simply react to the push and pull of the cosmopolitan paradigm that generates metaphors of success grounded only in the endlessly self-referential, technological, and superficial experience. My purpose here is to describe and understand the vital center of Cambodian culture as it inspires these men and women to live lives of promise and hope, and to document Cambodian culture as these families confront a more persuasive, pervasive cosmopolitan American culture.

I am aware that I have influenced this process insofar as I have intervened for the nearly ten years in the lives of these three families. I do not speak Khmer, nor have I grown up Buddhist. Only four (two adults and two adolescents) out of 18 members of these families have close contact with White Americans. I have assumed a variety of roles over the course of my relationship with them, from scientist/researcher, to student, teacher, mentor, elder, and extended family member. My respect for their culture and their insights has persuaded them to trust that I shall honor and respect their words and that I shall not betray their confidences.

The case studies are extensive because I am committed to allowing the members of these families to speak in their own words—to struggle with my questions, to contradict themselves, and to tell the story they want to tell. Perhaps it is one of the reasons most of the adolescents have asked me to use their real names in the text.

I discovered that questions around the meaning of success were intriguing to the adolescents and provided them an opportunity to explore some things they had taken for granted about themselves, their families, and especially their culture. Nonetheless, I recognize that my "categories of success" are infused with Western, capitalistic, Protestant norms where success is often measured by status and the accumulation of things. Although the Khmer talk about owning their own businesses, buying big houses and cars, and getting college degrees, becoming Americanized was not a goal for most of them. Over time I came to understand the distinction they made between an American concept of success and the norms of success embedded in Cambodian Buddhist culture. While I am privileged to have the final interpretation, the end result is something we have constructed together. I have been inspired and influenced in the process, as have they.

NOTES TO THE INTRODUCTION

1. Alejandro Portes, "Segmented Assimilation Among New Immigrant Youth: A Conceptual Framework," R. Rumbaut and Wayne Cornelius, eds.,

California's Immigrant Children: Theory, Research and Implications for Education Policy, (San Diego, CA: Center for U.S.-Mexican Studies, University of California, 1995), p. 72.

2. Ibid., p. 73.

3. Min Zhou, "Growing Up American: The Challenge Confronting Immigrant Children and Children of Immigrants," in the *Annual Review of Sociology*, 23, 1997, p. 75.

CHAPTER 1

Predicting Success for Southeast Asian Refugees

I respect the person that had nothing, kind of rags-to-riches story, had nothing and made something of himself. Do what he had to do; bettered himself in some way to make his life better, to make society a little bit better.

—MP

INTRODUCTION

In the fall of 1993, *Time* and *Newsweek* published feature articles on the widespread and increasing hostility toward America's new immigrants. The articles highlighted the debate between those who believed that immigration spurs new businesses and new taxpayers, and those who asserted that immigrants and their children "evade taxes and overburden local welfare, health and education systems."[1]

America's immigration history is a mixture of compassion, pragmatism, and xenophobia. Massive waves of poor immigrants from southern and eastern Europe flocked to the United States between 1880 and 1920. In 1920 fears of racial mixing and economic collapse effectively closed the doors to all but those immigrants from Germany, England, and Ireland. The period from 1920 until 1965 was almost completely free of immigration resulting in a foreign born population of less than 5 percent, 70 percent of whom were from Europe.

After the change in immigration laws in 1965, which ended the national origins quotas, and the 1980 refugee act, which redefined eligibility for political asylum, the picture of immigration changed. By 1992, just 15 percent of new immigrants came from Europe, while 37 percent came from Asia and 44 percent came from Latin America and the Caribbean.[2] Today, public perceptions have once again pushed policy-makers to define the pros and cons of immigration policy, and this has kept the pressure on scholars to document the degree to which immigrants are becoming either successful taxpayers or chronic burdens on a fragile social safety net.

Empirical and qualitative studies of Asians in the 1970s and 1980s were motivated by the need to document how these new immigrants were succeeding in American society. A lot of attention has been devoted to describing Asian groups whose socio-cultural traditions have supported their successful acculturation to *mainstream American values* such as superior educational achievement, individual self-reliance, and a willingness to delay gratification until time-on-task has resulted in social prestige and material rewards. However, the past decade of research focusing on different Asian and Southeast Asian groups has turned up a certain amount of disconfirming evidence. The following studies document the increasingly differentiated analysis of the ways in which America's Asian immigrants have approached the issue of assimilation and the ways in which the research community interprets their strategies as successful or not.

PREDICTING SUCCESS FOR ASIAN IMMIGRANTS

By the late 1980s and early 1990s, researchers were moving from macro-theories of immigrant adaptation strategies to micro-theories in which they attempted to clarify the evidence that not all Asians achieve according to American standards of economic or educational success (DeVos, 1973, 1983, 1975, 1980; Guthrie, 1985; Trueba, Guthrie, Hu, 1981; Trueba, Cheng, Ima, 1993; Tharp and Gallimore, 1988; Caplan,Whitmore, Cheng, 1989; Gibson, 1987, 1988; Haines, 1989; Rumbaut & Cornelius, 1995; Rumbaut & Ima, 1987, 1988, 1989; Kiang, 1990). These and other researchers focused on the diverse adaptive strategies of *East Asians* (Chinese, Japanese, Korean, Filipino), *South Asians* (Bangladeshi, Bhuanese, Burmese, Indian, Nepali, Pakistani, Sri Lankan, Sikimese), *Southeast Asians* (Hmong, Indonesians, Cambodians, Laotians, Malay, Mien, Singaporeans, Thai, and Vietnamese), and *Pacific Islanders*.

One result of this diversification has been to dispel the fairly universal stereotype of Asians as a "model minority" because of their reputation for hard work and rapid rise in social status. In reality, one third of Asian Americans fall below a number of indicators that American policy-makers use to determine the success of an immigrant group.[3] Trueba, Cheng, and Ima (1993) have attempted to describe and analyze the different strategies used by East Asian, South Asian, Southeast Asian and Pacific Islanders to achieve economic and educational success in the United States. Their study incorporates a decade of research on these groups prior to 1988, primarily in California. The analysis is wide-ranging, citing quantitative and case studies on the effects of economic and socio-cultural factors on the educational success and resilience of children in the schools.

> There is fast growing evidence that the 'model minority' has serious flaws; that is, not all Asian and Asian American students do well in school. Indeed some of the Asian American children are having serious academic problems.... Schooling is not easy for any Asian children, including Chinese children who come from families with high levels of literacy and intellectually stimulating environments. But for other Asian children, the challenge can be overwhelming. Not only does American schooling contradict their own cultural system, but it also basically undermines their sense of well-being and self-confidence. Their ethnic identity is tied to the group and the lifestyle they had in their home countries. In contrast, American schooling emphasizes independence and individualism, self-confidence and hard competitive efforts to excel and achieve.[4]

The concept of segmented assimilation (Portes, 1995) would suggest that only a few Asian immigrants will succeed in making it through the economic bottleneck to full integration into white, middle class society. The route for many Asian Americans then is to persist in acquiring economic self-sufficiency while deliberately preserving cultural traditions and ethnic solidarity. For Asian families who take this route, some of the benchmarks for success are congruent with white American aspirations—secure white-collar jobs, higher education for their children, home ownership, and comfortable retirements. Other standards of success have to do with the degree to which families persist in maintaining cultural traditions and norms, and these are highly differentiated for each ethnic group.

The majority of Trueba's study is a detailed, comparative analysis of America's Asian ethnic groups on a variety of economic, social, and educational scales. In the final chapter, Trueba et al. discuss sociocultural predictors of educational success—those cultural models inherent in families that support a child's achievement in the traditional American school system. In this section, they equate school success with cultural values toward education—over the long term—and the degree to which cultural values mirror American middle class values. Those families who seek out special tutoring and auxiliary educational opportunities for their children and who motivate their children to develop independent study habits such as critical thinking and inquiry skills will, the authors claim, ensure successful academic achievement for their children.

In fact, Trueba et al. observe that educational success is predicated on acquiring four interrelated competencies: academic, extracurricular, social, and the competence of parental support. The student who is striving to be successful in school, state the authors, must first of all demonstrate academic competency in all subject areas required by the school for promotion.

> The second type of success is extracurricular which involves student extracurricular activities such as student government, social clubs, volunteer work, sports and music. Success is measured by participation and popularity. The third category of school success is social. This may be measured by how popular the child is, how many parties he's been invited to, how many friends he has or what kinds of after-school social life he/she conducts. The fourth aspect of assuring school

success is parent participation where the parents support their child's education outside the school setting.[5]

Caplan, Whitmore, and Choy (1989) conducted a similar study of the "boat people"—Vietnamese, Laotian, and ethnic Chinese—comparing their socio-cultural values and the educational achievement of their children. Through a series of interviews and observations, they found that the degree to which cultural background reflects American middle class values is a powerful predictor of success for these refugee groups.

> We place great confidence in our explanation of the role of cultural values as implemented through family life-style. The values essential to promotion achievement are simple and direct.... What we find working for [these immigrant groups] in terms of achievement outcomes are the practical side of values they share in common with respect to spiritual, aesthetic and other values. These values of practical significance to achievement are, if not identical, congruent with what have been viewed as mainstream, middle class American beliefs about getting ahead.[6]

Like Trueba et al., the authors found a fit between American middle class values of hard work, delayed gratification in anticipation of high rewards, optimism, forward-looking 'can-do' attitudes, pride, persistence, and self-reliance with the cultural values cherished by this group of Southeast Asian refugees. However, not surprisingly, the Vietnamese, Chinese, and Laotians had their own interpretation for middle class values such as maintaining a strong respect for cultural heritage and past traditions, a willingness to face new challenges, the desire for comfort and security, and the willingness to delay gratification until the highest achievement was secured.

Caplan et al. also found that family characteristics that mirror middle class American norms contributed to economic self-sufficiency and high GPAs. They described the following child-rearing practices as strongly correlated with success for their children: equality in home decision-making and role sharing; parental involvement in reading to their children and helping with homework; strict discipline and control over children; and a strong sense of efficacy that located the control of one's destiny in the family not the individual.

TABLE 1: COMPARING FAMILY NORMS AMONG MIDDLE CLASS WHITES AND CAMBODIANS

White Middle Class (Caplan Sample)	Cambodians (Sample for This Study)
Dual-parent households.	Two female-headed households, one dual-parent household.
Both parents have white collar, upper-level jobs.	Parents have seasonal, manufacturing, or clerical job.
Both parents have college educations.	Two mothers have sixth-grade education and cannot read or write their own language; one mother is a part-time university student; one father has a college and a nursing degree.
Parents provide a rich learning environment, tutors, and auxiliary education when needed.	Parents require adolescents to assist with financial and childcare responsibilities; only two parents read English well.
Parents emphasize the development of inquiry, problem-solving skills.	Parents lecture children on respect to elders, responsibilities for the individual to community, proper behavior outside the home.
Parents instill a strong motivation to achieve status and recognition in school.	Parents instill values of self-reliance and persistence to do well in school and to withdraw when it becomes too stressful.
Parents expect commitment to academic efforts over long periods of time.	For most parents, schooling ends after high school or upon receiving a college diploma; then the productive stage of life begins by finding a good job and starting a family.
Parents expect children to achieve social popularity and participate in commitments outside of school.	Parents very restrictive with daughters, not allowing them to social date until after high school; sons have more freedom. Virtually all the adolescents in this study have part-time jobs and very little time for socializing.

From these two studies, I draw the conclusion that white, American, middle class norms are the dominant standard for success and the model for upward mobility in this society. One way of thinking about the socio-cultural values that are predictive of success for middle class white Americans is to see how the Cambodians in my study compare with the model offered by Caplan et al. Table 1 illustrates that comparison.

My findings will show that the members of these three Cambodian families have a good sense of what it takes to get ahead in American society. The families do not expect to integrate seamlessly into white middle class American society; neither do they expect to become part of the underclass, destined for permanent poverty. Most of the adolescents have persisted through high school as honor students; they have high aspirations and tremendous optimism about accomplishing their educational, occupational and personal goals. Two of the adolescents have dropped out of school. Still, they too are optimistic that they will be successful in life. For all of them, being successful involves a combination of acquiring enough money to live comfortable lives and finding work that makes a difference to society—work that allows them to give back to others. All but two of the adolescents are determined to hold onto their cultural identity—some through maintaining the language, others by staying close to their Buddhist faith. Their stories demonstrate that there is no culturally homogeneous path to success for Southeast Asian families and provide evidence both for and against the theory of segmented assimilation.

PREDICTING SUCCESS FOR SOUTHEAST ASIAN REFUGEES

While a deep commitment to ethnic solidarity and identity is not uncommon for immigrant groups, it is particularly salient for *refugees.* Refugees, unlike immigrants, have not prepared emotionally and practically to leave their homes and begin their lives in a new country. Instead they have left their homes and fled their country simply in order to survive. One of my assumptions is that ethnic solidarity is one of the few strategies that offer refugees some emotional and practical security in the host country.

Anthropologists use the push-pull theory to distinguish types of migration. On the one hand, refugees are *pushed* from their homelands largely by political factors that make it impossible to continue living there. This is in contrast to immigrants who are *pulled* away from their homes in search of greater opportunities in a new land. Given a choice, most refugees would prefer to remain in their home countries, and their reluctance to wholeheartedly embrace the host country partially stems from the belief that when things improve at home, they will return. Once having made the decision to leave their homes, refugees lose control over their lives and their futures; they have little to say about where they are settled or when. That decision is based on a set of abstract immigration laws and policies of the host countries which may give no priority to reuniting families.

In studying refugee adaptation and success, it is useful to remember that crises which result in refugees typically displace people in three waves: The first wave includes intellectuals, political officials, and the wealthy who arrive with sufficient human and social capital to make their way rapidly within the new society. The second wave comprises people from modest backgrounds who were employed as minor civil servants or merchants. Second-wave refugees are often family members who are leaving to be reunited with the family in exile. The third wave primarily consists of the rural poor, farmers, and manual laborers. They are the least educated—frequently even writing-illiterate in their own language. The refugees in the second and third waves are more likely to suffer poor physical and mental health due to the trauma surrounding their escape.

In 1982 Rubén Rumbaut and Kenji Ima began the Indochinese Health and Adaptation Research Project (IHARP), a major longitudinal study on Southeast Asian refugees in Southern California. Their rationale for studying this particular Asian population is as follows:

> The Southeast Asians (Vietnamese, Cambodians, and Laotians) predominate among refugee admissions. Over one million have resettled in the United States since the end of the Vietnam war in 1975 and they have exhibited the highest fertility rates among ethnic groups in the U.S. The Indochinese form the third largest Asian origin population in the country behind the Chinese and Filipinos. [7]

Rumbaut and Ima's report is one of three major longitudinal quantitative and qualitative studies done on Southeast Asians in the mid-1980s.[8] For the purposes of my research, I shall consider the IHARP study as the prototype for subsequent theories that predict which of these four refugee groups (Cambodians, Vietnamese, Laotians, and Hmong) will be the most successful in the United States.

A primary goal of the IHARP study was to be able to document those factors which influenced whether this predominantly *refugee* group would equal or exceed the upward mobility of older Asian immigrants primarily from China, Korea, Japan, India, and the Philippines. The surveys included questions about migration histories, social background, English proficiency, employment statistics, income, acculturation levels, and mental health.

For their research setting, Rumbaut and Ima selected San Diego, California (where 40 percent of *all* Southeast Asian refugees have settled), and collected data from Vietnamese, Chinese-Vietnamese, Cambodian, Hmong, and Laotian adults. After a year of preparation, 739 adults drawn from 9000 family sampling units between the ages of 18 and 71 were interviewed in 1983 and 1984 by native language speakers. In 1986-87 and 1989-90, the researchers assembled the children of these families, all of whom were enrolled in eleven high schools in the San Diego Unified School District. The majority of the students were born in their home countries and entered school in the United States as part of what the researchers called the 1.5 generation.

> [T]he design permitted the analysis of the effects of parental and family characteristics measured in 1983 on the children's academic achievement measured three and six years later.[9]

Rumbaut's 1995 article, "The New Californians: Comparative Research Findings on the Educational Progress of Immigrant Children," is an excellent review of this longitudinal study. As he points out, the research design intentionally covered successive waves of refugees from Vietnam, Laos, and Cambodia, and included the Hmong. The first reports focused on economic and socio-cultural adaptation of these groups. The results were compared against the standard set by earlier Southeast Asian refugees, primarily first-wave professionals from Vietnam. The characteristics of this cohort that could be tied to statistical indicators of upward mobility included the following:

1. The length of time in the U.S.

2. Whether parents had acquired English literacy prior to arrival.

3. Whether parents had high school diplomas prior to arrival.

4. Whether parents had prestigious or white-collar jobs in the home country.

5. Whether refugees effectively used ethnic networks to find jobs instead of depending on job training programs.

6. Whether refugees chose two-year associate college degrees or attended vocational/technical colleges instead of four-year college programs.

7. Whether family members pooled income and resources thus adding to the aggregate household income.

8. Whether parents sought to place their children in English immersion classes to speed up their acculturation to American schools and sought tutors to help their children achieve in school.

The following statistics summarize the way Rumbaut and Ima characterized the Cambodians in relationship, first to the Vietnamese, Hmong, Chinese-Vietnamese, and Laotians in 1983 and 1984, and later in relationship to Vietnamese and Laotians, plus Filipinos, Mexicans, Latin Americans, and East Asians.

To preface this analysis I need to state that Cambodian refugees do not precisely fit the wave theory of migration. Very few Cambodian elite had time to plan their future between the collapse of the Lon Nol government and the takeover by Khmer Rouge forces in 1975. Within a week, the vast majority of Cambodia's wealthy, educated classes (including the military, civil servants, teachers, and all Buddhist monks) were forced to leave their homes and resettle in the countryside. The few who managed to leave the country in 1975 had a choice of migrating to France, Australia or the United States. Most chose France.

By the war's end, 80 percent of Cambodia's intellectuals and artists had been killed. Thus, Cambodian refugees were primarily poor rural farmers along with some civil servants, merchants, and laborers from urban Phnom Penh or Battambang. Seventy percent of these were women with children. A significant number of Cambodian adolescents became refugees, resettling in America without any surviving relatives.

The statistics on 120 Cambodian adults from the 1983 and 1984 data set[10] shows that slightly less than half the respondents were from urban areas in Cambodia while the majority were from the rural areas (Table 2). The respondents averaged five years of education in their home country; only fifteen people out of 120 had high school degrees and over forty individuals were writing-illiterate in their own language.

TABLE 2: IMMIGRATION STATUS AND EDUCATIONAL INDICATORS AMONG CAMBODIANS VERSUS VIETNAMESE (RUMBAUT, 1989:144)

	Cambodians	Vietnamese
Immigration status		
Percent immigrated to U.S. during 1970s	14	35
Percent immigrated to U.S. during 1980s	86	64
Average years in the U.S. (1983)	3	5
Educational indicators (1975 time of arrival)		
Percent urban	45	95
Average years of education	5	10
Percent high school graduates	13	47
Percent writing-illiterate in own language	34	1
Percent adults speaking no English (1983)	63	31

The primary predictor of success, according to the research team, was English proficiency. Given that the Khmer population in this sample had been in the United States less than five years, it is not surprising that their English proficiency was statistically low. The language of instruction in Cambodia was Khmer except for middle class private schools which offered French. Cambodian refugees spent an average of three years in displacement camps where the schooling was extremely limited and where instruction was in Khmer. Upon reestablishing their families in the United States, Khmer parents were forced to balance success strategies against day-to-day survival needs, e.g., a father could only attend English as a Second Language (ESL) classes until he found a steady job; in the absence of work skills and extended family members to help with child care, many Cambodian women were unable to attend ESL classes at all; etc. Parents came to depend on their children to acquire enough English to act as their interpreters within the larger society.

The second predictor of success, according to Rumbaut and Ima, was economic stability and improvement (Table 3). Although the authors point out that 1983 and 1984 were years of a severe economic recession in the U.S, the number of Cambodians who were employed rose by 10 percent in one year to around 22 percent in 1984. Aligned with economic success is occupational status. Researchers found that for all refugees, the higher status jobs were found in refugee services as translators, job counselors, social service workers, teacher's aides, and native language facilitators. Since the majority of Khmer had low English proficiency and minimal education, 65 percent had acquired jobs in manufacturing and the trades. These jobs were described as "dead end" jobs, without access to promotion.

Household composition was a predictor of success both for economic self-sufficiency and indirectly for educational attainment. The study validates the finding that unmarried women—usually widows—headed a quarter of all Khmer households. (This percentage of female-lead households subsequently increased as women sought divorce which had been culturally suppressed in Cambodia.) The researchers connected the high rates of public assistance to single-parent families and reported that the Khmer sustained a higher dependence on welfare. Thus the statistics revealed that in 1984, 81 percent of the Khmer families were below the poverty line. Khmer mothers set a high priority on protecting and caring for their children and instilling proper beliefs and behavior until their children are married. The researchers concluded that for the Khmer, it was acceptable to balance public assistance with part-time work as long as it allowed them to care for their families.

TABLE 3: ECONOMIC INDICATORS AMONG CAMBODIANS AND VIETNAMESE (RUMBAUT, 1989: 144, 148, 150)		
	Cambodians	**Vietnamese**
Percent white-collar workers	7	33
Percent in sales	14	19
Percent blue-collar workers	8	11
Percent military	16	26
Percent farmers, fishers	54	11
Percent employed	22	47
Percent unemployed	38	22
Percent professional in private sector	0	11
Percent professional in public sector	15	12
Percent clerical/office workers	4	8
Percent in trades and services	15	18
Percent in manufacturing	65	51
Percent in jobs with no benefits	27	29
Percent in jobs with no promotion	85	46
Percent families with two wage earners	5	17
Percent families with no wage earners	65	39
Percent below poverty line	81	61
Percent on cash assistance	67	43

The authors state that each of these economic indicators can also be linked to a range of *educational* measurements that predict success for the next generation. In 1986 and 1987 Rumbaut and Ima surveyed second generation immigrant children attending eleven high schools in

San Diego Unified School District. The data included active and inactive students—those who entered high school in the ninth grade but dropped out of school or left the district.[11] A second study was conducted in 1989 and 1990.

TABLE 4: PERCENTAGE DISTRIBUTION OF GRADE POINT AVERAGES (RUMBAUT, 1989: 169)				
	Below 2.0	**2.0 to 2.9**	**3.0 and above**	**Total Students**
San Diego City Schools All 12th Grade Students, 1986-87				
Asian	11	37	52	169
Indochinese	12	48	40	460
White	19	47	35	3561
Hispanic	36	51	14	884
Black	43	48	9	858
IHARP-SARYS Sample 7th to 12th Grade Students				
All Indochinese	15	45	40	239
Vietnamese	13	33	53	54
Chinese-Vietnamese	18	33	49	45
Hmong	4	55	40	47
Khmer	11	68	20	35
Lao	24	43	32	58

The original 1983/84 data did not look at educational attainment of school-age youth, specifically grade point averages and the ratio of limited English proficient (LEP) to fluent English proficient (FEP) students. That changed in 1986 when IHARP added the Southeast Asian Refugee Youth Study (SARYS) to its data collection. (Thus the 1986 data set is referred to as the IHARP-SARYS sample.) In it, 92 percent of Khmer students seventh through twelfth grade were LEP as compared to 69 percent for Indochinese overall. The statistics for the

Khmer improved slightly by the 1989/90 survey, in which 78 percent of the students seventh through twelfth grade were LEP. This finding by itself is ambiguous except to suggest a certain diligence on the part of Cambodian students to improve their English skills over this three-year period.

The data on grade point averages for this cohort, however, is intriguing (Table 4). It shows that GPAs for Indochinese seniors are virtually the same as the GPAs for the Indochinese in the SARYS sample. If nothing else, this suggests that researchers such as myself can generalize with confidence based on the IHARP-SARYS data.

One revealing statistic is the fact that the percentage of Indochinese seniors with grade point averages of 2.0 to 3.0 is higher than their white, Hispanic or Black counterparts. As for the Khmer students in the SARYS sample, it is perhaps significant to note that most maintain grade point averages in the middle range, 2.0 to 2.9. That would seem to be consistent with their desire to seek a balance—not too high, not too low.

TABLE 5: PERCENTAGES OF LIMITED ENGLISH PROFICIENT AND FLUENT ENGLISH PROFICIENT STUDENTS DROPPING OUT OF SAN DIEGO UNIFIED SCHOOL DISTRICT 1989/90 (RUMBAUT, 1995: 38)

	Percentage of LEP Students	Percentage of FEP Students	Total Number of Students
East Asian	11	2	1050
Indochinese	11	4	3102
Vietnamese	11	4	1618
Cambodian	15	5	415

In the 1989/90 SARYS study, the dropout rate for the Vietnamese LEP students is at 11 percent and for FEP students it is 4 percent which is consistent with statistics for the Southeast Asians and East Asians overall. However, for Khmer students, 15 percent of the LEP students dropped out during this academic year, along with 5 percent for the FEP students (Table 5). My own findings confirm that high school is a watershed for Cambodian students who have not acquired a command of English. In my study, many Cambodian students who endured the stigma of ESL classes as well as the racial tension in the Forest City high schools, chose a path of least resistance: they dropped out and began working. Many completed their GEDs, passing the exam on their own. Some who attended GED classes flourished under the individualized attention of the instructors and the more purposeful intentions of the primarily adult students.

The outcome of these studies in 1983/1984 and 1989/1990 was a portrait of Cambodians, in comparison to the Vietnamese, Chinese-Vietnamese, Hmong, and Lao that looked like this:

- Cambodians had the second highest number of female-headed households.

- Cambodians were the second lowest in home ownership.

- Cambodians were the lowest in years of parental education.

- Cambodians had the highest percentage of parents who were unemployed.

- Cambodians had the highest rates of families living below poverty.

- Cambodians had the highest rates of welfare dependency.

- Cambodians were most likely to be attending inner city schools.

- Two-thirds of Cambodian children were classified as LEP.

- Cambodians had the lowest scores on the Stanford Achievement tests.

- More than 60 percent of Cambodian youth expected to finish college.

- *Cambodians scored the highest in self-esteem.*

- *Cambodians scored the highest on the optimism and satisfaction of life index.*

In 1990 Peter Nien-chu Kiang wrote about the college experience of Southeast Asian students (Kiang, 1990). From the perspective of these students, his review examined the literature on Southeast Asians, refugees, immigrants, and racial minorities. Kiang discovered that very little had been written about the educational persistence of

Cambodians, Vietnamese, or Laotians to enter institutions of higher education. Much of the literature he reviewed had a tendency to make claims for "Asians" as though they were a single, generic group. He points out that

> Southeast Asian students' expectations, learning styles, and
> performance in school may reflect traditional values and
> educational practices of their homelands. Differences, as well
> as similarities between each country and between regions
> within a single country in culture, language, history, religion
> and geopolitical development are significant.[12]

In one example Kiang describes the impact on refugees who encountered contradictory messages from displacement camp personnel who urged them to assimilate to American language and customs while implicitly conferring the stigma of minority group status. The majority of Southeast Asian refugees who spent from one to five years in displacement camps were taught to abandon their language, cultural customs, and aspirations in order to "make it" in the new society.

Kiang concludes his study by calling for more quantitative and qualitative research into the separate experiences of Vietnamese, Laotians, and Cambodians in order to better understand those factors which predict success or failure for their children. Specifically he suggests that the research be focused from the *point of view* of the ethnic group under consideration. He offers the following themes for further exploration:

- the roles of race, culture, and class in shaping the self-image, aspirations, process of adjustment and development of a minority group identity for Southeast Asian refugee students in college

- *the meaning of success* and the realities of survival as defined through the daily lives of immigrant and refugee students

- the roles and expectations of graduating students in relation to their families and communities. (my emphasis)[13]

The intent of my research is to provide a more complex picture of what it means to be successful from *within* the culture of these three Cambodian families. As noted above, the parents and the adolescents in these families are able to make choices about their future that might not have been conceivable in their own country. Two of the mothers have divorced abusive husbands; one is completing her college education—something she could not have easily done in Cambodia. The other mother has delayed her own schooling in order to manage the educational careers of her five children and care for her elderly parents. She takes advantage of public assistance to supplement her part-time, seasonal income because she insists on being a full time caretaker for her family.

Two of the young men have dropped out of school and are working for local factories. Two of the young men are freshman in private universities, and their sisters will attend college in the fall of 1999. While all of them consider themselves on the path to success, they are very realistic about the racial barriers they face in mainstream society. It may or may not be the reason all but one of them earnestly desire to maintain their cultural identity, specifically as it is embodied in Buddhism. Over the three years that I spent with them, I watched them struggle with the knowledge that the price of success in the "American Way" meant separation from their families and their community. Only one was willing to make a permanent break with her family. Furthermore, the parents commented that as their children got older, they seemed to become more interested in the language, the customs, and their bonds to the family.

Kiang anticipated my study by almost a decade by recognizing that data on immigrant Asians was likely to generalize positive or negative findings to the entire group without regard to the different ethnicities within the "Asian origin" category, their specific migration status, or their socio-cultural differences. He then rightly predicts that members from each Asian group may view the meaning of assimilation, acculturation, and success from different conceptual models.

PREDICTING SUCCESS: CAMBODIAN PERSPECTIVES

Bo Chum Sin (1991), who is a bilingual Cambodian native, wrote her doctoral thesis on case studies of fifteen Cambodian students in

Oregon, California, Washington, and New York. Sin's study looks at psychological, linguistic, and socio-cultural influences on academic success for these adolescents. Although her research focused on students, her findings highlight the cultural models inherent in Cambodian families. She theorizes that Cambodian families tend to adopt one of three different strategies for a life-path: high achievers, financially concerned, and underachievers.

High achievers come from families that possess sufficient cultural capital to compete and succeed on their own in America. The parents remain open to communication with their children and selectively add new behaviors that are influenced by American culture, while maintaining core Cambodian norms and traditional beliefs. In the face of residual psychological trauma and daily experiences of racism and discrimination, the family "solicited understanding and cooperation from their children in working together to survive the common hardships."[14] Once the mutual respect and trust is established between parents and children, the children tend to remain in school longer and strive to compete at higher levels.

Other families, Sin states, struggle to reconcile their experiences of violence and greed in the refugee camps and the persistent daily racial discrimination they face in school and the wider society. Sin labels these families *financially concerned.* The families turn away from cultural values that stress education and Buddhist norms and put their energies into accumulating wealth and possessions. A few justify their choices by pointing out that the first people to be killed by the Khmer Rouge were those with a lot of education. The sentiment might be summarized, "What good is an education if you can't survive?" According to Sin, these families pressure their children to leave school at age eighteen or if school becomes too difficult for them, and to get jobs in order to help with family expenses. "Some parents generally did not view education as an important tool for their children's future. Education was viewed only as an immediate or short term goal."[15]

Finally, Sin describes families which have disintegrated in the face of poverty, dislocation, and continuing psychological trauma. Labeling them *underachievers,* Sin states that the children tend to drop out of school, often forming gangs trying to recreate a sense of belonging and family with their peers. In the larger Cambodian communities, the temple and the monks stand in as surrogate parents and role models for these troubled youth. Monks command respect from the most alienated young person. Because of their training, moreover, monks are often able to teach both educational knowledge and proper cultural norms.

Sin describes conceptual models of success that Cambodian students draw on and the different paths they take to achieve their goals. One such model is referred to as "the three stages of life." Parents and grandparents teach their children that life exists in three stages: The first is the time for completing one's education, which is important but has a finite limit not to extend beyond college for those fortunate enough to attend. The second stage is equally important as it concerns marriage and starting one's family. As the ideal, people in the second stage of life bring "pride and happiness to the family through marriage, having children, and becoming successful in their lives."[16] Retirement, the third stage, is important because during it elders have time to give to the temple, help out in the community, and care for their grandchildren.

Sin confirms other studies that show the parents' socioeconomic status does not influence students' achievement in school as long as the cultural values are emphasized in the home.[17] She found that children tended to do well in school and in the society even if parents were unable to read or write their own language so long as parents talked with their children and trusted them to be both respectful of cultural norms and to limit their acceptance of certain American behaviors.[18] The parent who was also able to show a positive attitude toward both cultures helped his or her children to develop strong ethnic resilience. She discovered that the child who demonstrated a strong ethnic self-concept had the self-confidence to compete with American students to the level of his or her intellectual abilities.

> Personal drive, self commitment and ability to achieve a
> balance between home and school cultures were a prerequisite
> for [my] respondents. Those who accepted the mismatch
> between the old and new culture were able to concentrate on
> their learning rather than worry about being alienated from the
> mainstream culture.[19]

Usha Welaratna's 1993 ethnography of nine Cambodian refugees is a revision of her master's thesis. She is a native of Sri Lanka and a

Theravada Buddhist who became fluent in Khmer for her study. Welaratna gives us an account of nine individuals who survived the Cambodian holocaust and shares their stories of success and failure. At the end of the book, she addresses the interpretation of the Cambodian personality presented by Rumbaut and Ima in their 1988 publication. Welaratna offers an alternative philosophy of success for Cambodian families rooted in their belief in *karma*, the precept that holds that one's actions always have consequences for good or evil in the next life. She points out that acts of generosity, kindness, and compassion bring great merit to individuals and enable them to attain good lives when they are reborn.

Welaratna states that the Buddhist worldview differs from a middle class Western tendency to believe in wealth and possessions as a measure of personal success. The recognition that most rural Cambodians sought was that of a person who followed Cambodian norms, i.e., a person who was generous of his or her time and resources within the community and to the temple.

> Cambodians obey rules of behavior based not on competition and aggression, but on cooperation and consideration for others.... Cambodians cooperate not because of passivity, but because their adherence to these values ensured the welfare of the family and the community.... Aggressive speech and behavior create not success and social unity, but failure arising out of conflict.[20]

Moreover, she argues,

> The emphasis the Khmer place on emotional fulfillment rather than commitment (to a career) is seen as another reason for their lack of success.... For the Khmer to have commitment one must find emotional fulfillment, financial fulfillment alone does not suffice.[21]

Welaratna introduces the complexity which characterizes the Theravada Buddhist worldview and how nine survivors have interpreted and internalized their worldview within the context of the United States.

The work of Sin and Welaratna provides evidence that Cambodians possess a variety of strategies they claim lead to successful lives. As a way, perhaps, of illustrating the concept of segmented assimilation, Sin identifies three strategies Cambodians frequently take to move ahead in American society. One is the family which stresses cultural norms while adding American norms that appear to ensure success for their children. However, when the pressure of competition becomes too stressful for the adolescent, some parents encourage withdrawal. As Welaratna emphasizes, the goal in life is to maintain a balance between the pressure of getting ahead and the value of achieving emotional fulfillment in life.

SUMMARY

Researchers who are out to compare the rates at which different immigrant groups become self-sufficient in American society are inevitably drawn to use middle class values and characteristics as the baseline for success. Thus, the student who will "make it" on this playing field, must first have parents who are prepared to be proactive on her behalf, both in school and in the wider community, providing supplemental activities and training that prepare her to stand out or compete. The student, in addition to achieving high marks in all academic areas, must also be active outside of the classroom, becoming involved in clubs, sports, service projects, or the arts. Finally, the student must demonstrate that she is popular, sought after as a friend and teammate. This is the standard of success that is implicit in most classrooms in the United States; it is the standard by which immigrant children are measured regardless of whether it is a standard they understand or embrace.

For those who meet or surpass the standards set by the educational environment, the next step on the path to success is to find a career. From then on, as Robert LeVine states, "One's life course is the preparation for the career, pursuit of the career and retirement from the career."[22] It goes without saying that this experience is a solitary, competitive, and frequently stressful one. The individual is measured by the status of the career, her performance rating within her profession, her income level, her promotion rate, and so on.

The foregoing synopsis is a description of an American cultural model—the paradigm that is perpetuated by many white, middle class families, suburban public school systems, the media, and the legacy of our cultural epistemology. For some theorists, this model stands in opposition to the model of cultural deprivation described by Suárez-Orozco (1989),

> [The cultural deprivation] model would suggest that the Mexican American family hinders school achievement by creating asphyxiating "ties" that retard independence and thus achievement. A major weakness of [the cultural deprivation] model is that it seems to utilize certain White, middle class traits as the yardstick for "normalcy," branding as pathological any ethnic departures from this preconceived, arbitrary standard.[23]

The Cambodian youth in both the SARYS study as well as my own do not, as a rule, conform to the middle class model mentioned above. Cambodians remain close to their communities and their families. They prefer a more balanced approach to school and work, opting for happiness and fulfillment over striving and stress. Kiang, Sin, and Welaratna seem to indicate that understanding what it means to be successful to the Khmer requires setting aside conventional standards of measurement and reconstructing the world from their point of view. For the Khmer, maintaining their culture is their most important goal. Along with that is the need to keep their language alive and to be sure their children know about and participate in the Buddhist ceremonies and traditions. The duty of the parents, then, is to teach their children what they need to know to be successful Khmer.

American schooling is an instrumental goal for most of them—it is the key to getting a secure job which can support one's family. The duty of the school, then, is to teach their children English and whatever academic content they need to progress through school. The responsibilities of the parents are no less important than the American teachers. As Pirun, the key informant for my study, has put it, both the teachers and the parents are required to bring the child up to be a "full human being."

NOTES TO CHAPTER 1

1. Bruce Nelan, "Not Quite So Welcome Anymore," *Time* , Fall, 1993, p. 10.

2. Ibid., p. 13.

3. Indicators of economic success predictably include aggregate household income, level of welfare dependency, occupational status (manual to professional), home/car/telephone ownership, salaried or self-employment criteria. Educational success is invariably measured by grade point averages, standardized achievement test scores, English proficiency, post-secondary enrollment, and the degree to which students mirror middle class values for achievement (effort, time on task, competitiveness, independence, and delayed gratification).

4. Henry Trueba, Lilly Cheng, Kenji Ima, *Myth or Reality: Adaptive Strategies of Asian Americans in California*, (Washington, DC: The Falmer Press, 1993) p. 39.

5. Ibid., p. 127.

6. Nathan Caplan, John Whitmore, Marcella Choy, *The Boat People: A Study of Family Life, Hard Work and Cultural Values*, (Ann Arbor, MI: The University of Michigan Press, 1989), p. 178.

7. Rubén Rumbaut and Wayne Cornelius, eds., *California's Immigrant Children: Theory, Research and Implications for Educational Policy*, (San Diego: Center for U.S.-Mexican Studies, University of California, 1995), p. 20.

8. See also Baizerman, Hendricks, Hammond, Neale, Nguyen, "Study of Southeast Asian Refugee Youth in Minneapolis," and Heather Peters, "Study of Southeast Asian Refugee Youth in Philadelphia," United States Government Printing Office, 1987.

9. Ibid., p. 50.

10. The following analysis of Cambodian adults and students is drawn from Rumbaut and Ima, 1988, Rumbaut in Haines, 1989, and Rumbaut in Rumbaut and Cornelius, 1995.

11. Rumbaut and Cornelius, op. cit., p. 35.

12. Peter Nien Chu Kiang, "New Roots and Voices: The Education of Southeast Asian Students at an Urban Public University," Unpublished doctoral dissertation, Harvard Graduate School of Education, 1991, p. 42.

13. Ibid., p. 48.

14. Sin Bo Chum, "Socio-cultural, Psychological, Linguistic Effects on Cambodian Students' Progress Through Formal Schooling in the United States," Unpublished Doctoral dissertation, University of Oregon, 1991, p. 256.

15. Ibid., p. 258.

16. Ibid., p. 250.

17. Marcelo and Carola Suárez-Orozco, "Some Conceptual Considerations in the Interdisciplinary Study of Immigrant Children," in E. Trueba and L. Bartolomé, eds, *Immigrant Voices: In Search of Pedagogical Reform*, (Lanham, MD: Rowman and Littlefield) in press.

18. Ibid., p. 264.

19. Ibid., p. 292.

20. Usha Welaratna, *Beyond the Killing Fields: Voices of Nine Cambodian Survivors in America*, (Stanford, CA: Stanford University Press, 1993), p. 265-266.

21. Ibid., p. 274.

22. Robert LeVine and Merry I. White, *Human Conditions: The Cultural Basis of Educational Development*, (New York and London: Routledge and Kegan Paul, 1986), p. 196.

23. Marcelo Suaréz-Orozco, *Central American Refugees and United States High Schools: A Psychosocial Study of Motivation and Achievement*, (Stanford, CA: Stanford University Press, 1989), p. 31.

CHAPTER 2

Patterns of Culture—Elements of a Worldview

I fear the popular notion of success stands in direct opposition in all points to the real and wholesome success. One adores public opinion, the other private opinion; one fame, the other desert; one feats, the other humility; one lucre, the other love; one monopoly, and the other hospitality of mind.[1]

—*Emerson*

INTRODUCTION

The perspective advanced by Caplan et al., among others, is to focus on the influence of cultural values as more predictive of success. The authors focus specifically on the Southeast Asian family (Vietnamese, Chinese, and Lao) and the "cultural compatibility" between their values toward hard work, education, self-reliance, persistence, and respect and American prerequisites for success.[2] Caplan et al. notice that, regardless of prior educational attainment or socio-economic status, the parents who consistently connect cultural values to the present situation enable their children, often within one generation, to level the playing field between themselves and their American peers. Nonetheless, the authors admit that researchers do not fully understand the synergy between family transmission of cultural models and successful social outcomes.

> [T]he family does more than maintain the culture core; it also connects the cultural values to the living present through the development of strategies to survive, to get ahead, guided by the ethical and practical doctrines embedded in the culture. We can only infer obliquely how these strategies evolve, but we have learned something of the characteristics of the families that function best in using the cultural heritage to make the most of available opportunity.
>
> An educationally competent family depends for its effectiveness on a life-style within the home, premised upon a set of cultural values, the implementation of which allows for a good fit or interface with the available educational opportunity. The same applies for the achievement of economic status. It is the family's ability to translate cultural values into a life-style, not its surface of demographic features, that helps its members to confront adversity and prepares them for future success.[3]

Most of the studies I have read which document and analyze the achievement of Southeast Asian students over time refer to the distinctive differences in cultural epistemology among each group: Cambodians, Laotians, Thai, and Burmese are Buddhists in the *Theravada or Indian tradition*; Vietnamese, Hmong, and Chinese are Buddhists in the *Confucian tradition*. While to the average Westerner these differences may appear moot, the cultural realities which are constructed out of these two philosophical traditions are significant. When combined with history and geography, these differences have an enduring influence on the way individuals understand their world and conform their actions to that world.

In order to set up the following discussion, I shall define my use of the terms *culture, epistemology,* and *cosmology* since they are central to my thesis and I cannot assume that each of my readers understand their conventional definitions, nor the ways in which I am using them.

Culture is broadly used in a cosmopolitan sense to refer to the artifacts of civilization—art, music, literacy and other attributes of high status individuals, and connotes wealth, privilege, and elitism. However, in a religious context, culture may refer to practices that are organized around some construction of a metaphysical universe and a Creator. In this context, culture then provides humans with answers to the profound questions of life: How are we to live? Who are we to marry? What makes meaningful work, play, and relationships? What happens when we die? On some fundamental level the answers to these questions become taken for granted, even though the pragmatic day-to-day behavior may change from generation to generation. Each society devises different symbols, patterns, and rationales for the choices it makes and thus perpetuates a range of potentialities which, depending on the context, are also subject to change. Language is the most enduring symbol of culture and embodies the full range of behaviors and beliefs that characterize a distinct culture.

Oliver (1989) refers to the foregoing as "deep enculturation" and opposes it to "shallow culture." Shallow culture, he states, is the cosmopolitan culture represented by technology and popular taste. It is the culture that is recognizable as affinity, political or lifestyle groups such as "student culture," "corporate culture," "football culture," "rap culture," and so on. This concept of culture has specific practical uses in modern society and provides cultural groups with "strategies" for the problems of adaptation and survival.

> From this perspective the more basic quality of knowing is the practical, the "smart." Rituals and myths are built to make sacred or to 'fix' those smart and adaptive practices that work.... [C]ulture has two rather contradictory jobs to do: 1. to solve external, adaptive problems that demand smart solutions, and 2. to solve internal self-awareness problems [of] properness and goodness.... Behaviors defined as "smart" became "good" when they had "proved" their adaptability, effectiveness and efficiency to the satisfaction of community members.[4]

Epistemology is the study of knowledge and how we come to know what we know. In most constructions, epistemology is synonymous with the nature of truth, thus a "feminist epistemology" defines the nature of women's knowledge—not as some universal index of *a priori* truths, but as knowing that is grounded in the bodily, geographical, historical, and social experiences of particular women.

My own theoretical position on the discussion of epistemology is that some knowledge is universal and verified by certain empirical processes—cuts in the flesh bleed, fire burns, and human infants must be loved in order to flourish. Some knowledge is sensitive to cultural constructions of reality as indicated above. Metaphor frequently calls up this deep epistemology by utilizing language to embed cultural truths in everyday beliefs and behaviors.

Cosmology represents the whole cultural system. It incorporates all the fields of knowledge—scientific, religious, historical, institutional (kinship, community, work, education), and metaphysical. A cosmology is inherently an *emic* construction,

> The cosmologist speaks from the inside showing how beliefs are plausible, how inconsistencies can be resolved. She or he is an artist working on the adequacy, comprehensiveness and coherence of his or her own meaning system. In short, the cosmological point of view is involved in an effort to integrate reflection, a broad historical philosophical perspective, with personal commitment, meaning and prudent action.[5]

Anthropologists see their work as documenting and describing cultures and their cosmological constructions. They note the consistencies and contradictions, frequently in relationship to some other normative cosmological standard. It is the rare anthropologist who is able to set aside her own internalized cosmology and understand what is going on from within another cosmology. Nonetheless, when it comes to answering questions about meanings of success, this is the critical task one must undertake. The following authors provide insights into methods and rationale for understanding "the native's point of view."[6]

There are two important specializations in anthropological research which inform the study of culture. One is in psychology which studies the mental or cognitive *processes* that operate in response to a cultural epistemology. Another is philosophy which studies the symbolic meaning systems and institutions that *represent* the cultural cosmology. Another way of framing the distinction is to ask whether culture is in a person's mind or whether culture is in the external evidence of a person's actions, artifacts, language, and traditions. While these categories frequently overlap, most anthropological research privileges the interpretation of *emic* perspectives on phenomena as expressed and defined by the actors themselves, or the interpretation of *etic* perspectives on phenomena which is gathered by intentional, outside observers.

Historical antecedents of the two approaches in anthropology can be found in the work of Ruth Benedict (1934). Benedict's research was among the first to describe social behavior and beliefs that were in line with a cultural cosmology which was internally coherent, and which provided formulas for what was considered to be normal and, by implication, successful behavior. In Benedict's day the concept was framed in the language of "cultural patterns." Later, cultural psychologists (Holland and Quinn, 1987; D'Andrade, 1987; Strauss, 1992; Shore, 1996; Clarke, 1996; Holloway, 1997) would come up with the concept of cognitive models or schemas which are believed to carry the basic prototypes of ethnic identity. Anthropologists and sociologists (Shweder, 1991; Geertz, 1983; Berger & Luckmann, 1980; Bellah, 1985, 1991; Fernandez, 1991; Durkheim, 1964/1915; Weber, 1958; Oliver, 1989) who take a philosophical approach to culture view the creation of cultural models as an intentional activity carried out by a particular group in response to a complex and formal cosmology. Given that my research is focused on what these Cambodians *say* about the meaning of success and how they act in society, the literature in cultural models is useful in describing how these models are defined and used in constructing theory.

HISTORICAL AND CONTEMPORARY SCHOLARSHIP IN INTERPRETIVE THEORY

In 1934 Ruth Benedict published *Patterns of Culture* which introduced the idea that cultures could be distinguished from one another, not just by outward features of language, dress or living arrangements, but by a coherent system of internalized meanings. The culture, she suggested, intentionally established patterns of behaviors that represented their particular version of reality.

> This mental pattern was not a set of specific traits, but instead
> a perspective of vision which provided for choosing among
> cultural traits amenable to it, modifying clashing traits to
> conform with it, and creating new traits from within according
> to its parameters. This psychological mind-set served as the
> *ideal* for the culture, providing the standard or norm for the
> group around which individual variations inevitably occurred.
> Moreover the pattern allowed to individuals differed from
> culture to culture as the underlying viewpoint of the cultural
> ideal changed.[7]

In writing *Patterns of Culture,* Benedict went to great lengths to
illustrate her theory that culture was simply "personality writ large,"
and described the rewards for individuals who were able to conform to
the "normal" expectations of a society and the stigma for those who,
for whatever reason, could not conform and thus were labeled
"abnormal."

Benedict's marriage of anthropology, humanism, and psychology
was at times a rocky one. Ultimately her observations, while intuitive,
would be discounted by later anthropologists who resisted the impulse
to generalize personality traits such as paranoia to entire cultures.
Nevertheless, researchers did begin to fill out the picture composed by
Benedict of an American society consisting of a *cosmopolitan culture*
that is recognizable as American in virtually any part of the globe, and
a plethora of *local cultures* embedded in ethnic enclaves and exhibiting
traits that are relevant to that group alone.

Richard Shweder is a philosopher and psychological
anthropologist. In his book *Thinking Through Cultures* (1991),
Shweder expands Benedict's work by a much deeper analysis of the
distinctions between cosmopolitan and local cultures. Shweder begins
with the premise that all cultural groups live in intentionally
constructed worlds, each one different from the other. He grapples
with the notion that because each human culture or community is
context specific, and humans can only function rationally within this
context, there is no common, universal authority which can mandate
the proper way to die, design a language, or be successful.

Shweder states that humans cannot define themselves separately
from their own intentional contexts and that what is true in one context

will not be true in another. Cambodian concepts of reality are grounded in the geography, history, and religious context of Cambodia. For instance, while most Cambodians in the U.S. have had to adjust to American practices around death and dying, their beliefs about death and reincarnation and the practices that accompany these ideas follow from their traditional worldview which is based on a blend of Theravada Buddhism and animism.

Shweder challenges the positivist position which asserts that the concept of psychic unity proves that human beings are all products of the same "reality." Shweder states that psychic unity is not what makes us the same; it is what makes us *imaginable* to each other. In other words, local cultures and their constructions of reality have the power to "astonish" us. The "reality" we experience as ours is usually, if not always, different from the "reality" experienced by others. Therefore the only way to understand what is going on in another culture is to practice seeing reality from another's point of view.

Clifford Geertz describes himself as a "meanings and symbols ethnographer."[8] Geertz has written extensively on the need for anthropologists to practice seeing things from the native's point of view. This, according to Geertz, does not require the anthropologist to *become* a native, but rather to describe fully their concept of reality and account for meaningful behavior and expectations within that reality.

> The trick is not to get yourself into some inner correspondence of spirit with your informants. Preferring like the rest of us to call their souls their own, they are not going to be altogether keen about such an effort anyhow. The trick is to figure out what the devil they think they are up to....
> The notions of what persons are may be, from our point of view, sometimes more than a little odd. The Western conception of the person as a bounded, unique, more or less integrated motivational and cognitive universe, a dynamic center of awareness, emotion, judgment and action organized into a distinctive whole, set contrastively against other such wholes and against its social and natural background...is a rather peculiar idea within the context of the world's cultures.[9]

Geertz's point, which supports my own thesis, is that in spite of individual variations within a society, cultures arrive at an understanding of what represents a successful person or a successful life that is internally coherent with the model of success an individual has in her head and the successful behavior that is rewarded in the society. The trick for the researcher is to be vigilant about maintaining a separation between what passes for success in the local culture and what is taken for granted in the cosmopolitan culture. An account which privileges the Cambodian perspective, according to Geertz, must come as close as possible to describing the cultural model of success from within the Cambodian context. For example, if the researcher does not accept the implications of *karma*, then she will not understand that the responsibility of the good son to ensure his parents' rebirth after death is perhaps as important as whether he gets accepted into a high status university.

Another perspective on cultural models can be found in Berger and Luckmann (1980). Berger and Luckmann are sociologists of religion. They argue that most modern societies are pluralistic which to them means that all humans share a cosmopolitan universe in which things like traffic laws and the rules of baseball are taken for granted. Simultaneously, they assert that humans live in partial universes which coexist "in a state of mutual accommodation."[10] The authors refer to these as "symbolic universes." The symbolic universe is composed of a physical place, a history, social institutions and roles, and the operating rules of behavior for each individual. "The symbolic universe also orders different phases of biography.... To be a child, an adolescent, an adult is legitimated as a mode of being in the symbolic universe."[11]

Berger and Luckmann state that a major occasion for making a symbolic universe concrete is when one society is confronted with another society that has a different history and a different set of symbols. While the contact is often beneficial to both, it occasionally results in the insistence that some traits or beliefs of one culture are superior to those of the other culture.

Berger and Luckmann's insight into what happens to a cultural epistemology upon contact is critical. As stated in Chapter 1, refugees are usually torn violently away from their homes, their history, and eventually their language. The response is predictably to become *more explicit* about cultural models that distinguish the refugee culture from the host culture. Simultaneously, there is a readjustment in assessing which routes lead to success and security in the new life. Individuals at every level of the society engage in a process of negotiating between expressive demands to maintain cultural identity and pragmatic strategies for fitting into the new society.

In one example, the Cambodians in Forest City had to adjust the seasonal Buddhist ceremonial calendar to fit into the five-day American workweek in order to allow the majority of working adults to attend. Ceremonies that traditionally would have begun on a Tuesday or Wednesday and last for five days, were confined to a two-day weekend. The result is that Cambodian families, at least in Forest City, attend temple infrequently as opposed to every day. Life cycle ceremonies, particularly for young men, are simplified to the point that they no longer have the time to acquire the religious knowledge that guides them in bringing merit to their families. Annual ceremonies also take on a heightened importance and come to incorporate a constellation of cultural rituals rather than just one. There is a subtle urgency to become even more Cambodian as language disappears and intermarriage dilutes family unity.

Holland and Quinn (1987), D'Andrade (1987), D'Andrade and Strauss (1992), Clarke (1996), and Holloway (1997) discuss cultural models within the literature on culture and cognition. D'Andrade refers to cognitive schemas as "folk models of the mind" which contain common-sense knowledge about the "way things are."

> The folk model of the mind is composed of a variety of mental processes and states, e.g. perceptions, belief/knowledge, feelings/emotions, desires/wishes, intentions, resolution, will or self control...and seems to act as a standard for determining 'normality.'[12]

Like Geertz, D'Andrade asserts that these schemas are rarely explicit because they are so much a product of everyday life. The folk models of the mind are composed of beliefs about the world, as well as explanations for what constitutes an object such as a cat, a tree, or a bicycle. As indicated above, most Cambodians share the concept of *karma*, yet depending on the level of social status or religious education, most people are not able to give a "textbook" description of how it operates. D'Andrade's point which is relevant to this study is that the individual does not need to know explicitly how concepts or objects "work" because, according to the author, they are imprinted in the brain as the shape and substance of this particular reality. Thus, it is possible the Cambodians in my study may never conceive of the solitary millionaire as their role model for success because of a deeply salient cultural model which teaches that excessive wealth is as unfulfilling as excessive poverty.

Holland and Quinn's (1987) definition of cultural models is widely quoted as a way of describing patterns of cultural behavior:

> Cultural models are presupposed, taken for granted models of
> the world that are widely shared by members of a society and
> that play an enormous role in their understanding of that world
> and their behavior in it.[13]

In this theoretical perspective, the authors are more interested in describing the cognitive processes that are revealed through the actions of individuals in the culture. For instance, they state that culturally shared schemas are like tools which are used in appropriate situations and set aside when not needed. One of the teenage daughters in my study exhibits behavior that is appropriate to a "normal" middle class American teenager when attending classes at an exclusive private Catholic girl's high school. However, once she is home her behavior shifts to accommodate the needs of her grandmother, her mother, her sister-in-law, and her three siblings. She is aware both that she uses two different cultural schemas which influence her actions in different contexts and that she is constantly balancing her family's expectations for success with the expectations imposed by the school.

The significance of these theoretical perspectives is the strength they give to the philosophical concept of separate and integrated cultural layers. This research demonstrates that cultural models, even when they contradict a more dominant, cosmopolitan cultural model such as success, are highly resistant to revision.

> [T]acit and unexamined, the models embed a view of "what
> is" and "what it means" that seems wholly natural.

Alternative views are not even recognized let alone considered. These models grant a necessity to how we live our lives.[14]

It is this insight which supports my position and Kiang's challenge that in order to judge the "success" of one group against another, it is critical to understand what being successful means within the context of the cultural epistemology and how individuals within that culture are constructing models of success for themselves. It may be that Cambodian models of success do not align with the measurements of success that are consistent with American models of success. If we return for a moment to the concept of ethnic resilience as it is used by Bo Chum Sin, she found that Cambodian students who maintained cultural values and traditions while accommodating certain cultural values from the new society experienced the highest level of academic success. In view of the foregoing discussion of cultural models, it is likely that ethnic resilience in the Cambodian context is synonymous with an intricate set of cultural schemas which are held in the mind and which govern the laws of their symbolic universe. Without this structure, a Cambodian does not know how to greet a stranger, instruct her daughter, or plan for her future. While some cultural patterns, such as the number of years one should attend school, are subject to radical shifts in a new culture, most Cambodians will select from a predictable and proven treasury of culturally patterned options that the culture defines as successful.

APPLYING INTERPRETIVE THEORY TO RESEARCH ON SOUTHEAST ASIANS

One way of applying this theoretical perspective to Rumbaut and Ima's research would be to analyze the way they interpret Khmer success in school and careers as reflective of cultural beliefs. Part II of Rumbaut and Ima's (1988) longitudinal study on Southeast Asian refugee youth was designed to support the quantitative data in Part I. While their field researchers were native language speakers expected to understand an *emic* perspective, it was the authors who constructed the interview protocols according to questions that emerged from the statistical data. Rumbaut and Ima wanted to find "ethno-cultural clues" that somehow explained the implications of the results for the Vietnamese, Khmer, Lao, and Hmong. The most and least "successful" groups were already defined by their economic and educational achievements, and so the qualitative data was collected with the intention of filling out that story. They concluded that,

> for all their diversity, as refugee youth go about the process of selecting occupational goals, making plans for schooling and careers, "learning the ropes" of the American settings they try to adapt to, and dealing with Americans and with authorities, *they exhibit approaches to problem solving which are patterned and predictable.*[15]

In summarizing the interview data, Rumbaut and Ima characterized each of the four Southeast Asian refugee groups according to a set of psychological orientations which defined each refugee group with a "distinct ethno-cultural adaptive style":

1. *Self vs. Collective Orientation*: Do they take themselves as individuals or their family or other collective as the major reference point in their adaptive strategies? Will they be principally preoccupied with their personal feelings and well being over that of their family, clan, or other collective, or will it be the reverse? What takes precedence in guiding their goals, plans, and actions?

2. *Instrumental vs. Expressive Orientation*: Do they approach their adaptive tasks with an instrumental or an expressive focus? That is, are they mainly concerned with achieving specific goals by performing practical, affectively neutral tasks, or are they more affectively rather than instrumentally concerned with maintaining harmony in social relationships?

3. *Active vs. Passive Orientation*: How do they engage others in the process of adaptation and in the pursuit of self-sufficiency? Will they be active or passive, aggressive and competitive or withdrawn and perhaps even wanting to be "invisible?"

4. *Short-Term vs. Long-Term Orientation*: Are their plans and problem solving strategies geared to short-term or long-term solutions? What is the temporal dimension that is reflected in

their approaches and calculations? Are they carefully calculating their current activities on the basis of long-term future goals, or are they almost solely preoccupied with the immediate requirements of the present, to the exclusion of long-term planning?[16]

In reading these descriptions carefully, one notices the language of "individualism," "achievement," "goal orientation," "self-reliance," "competition" and "long-range planning." As noted in Chapter 1, this language reflects dominant middle class values that some scholars equate with success and status mobility. For instance, Rumbaut and Ima characterize the Vietnamese coping strategies as a "family oriented collective instrumental competitiveness with a long-term orientation to goal setting and planning."[17] They use the following words to characterize the Khmer coping strategies: "passive, unhurried, unambitious style which we call individual expressive withdrawal" with "non-competitive, short-term goals." Given the variation on economic and educational measures reflected in the statistical data, these characterizations would seem to explain the highly successful Vietnamese and the less successful Khmer.

Rumbaut and Ima, working with this template, fill in their picture of Cambodian culture. When asked about occupational goals, the authors state that the Khmer tended to name occupations which were of "lesser status and more likely to entail human services—nursing, clerical assistance, engineering, social services."[18] Using a familiar Cambodian metaphor, the authors describe the strategy of a Khmer informant as taking a "step-by-step," short-term approach to her education which prepares her for a career in social services—possibly as a counselor or a nurse. Rumbaut and Ima observe that each "step" is an end in itself, and a number of interviews revealed that the informants were reluctant to tie themselves to a long-range commitment in the event they chose not to pursue that particular path.

Rumbaut and Ima link this attitude to a Khmer folk theory which states that each person enters this life with a particular destiny and an innate talent that will unfold over time. The patient, step-by-step approach to selecting and preparing for a career is complimented by the profoundly important belief that the goal in this life is to do good deeds in order to earn merit for future lives. In contrast with an American cultural stereotype which links self-interested, goal-oriented ambitious striving to successful outcomes in education or career advancement, the authors describe the Khmer as more motivated to enjoy life with a minimum of stress and competition.

> The Khmer are typically non-aggressive and non-competitive, seeking gratification as an extension of one's natural inclinations in a more relaxed unhurried and leisurely way. We suggested earlier that this may reflect a Buddhist-Karmic religious worldview, as well as parental values and possible overprotective child rearing practices which encourage longer dependency on the mother and which lower the standards and pressures for achievement by the child.... The main concern of these groups is with personal happiness and fulfillment which often...involves doing good deeds and accumulating merit by helping others.... The Khmer approach to achievement—in moderation and at a slow pace—is typically less ambitious.[19]

Withdrawal is a coping strategy which Rumbaut and Ima connect to the Cambodian tendency to walk away from pressure and stressful situations. They observe that the high number of high school dropouts among the Khmer population is likely due to their way of handling problems by withdrawing to the background. This is further complicated by the Khmer belief that each individual is responsible for his or her own actions in this life. This often means that the young Cambodian will try to resolve the situation on his or her own before turning to his or her family for support.

Finally Rumbaut and Ima comment on the Cambodian openness to American culture. Their conclusion is that the lack of a strong ethnocentricity among Khmer informants leaves individuals open to rapid acculturation. Since their analysis asserts that ethnic resilience "is likely to be associated with academic success while 'Americanization' is likely to undermine it," the implication is that the Khmer will achieve neither a strong ethnic identity nor a high status position in the society.

This study provides some evidence that confirms Rumbaut and Ima's conclusions. As the second-generation adolescents begin their college careers, they experience an initial separation from their families and begin interacting with a self-selected cohort of peers most of whom have bought into the belief that a college and post-graduate degree are fundamental to success in American society. These young people also find that academic and social expectations are quite complex, and there are few supports to scaffold them through the process. While the Cambodian community takes great pride in sending its young people to college, they do not stigmatize the person who withdraws to seek another path. The Khmer interpretation of what it means to be successful is drawn from the concept of balance and flexibility and it is this perspective which, I believe, sheds a different light on Rumbaut and Ima's findings.

SUMMARY

In trying to explain why some immigrant groups outperform others in academic achievement and go on to professional careers while some groups do not, scholars have searched for clues in cultural worldviews. The implication is first that the cosmopolitan culture sets the standard for success for all individuals regardless of whether this standard is perceived as either attainable or desirable. Second, that local culture is different from cosmopolitan American culture on some important indicators. Finally, when local cultural models fit with middle class cosmopolitan models around attitudes and behaviors which predictably lead to success in economic or educational terms, then the prediction is that this cultural group is or will be successful in the society.

The concept that ethnic resilience is linked to successful outcomes in school and work presents a paradox for scholars since the evidence indicates that some cultural models do *not* fit with middle class values of success. The literature in cultural model theory offers insights into this paradox by making explicit the enduring potency of local cultural models.

Benedict in the 1930s changed the way anthropologists studied cultures by shifting the focus from a detached and implicitly ethnocentric description of cultural behavior, to a recognition that cultural behavior could be connected to complex and meaningful patterns. Shweder challenged the idea that at some fundamental level all cultures are the same by demonstrating that each cultural context represents a reality which can only be imagined by someone outside that context. Geertz has spent a lifetime observing and attempting to understand the symbols and the meanings that characterize particular cultures from the point of view of the people within the context. Berger and Luckmann return to the distinction between cosmopolitan culture and local culture in describing the process by which symbolic universes are institutionalized and perpetuated. The tendency for local cultures to sustain their singular identities is triggered by the experience of confronting a different cultural reality. Local cultures respond, they assert, by becoming more explicit about cultural beliefs, traits, and behavior in the face of this confrontation. Finally, D'Andrade, Holland et al., and Shore, place the genesis of cultural epistemology and ontology deep in the mind. As a result, they suggest, certain cultural constructions remain resistant to revision even in the face of contradiction and discrimination.

Rumbaut and Ima along with other authors in immigrant studies have been very successful in shattering the global stereotype of the model (Asian) minority. We know that not all Asians graduate *summa cum laude* or move into scientific careers. But a great deal of this analysis continues to perpetuate the hegemonic ideology that stigmatizes some groups for their lack of success in acquiring middle class values and aspirations.

In order to understand what success means to a Cambodian, one must know something about the geography, history, and religion of Cambodia. If success in this context diverges from an American standard, does it nevertheless sustain cultural identity and encourage life choices that are consistent with the Cambodian worldview? If respecting one's family and serving one's community is considered worthy of high praise in Cambodian epistemology, then how do today's adolescents measure up to that criteria? If happiness and fulfillment in life are highly sought as a way to live a balanced life, how would one judge the young person who maintains average grades and a low-stress approach to her schooling?

Notes to Chapter 2

1. Ralph Waldo Emerson, *The Works of Ralph Waldo Emerson: Society and Solitude*, (Boston and New York: Fireside Edition, 1870, 1898), p. 290.

2. Caplan, et al., op. cit., p. 145.

3. Ibid., p. 147-8.

4. Donald W. Oliver and Kathleen Waldron, *Education, Modernity and Fractured Meaning: Toward a Process Theory of Teaching and Learning*, (Albany, NY: State University of New York Press, 1989), p. 40-41.

5. Oliver, op. cit., p. 57.

6. Clifford Geertz, *Local Knowledge: Further Essays in Interpretive Anthropology*, (Basic Books Inc., 1983), p. 55.

7. Margaret Caffrey, Ruth Benedict: *Stranger in This Land*, (Austin, TX: University of Texas Press, 1989), p. 155.

8. Geertz, op. cit., p. 69.

9. Ibid., pp. 58-9.

10. Peter Berger and Thomas Luckmann, *The Social Construction of Reality: A Treatise in the Sociology of Knowledge*, (New York: Irvington Publishers Inc., 1980) p. 115.

11. Ibid., p. 92.

12. Roy D'Andrade, "A Folk Model of the Mind," in D. Holland and N. Quinn, eds., *Cultural Models in Language and Thought*, (Cambridge: Cambridge University Press, 1987), p. 114-5.

13. Dorothy Holland and Naomi Quinn, eds., "Culture and Cognition," in *Cultural Models in Language and Thought*, (Cambridge: Cambridge University Press, 1987) p. 4.

14. Ibid., p. 11.

15. Rubén Rumbaut and Kenji Ima, "The Adaptation of Southeast Asian Refugee Youth: A Comparative Study," Final Report to the Office of Refugee Resettlement, Department of Sociology, San Diego, CA, 1988, p. 106.

16. Ibid., p. 106-107.

17. Ibid., p. 107.

18. Ibid., p. 108.

19. Ibid., p. 112.

CHAPTER 3
Context and History
Cambodian Cosmology

The Khmer have been a majority group throughout history with ties to a long-past position of power, and the heritage of a high civilization. The Khmer have never had to deal with minority status in a different culture. The teachings [of Khmer culture] reveal little about how to avoid conflict and turn aside ill treatment by others who view them as a minority.[1]

—Lan T. Pho

INTRODUCTION

Each family in this study has lived in the United States since 1981, and during this time the older generation has instilled in the younger generations the language, behaviors, attitudes, and beliefs which define them as Khmer. Each family has relatives and friends still living in Cambodia as well as relatives and friends living in different parts of the United States. Two of the families maintain a strong connection with Buddhist institutions and the yearly celebrations, and members of each family are making their way within American schools and workplaces. When considering what it means to be successful, to be a good person, to receive the commendation of "high praise," or to acquire merit, Cambodians refer to cultural models that are full of geographical,

45

historical, and religious significance. Their illustrations are full of metaphor which conjure images of mountains, forests, animals, rivers, rice fields, and pagodas. It is inconceivable for a Cambodian to discuss the ideal person separate from references to religion, family, or community.

Just as native-born Americans are defined by the geography, history, and ideology of the United States, so too are Cambodians the product of their unique context and ideology. In order to place Cambodian cultural models into their proper setting, then, I must begin with a discussion of Cambodian culture and its distinctive relationship to the context in which it developed.

In 1968 May Ebihara completed a detailed ethnographic study of a small village in central Cambodia for her Ph.D. thesis. In 1993, twenty-five years later, Ebihara returned to the same village to try and understand the impact on Cambodian culture since the Khmer Rouge holocaust. Her book *Cambodian Culture Since 1975* (1994) contains essays prepared since the mass genocide and diaspora of nearly three million Cambodian citizens. The authors offer profound insights into the experiences of Cambodian refugees as they attempt to reconstruct their culture, their language, their history, and their religion in exile.

> [The Khmer] are using key symbols and cultural scenarios
> restated as "tradition" to adapt to new situations. The very
> thought that the events of the Democratic Kampuchea years
> constituted the end of a Buddhist era, brings the Khmer to
> reexamine basic cultural concepts. In general, they have a
> heightened awareness of culture. [2]

Ebihara is careful to point out that the Khmer who now reside in California, Massachusetts, Rhode Island, and Indiana are more than simply bicultural people who have transplanted their culture intact into a new setting. Being Khmer, she states, is the product of Khmer individuals and families co-creating their culture within a new community of other Cambodian individuals and families, most of whom were complete strangers prior to the refugee camps and resettlement in the host country. Cambodian identity is no longer simply the history of the village in which generations of one's family have lived and died. Today, the identity of the Cambodian refugee includes being a survivor, a person who fled his or her country, a resident of resettlement camps, and a displaced refugee often in an urban center of a Western (primarily Christian) industrialized nation.

> Khmer Buddhists now coexist as a tiny, relatively powerless minority among Christians. Cambodians may have known that such people (who did not hold the same belief system) existed, but they seldom encountered them, were not surrounded by them, and were not forced to adapt to their ways to survive. [3]

CAMBODIAN GEOGRAPHY AND HISTORY

Today, the country of Cambodia comprises 70,000 square miles. It is bordered in the north and northwest by Laos and Thailand, in the east and southeast by Vietnam. The western edge of the country sits on the Gulf of Siam but is separated from the interior of the country by the Cardamom Mountains.

History, geography, and convention divide Cambodia into a land kingdom and a water kingdom. The land kingdom consists of dense forests made up of evergreen trees at the higher elevations and deciduous trees in the monsoon forest. Even today the forest is home to many species of tropical birds, monkeys, tigers, boar, snakes, and crocodiles. Virtually all the refugees' stories of escape include a narrative about their journey through the forest and mountains, a wilderness landscape that sets a dominant theme in Cambodian myth and proverbs: "In the wilderness were unknown and dangerous spirits that dwelled everywhere in the natural environment and are fundamental to an understanding of the mental universe of the Khmers."[4]

Cambodia's water kingdom includes the Great Lake Tonle Sap in the northwest interior which gives rise to the Tonle Sap river. This river intersects at right angles with the Mekong River which flows out of Laos to the north through Cambodia and southern Vietnam to the Gulf of Siam. Phnom Penh is located at the exact point of intersection of the Mekong and Tonle Sap rivers. From December to April, the climate is hot and dry causing the soil to compact and erode as a result of generations of slash and burn agriculture. Starting in May, the monsoon rains begin which, joined with melting snows from the Himalayas, surge into the Great Lake and down the river. For approximately six months, the surge of water is sufficient to reverse the course of the Tonle Sap river, flooding the entire watershed and increasing the area of the Great Lake from 2,700 square kilometers to 10,000 square kilometers.

This natural phenomenon has influenced the settlement and development of the Khmer culture since the Bronze Age of about 1000 BCE. Most prehistoric Khmer settlements have been found in this fertile watershed area along the two rivers. To this day, the majority of Khmer people are farmers and fishermen. (A small percentage of the Khmer population lives in the mountains and makes their living from forest products and in the mining of precious gems). For the most part, the technological expertise of the Khmer can be seen in the extensive development of their water resources. During the Angkor period (900–1400 CE), the irrigation system supplemented the national highways. Canals tied the kingdom together and carried the traffic of society.[5] The measure of their success in turning the interior of Cambodia into an agricultural paradise is the fact that until the 1970s, Cambodia was able to supply its population with more rice per person than any other country in Southeast Asia.[6]

The language of the Khmer people is part of the Austro-Asiatic family of Northeastern India and Southeast Asia. "Mon and Khmer are spoken by comparatively large and dense populations of agriculturalists …and small minority communities."[7] The vocabulary and grammar have no completed verb tenses, articles, or gender identification. The bureaucratic written language is derived from Sanskrit; the religious written and spoken language is Pali, which was imported by Buddhist monks from India via Sri Lanka. The verbal form of the language has three distinct and unintegrated levels: "words used in speaking to or about royalty, words used in speaking to or about Buddhist monks, and words used in common discourse among ordinary people."[8] Within the last discourse there is a further distinction between formal and common Khmer.

According to Mabbett and Chandler, the first organized political Khmer kingdom was named "Fu-nan" by Chinese travelers and archivists who began traveling to Southeast Asia in the second century BCE. Their records indicate that Fu-nan comprised the current territory of Cambodia as well as southern and central Vietnam. The Chinese and Indian traders related local legends which stated that the Khmers were the descendants of a native princess and an Indian prince whose descendants became the "sons of Kambu, in the country of Kambuja."

In the first century of the Common Era, traders from India began infiltrating Cambodia and setting up trading stations at the mouth of the great Mekong river. They discovered that a well organized and sophisticated civilization already existed in the interior which was prepared to exchange gold and forest products for goods from India and China. Mabbett and Chandler believe that this exchange of goods and ideas over a long period of time, without evidence of military intervention, indicates that the two cultures "were on an equal level and the relationship between South Asia and Southeast Asia was one of convergence not domination."[9]

However, the authors describe a long period of conflict within Cambodia among clan or tribal chiefs whose lifestyles were lavish, displaying a taste for gold, gems, clothing, royal ceremonies, and the esoteric philosophies of Sanskrit religions. During this period the country was divided between the inland northern areas and the southern water areas. According to Chou Ta-Kuan, a Chinese traveler and historian in 550 CE, Jayavarman I, a "feudal king" invaded and ultimately eclipsed the territory of Fu-nan. Upon his death, the kingdom was split into "Land Chen-la and Water Chen-la"

The unification of Cambodia in 801 CE occurred when Jayavarman II reunited the two kingdoms of Chen-la under his rule. Borrowing from elements in the Brahmin ideology, Jayavarman instituted the cult of the *devaraja* which he interpreted as the "god-king." His success is partially explained by the syncretization which occurred between Hindu myth and Cambodian folk lore: "The cult of the *devaraja* had to take place within the universe of Khmer religious thought as a patron saint with protective power like the *nak ta*."[10] One hundred years later, Jayavarman VII was able to transform the concept of the god-king and Hindu ideology into Angkor Wat, an unmatched architectural achievement.

Over a period of fifty years, thousands of laborers built the great capital city of Angkor Thom which was enclosed inside a wall measuring over three kilometers on each side. Angkor Wat, or temple of the gods, was constructed to represent Mt. Meru, the holy mountain of Hindu myth. Hindu icons decorate this massive structure and are stone reflections of the culture that gradually became synonymous with Khmer royalty. The art, literature, music, and dances of Cambodia are in many ways elegant transformations of this great period of Indian civilization. Angkor Wat and its miniature replications throughout the countryside also include Buddhist iconography which was introduced into Cambodia at this time by missionaries from Sri Lanka.

At its height, Angkor Thom was home to over one million people who benefited from the codification of native law into Sanskrit forms, a centralized government, luxuries, and wealth from most of the known world. The king ordered the construction of an extensive irrigation system which turned thirteen million acres into fertile and productive rice fields. Probably the most significant outcome of the building of Angkor Thom and the centralization of the political institutions of the country was the simultaneous synthesis of Hinduism, Buddhism, and the ancestral spirits of the *nak ta*. Ironically, during the demise of the Angkor empire, the Buddhist monks, preaching the Indian variant Theravada Buddhism, found enthusiastic converts among the village people. In complete rejection of the warring, ambitious, and decadent royal classes, the common people "converted en masse to this new faith that offered social tranquility without striving for material gain or power."[11]

The Angkor era lasted only 600 years, and its monumental city eventually was lost. Angkor was rediscovered only in 1850, and then by a French naturalist who found it inconceivable that the simple Cambodian farmers and fishermen he encountered were descended from the architects of Angkor. Nonetheless, the impact on a new generation of Cambodian royalty caused by the resurrection of this ancient monument was to transform Angkor into a deeply significant metaphor which has inspired the Cambodian people and this royal dynasty for over one hundred years. Since its rediscovery, Cambodian kings have anchored their authority in symbols from Angkor.

The Khmer realm was an artifact. It was a constellation of communities sustained by stretches of water; it was contained within a larger community of people who spoke mon-khmer dialects.... The powerful spiritual energies of the great gods made them *one*, and upon these gods depended the careers of a succession of kings.[12]

The modern history of Cambodia begins in 1860 with the dynasty of King Norodom, grandfather of Norodom Sihanouk. After the decline of Angkor, Phnom Penh became the capital of the country. Elizabeth Becker, in her definitive study of the events leading up to, during, and after the Cambodian revolution (1986), describes a Cambodia which was governed by an opportunistic monarch and a population weary of territorial battles with the Vietnamese to the East and South. The French, having successfully set up a colonial government in Vietnam, told Norodom that he could continue to "govern" his country in exchange for "protection" against Cambodia's ancient enemies, the Vietnamese. Within twenty years, the French effectively controlled the political and economic institutions in Cambodia, implementing repressive taxes on rice and other exportable goods.

Most of the population continued in their traditional roles as farmers and minor civil servants. Those Cambodians fortunate enough to be part of the upper middle class were funneled into education. Pampered and isolated from the economic and political life of the city, the Cambodian middle class attended French universities and returned to Phnom Penh to found lycées, teach at the university, and maintain the life of the intellectual. "In the hierarchical world of Phnom Penh, pedigrees, diplomas, and royal patronage were essential for social mobility."[13] In time Phnom Penh acquired a cosmopolitan sophistication where Cambodian artists and scholars selectively added elements of French culture.

The real power as far as the people were concerned resided in the Buddhist monks and the *sangha*. The monks or bonzes were involved in every aspect of family and community life from marriage to instruction of the young to burials of the dead to ceremonies and festivals honoring the ancestors and the life of Buddha. "The bonzes taught the children, raised the orphans, set the moral and social standards of the country.... They filled the pagoda coffers and became the most important source of charity in the country dispensing food and funds to the poorest of peasants."[14] The Buddhist *sangha*, from the village temple to the most venerable leader of the nation, was democratically organized and functioned as an autonomous institution alongside the royal family and Cambodian parliament. It was widely understood that the *sangha* and the monks were responsible for protecting the country's values and culture.

Under the French protectorate, the city of Phnom Penh became racially divided. Believing that Vietnamese and Chinese were superior to Cambodians in industriousness and modernization, the French employed them as bureaucrats and allowed them to hold monopolies in business, trade, and informal banking.

> The French decided that the Vietnamese were the industrious race of the future and the Khmer a lazy, doomed people grown decadent on Buddhism and the rule of their opulent monarchs. The Vietnamese accepted modernity and seemed unfettered by a demanding, all-consuming faith. Taoism seemed an atheist's philosophy compared to what the French saw as the peculiar, otherworldly Buddhism of the Cambodians.[15]

The result was to deepen the ancient hostility between Cambodia and Vietnam, a fact that the internationally minded communist movements in both countries were able to turn to their advantage. Vietnamese communists, allied with and trained by the Maoist Chinese, were engaged in unifying their country under Ho Chi Minh. Khmer communists, who sought independence for Cambodia from the French and from the royal family, turned to the North Vietnamese for training and support. The political situation also spurred the rise of small fascist organizations within the Cambodian military. The rest of the population, suffering under oppressive taxation, "turned ever more enthusiastically to the symbol of the king, the anchor of the nation.... The people worshiped the symbol, not the power running the country, a habit that fed illusions and quashed rebellion."[16]

In 1953 after years of unrest, France transferred its colonial power over to Prince Norodom Sihanouk who declared himself the father of Cambodian independence. The rule of the "god-king" thus passed from father to son as Cambodia entered the future free from all colonial interference. For the next twenty years, Sihanouk ushered in a Cambodian renaissance reminiscent of the Angkor era. He heavily subsidized the symbols of the royal court—the ballet corps, royal musicians, the palace, museum and public antiquities. The Royal Cambodian Dance Company became the symbol of Cambodian culture and national pride.

Sihanouk resisted all attempts to industrialize his country and instead turned his attention to building an infrastructure of roads, railways and a seaport. By the 1960s three fourths of the country's population still lived in villages, but twenty-five percent of the national budget was spent on education and social improvements designed to maintain the traditional Buddhist character of village life.

> The Prince believed that "agricultural pursuits ran highest in production, while commercial and other service activities are looked upon as more or less parasitic...." He discouraged large industrial schemes and foreign commercial ventures that might have attracted Cambodia's villagers to Phnom Penh.[17]

Becker makes an interesting analogy between Southeast Asian countries in the early part of the 1970s and cultures of Europe. She equates the Cambodian temperament with "artistic, Latin culture", slow moving, fun-loving and captive to the mandates of the Buddhist universe and dependent on the solace of magic. The Vietnamese, by contrast resemble the northern temperament—aggressive, competitive, and grimly determined to liberate their country from the domination of their ancient colonizers the Chinese and the French.

In 1970 Sihanouk was ousted by a military coup. Lon Nol, an extreme right-wing fanatic, persuaded the country that Sihanouk, a communist sympathizer, was preparing to deliver Cambodia into the hands of the Vietnamese and the Americans. Lon Nol's government was a disaster for Cambodia, bringing the Vietnamese War within Cambodia's borders and providing a unifying catalyst for Cambodian communists. By 1975 the Cambodian population was seeking liberation from Lon Nol by welcoming the Khmer Rouge led by Solath Sar, a young intellectual whose vision of a new Cambodian society was an extreme version of Maoist revolution and cultural catharsis. Over the next four years, Solath Sar—better known to the world as Pol Pot—crafted a social revolution that was to destroy over 35,000 Buddhist monks and their temples; an entire generation of Cambodian intellectuals, teachers and civil servants; the Cambodian military; and virtually all of the country's artists. Close to three million Cambodians died of starvation, torture, overwork, neglect, disease, and escape attempts before the Vietnamese army "liberated" Cambodia from the Khmer Rouge genocide.

The Cambodian diaspora, which began in late 1978, included a first wave consisting of a small number of middle class, educated citizens who fled to Thailand and were settled in France, Canada, Australia, and the United States. The second and largest wave consisted of villagers from all over the interior who waited for years in Thai resettlement camps until international agencies located sponsors willing to take responsibility for their housing and employment needs. This second wave of refugees came to the United States between 1981 and 1983. Subsequent, smaller waves of refugees from Thailand and Cambodia have occurred to reunite families separated by the holocaust. More recently, a second migration is occurring within the United States as Cambodian families seek smaller communities safe from gangs and violence. They settle in cities where enclaves of Cambodians have established Buddhist institutions and where community networks provide information about or access to entry-level jobs for non-English speaking adults.

CAMBODIAN SOCIETY AND DAILY LIFE

The Cambodian population remained largely insulated from significant modernization until the reconstruction of the country's religious, political, and economic institutions in the mid-1980s. It would be safe to say that the mental universe of the average Cambodian remained fixed in the structure and rituals of village life. May Ebihara's Ph.D. thesis (1986) is a definitive study of village life in a time of relative political stability. A complete analysis of Khmer society and village patterns is beyond the scope of this study; nonetheless, I believe it is important to describe the day-to-day context in which each of the adults featured in my case study would have been raised or spent time.

The dominant form of a Cambodian village is located in the lowlands near a source of water. The primary agricultural economy is rice growing, with most families engaged in some cultivation of vegetable, fruit, and fiber crops. The secondary economy is fishing. Villages might contain from 200 to 1,000 inhabitants and commonly include some form of political authority, roads or railways connecting the village to larger metropolitan areas, and at least one Buddhist temple housing a primary school.

Ebihara reported that most communities had popularly appointed leaders; some commanded great respect depending on the degree to which they served their constituents. Rich people were those who had a number of rice fields, a nice house, good clothes, and gold jewelry. People who were well off had a few rice fields and enough to eat through the year. Poor people were those who had only one rice field and had to purchase food by the end of the year, and poorer than poor people had no land on which to grow food and depended on the community for daily subsistence.

The author points out that wealth and possessions alone did not confer prestige or status on the individual villager; rather, it was good character and personality that the community judged as worthy of great respect.

> The major characteristics of "good character" are generosity
> and selfless concern for others; warmth and good natured
> temperament; abhorrence of fighting, drinking, fornication and
> other sins; devotion to family; industriousness; religious
> devotion; and honesty.[18]

According to Ebihara, most Cambodian villagers choose to live in nuclear family units in their own homes. The preference is to cluster family units together in neolocal arrangements which usually arise as children marry and begin their own families. However, it is common for newly married couples to live with the parents until they can afford their own home, as it is customary for grandparents who can no longer maintain a separate home to move in with one of their children. (Alternately, a widowed grandparent will frequently move into the Buddhist temple and spend their retirement years serving the monks). Cambodian extended families also include relatives and non-relatives as part of the living enclave, and it is common for a child who loses both parents or who does not get along with his or her parents to be "adopted" by other relatives or friends of the family.

Occupations do not distinguish most villagers from one another since virtually everyone is a farmer or fisherman. Some villagers develop a talent for craftsmanship either as a builder or as an artisan. A few villagers study to be healers and function as lay physicians (*kru Khmer*), while a few villagers study Buddhism and function as part-time lay monks (*achaa*). Both of these avocations command great respect and prestige within the community.

The Buddhist temple is the moral and social center of the community. "The temple and its monks not only exemplify and disseminate the Buddhist teachings, but also offer various opportunities for laymen to earn merit."[19] The Buddhist festivals throughout the year are the motivation for social gatherings and a source of entertainment. The festivals occur in accordance with the agricultural calendar and to celebrate significant events in the life of Buddha. Attendance provides a place for young people to interact, an opportunity for villagers to accrue merit for their next life, and an important break from daily work. The New Year festival in the spring can run as long as a week which is followed in importance by the Ancestor's festival in the fall.

THE ROLE OF EDUCATION IN CAMBODIAN LIFE

Prince Sihanouk regarded education as his highest priority, and by 1970 more than three quarters of eligible young people were students. "The enrollment in high schools went from 5,000 to 118,000 and the number of teachers increased from 7,000 to 28,000."[20] During the French protectorate, the French language was introduced, but the basic curriculum, which included reading, writing, mathematics, and the study of Buddhist philosophy, was not altered. Education was (and is) highly valued among Cambodians, as is the profession of teaching. Buddha is considered to be the greatest teacher and thus serves as a prestigious role model for this profession.

According to Pirun, the key informant of this study, public elementary schools in the villages are day schools and go from grades one to six, with children starting school when they turn seven. In farming communities, most boys and girls attend these schools for three years, but in cities, boys and girls might be schooled for six years. The American idea of "social promotion," i.e., passing children from grade to grade with their age group regardless of whether they have mastered the curriculum, is completely foreign to Cambodian education. A student could stay one, two, even three years in each of the elementary grades, especially in the provinces. Thus should a student actually reach grade six, it would not be uncommon that she or he be older than thirteen and have quite a bit of schooling. In order to attend high school, students must pass a national examination. The children of the elite in Phnom Penh were often sent to private schools and universities in France and Canada, where they trained to be teachers and, to a much lesser extent, engineers or bureaucrats.

In contrast with *public* schools which are day schools and comprise grades one to six, *temple* schools comprise grades three to six and students live full-time at the temple. Theoretically only boys may enroll as full-time students, but some Khmer have told me that girls could attend classes but not live at the temple.

The courses in the temple schools include Pali language, Buddhist rules and doctrine, government, and academic subjects. The student must pass two subjects in order to advance. At the end of six years, temple school students can take the exam to enter high school just like public school students. At the end of high school in the temple school as well as the public school, another set of exams determines who can enter the university. An entering university student is usually age nineteen or twenty.

Sihanouk's emphasis on schooling during the 1960s transformed the status mobility system. Access to education meant access to non-farming occupations, and families who could spare their sons sought to give them this opportunity. Prior to 1975, only people with high school degrees and above could apply for security positions with the government. These were highly coveted jobs because an individual could hold the job for life. The office holder received a salary which had incremental levels depending on marital status and the number of children, and the individual received the salary regardless of whether or not there was work. This provided Cambodians with a great deal of incentive to complete high school. Nevertheless, the tradition held that once an individual had reached the age of 18 to 20, the first stage of life was ended.

SUMMARY

The foregoing description of Cambodia and Cambodian history reveals the shape and substance of a cultural epistemology that continues to be salient in the language and metaphor of Cambodian refugees today. Cambodian language is structured in three levels of status – royalty, religious, and common. These levels carry the historical concept of the *devaraja* or god-king which is syncretized with the folk spirit of the *nak ta*. The god-king protects his people from enemies both physical and metaphysical. The god-king is also a direct link to the mysterious and glorious Angkor era, evidence that the Khmer civilization was once superior to any in Southeast Asia.

The language of Buddhism is the symbolic or religious language. Infants learn it while their families attend weekly events at the temple. The religious teaching is inculcated in abundant stories about the life of Siddhartha Gotama and his various reincarnations. The language establishes the value structures of the culture and internalizes these concepts as an unchallenged natural order.

The folk-tales which are used extensively as an educational curriculum from primary school through high school are based on concepts drawn from the Cambodian context—wilderness, mountains, beasts, farming, fishing, and water. The stories reflect elements of Cambodian character such as cleverness, generosity, quick thinking, honesty, and even opportunism that are valued and respected. They are also used to explain mysterious or tragic events in daily life.

The history which is embedded in Cambodian cosmology defines a divided society existing in parallel universes, not unlike a European feudal society. The Khmer royalty have for centuries ruled over a large, agricultural peasant class. In contrast with the ambitious power struggles of the elite, the peasants conformed to a religion that emphasized harmony and moderation. In the best of feudal traditions, the royal family resisted external demands to industrialize the country, preferring instead to keep their "children" protected from the stresses of modern life.

For nearly 100 years, Norodom's descendants defined the Cambodian identity as intellectual, artistic, and agricultural. For most Cambodians seeking a better life, the highest status was as a university professor, a royal dancer, a monk, or an owner of rice fields. By contrast, it was the colonial powers—the French, Vietnamese,

Americans and Chinese—who were perceived as parasites and barbarians, aggressive, war-like, ambitious, and modern. They were condemned even as they were feared, and only a portion of the Cambodian middle class sought to emulate their culture. (A tragic irony is that the ambitious, the over-educated, and members of the military did not survive the Khmer Rouge revolution. During the four years of Khmer Rouge domination, it was better to be a poor, simple villager.)

Village life in Cambodia through the 1980s was an enduring reflection primarily of Buddhist epistemology. Wealth was defined by the number of rice fields one owned and the amount of food a family had. High status and respect accrued to those with good character, which included qualities of generosity, selfless concern for others, devotion to family, and devotion to religion. The Buddhist temple was the center of village life for all ages and represented the social and religious universe.

Education, while highly valued by the national government, was primarily for males, and the curriculum included academic subjects along with religious doctrine. A person's path through life proceeded through definite stages, one ending before the other began, so education was primarily for the young. The productive years were spent raising a virtuous family and securing sufficient affluence so that the retirement years would allow the individual to accrue merit for the next life.

As Ebihara suggests, the cosmology that has always defined Cambodian culture has undergone transformation in the diaspora. In the United States, Cambodian families must send all of their children to school regardless of whether they are needed to supplement the family income. Whereas in Cambodia a high school diploma assured access to a good civil service job, in America, one must acquire a college diploma to be eligible for a good job. Many Cambodian women, inspired by American feminist ideology, have taken action to divorce abusive or alcoholic husbands. Mothers and daughters face an enormous cultural gap. Traditionally the daughter's reputation in the community reflects on the good character of the family, and in particular the mother. In America, the Khmer daughter wants the freedom to progress through school, to date, to plan on a career, and marry whom she chooses. Nevertheless, and as this study bears out, most Cambodian enclaves in the U.S. have managed to reestablish a variant of the village complete with religious institutions and social sanctions for everything from divorce to dating.

NOTES TO CHAPTER 3

1. Lan T. Pho, "Educational Background of Khmer Refugees," in Mory Ouk, Franklin Huffman, and Judy Lewis, *Handbook for Teaching Khmer-Speaking Students*, (Folsom,CA: Folsom Cordova Unified School District and Southeast Asia Community Resource Center, nd), p. 1.

2. May Ebihara, Carol Mortland, Judy Ledgerwood, eds., *Cambodian Culture Since 1975: Homeland and Exile*, (Ithaca and London: Cornell University Press, 1994), p. 7.

3. Carol Mortland, "Khmer Buddhists in the United States: Ultimate Questions," in Ebihara, et al., p. 88.

4. Ian Mabbett and David Chandler, *The Khmers*, (Cambridge, MA: Blackwell Publishers, 1995) p. 26.

5. Elizabeth Becker, *When the War Was Over: The Voices of Cambodia's Revolution and Its People*, (New York: Simon and Schuster, Inc., 1986), p. 48.

6. Mabbett and Chandler, op. cit., p. 37.

7. Ibid., p. 4.

8. May Ebihara, "Svay: A Khmer Village in Cambodia," Unpublished doctoral dissertation in Anthropology, Columbia University, 1968, p. 197.

9. Mabbett and Chandler, op. cit., p. 64.

10. Ibid., p. 90.

11. Becker, op. cit., p. 57.

12. Mabbett and Chandler, op. cit., p. 93.

13. Becker, op. cit., p. 107.

14. Ibid., p. 57.

15. Ibid., p. 52.

16. Ibid., p. 53.

17. Ibid., p. 24.

18. Ebihara (1968), op. cit., p. 197.

19. Ibid., p. 382.

20. Becker, op. cit., p. 24.

CHAPTER 4

Religion as a Social System
Cambodian Cosmology

The Buddhist religion and the Cambodian society—the two wheels don't spin in the same direction.

—Pirun

INTRODUCTION

The previous description of Cambodian history and society is meant to give the reader an understanding of the *contextual* elements of Cambodian cosmology. But Cambodians also live with an equally potent *spiritual* cosmology which combines centuries-old beliefs in folk wisdom and magic with the simple message of Buddhism. In this aspect of their worldview, the truly moral person is one who abandons the pleasures of the ego and lives a life balanced between wisdom and compassion. The successful person is the individual who rules herself or himself instead of others:

> To rule the universe you must first rule yourself. To rule yourself, you must be able to rule your own mind.... The world is created by the mind. If we can control feelings, then

we can control the mind. If we can control the mind, then we
can rule the world.[1]

This chapter is a discussion of Cambodian cosmology and the ways in
which the religious systems of folk religion and Buddhism are
connected to contemporary concepts of being successful.

RELIGION AS COSMOLOGY

For most Cambodians the folk religion is the oldest and most powerful
representation of the Khmer sacred universe. Religion explains things
and for the average Cambodian, the mysteries of the dark and
dangerous forest, the capricious weather, sudden illness or death can be
explained by the behavior of a pantheon of natural spirits. Every
village and every family believe in the local spirits of the *nak ta*
(ancestral spirits of the neighborhood), the *smauit* (ghosts of several
kinds), the *meba* (ancestral spirits of the family), and the *cmnieng ptea*
(house spirits).[2]

Every family also knows the rituals of propitiation which comprise
the laws of common sense and function as personal insurance policies.
For instance, some Khmer believe that illness is caused by rain falling
on one's skin. If this should happen, the victim is immediately
subjected to abrasion with a copper coin which draws the illness from
the body and heals the spirit. Daily rituals which honor and appease
one's ancestors are also commonplace in that they guarantee the
harmonious functioning of family life.

The intriguing part about the sacred Cambodian universe is its
ability to provide psychic insurance on many different levels. The folk
religion plays an important and functional role in village and family
life—it does not have to answer the great metaphysical questions about
being and non-being. On another level, however, the Cambodian elite
appropriated the sacred cosmology of India, and these gods assured the
success of the country's rulers. When Theravada Buddhism arrived in
the 13th century, its philosophical structure merged with the sacred
universe of both classes. Ultimately, Hinduism, Buddhism, and the
indigenous folk religion evolved into a national religion that became
identified forever as Cambodian culture, as Mabbett and Chandler
describe using a long quotation from Thierry:

No gulf was fixed between powerful local spirits and abstract Hindu-Buddhist images. One took over where the other left off.... "the syncretism is powerful, being deeply embedded in the conduct of ceremony; it is also flexible and diffuse, leading to local variations and diverse interpretations. The Cambodian is not bothered by the contradictions: he knows, if he has acquired some Buddhist ideas, that the individual soul has no existence, but he knows also that he has nineteen souls, nineteen 'vital spirits' which make up his individuality and if one or another of them is lost, he will fall ill. His various beliefs making up his spiritual and religious culture are all on an equal footing."[3]

Today, Cambodians consider their culture as well as themselves to be Buddhist. Buddhism is the national religion, and the Buddhist theocracy is responsible for the maintenance of Cambodian culture and moral values. However, the Buddhism which substitutes for a social system in Cambodia, is *distinct to only five nations in Southeast Asia.*

For most Westerners, Buddhism denotes a single religion whose followers are predominantly Asian. Buddhism was founded by an historical individual: Prince Siddhartha Gotama, who lived in Northern India between the sixth and fifth century BCE. After gaining enlightenment, the Buddha remained on earth to teach his followers the process by which they, too, could achieve spiritual transformation. He did not believe in a god, nor the existence of a soul; his central message preached a middle way. Buddha warned against the extremes of self-indulgence and pleasure as well as the extremes of ascetic discipline.

Today there are three great traditions of Buddhism which are distinct geographically, historically, and philosophically. Eastern or *Mahayana Buddhism* is practiced in China, Japan, Korea, and Vietnam. Some scholars estimate that Mahayana Buddhism has a following on the order of 1.2 billion. Northern or *Tibetan Buddhism* is predominant in Tibet, Mongolia, and the Himalayas with approximately 10 million adherents. The tradition with which this study is most concerned is Southern or *Theravada Buddhism.* It has about 100 million adherents, most of whom live in the five countries of Southeast Asia: Sri Lanka, Burma, Cambodia, Laos, and Thailand.[4]

Melford Spiro's study of Theravada Buddhism (1970, 1982) explains that the tradition of Theravada diverges from the other Buddhist traditions in significant ways. Originally meant for an elite group of highly educated men, Theravada became the Way of The Elders. The monks who chose to follow this path were committed to a spiritual discipline that would ultimately release them from the cycle of rebirths (*samsara*) into a state of non-existence or *nirvana*. One's salvation from *samsara* depends entirely on the individual—there is no God, nor are there saints or angels who will intervene on the individual's behalf.

Spiro's field research since 1961 has been in Burma. His book contains an interpretation of Theravada eschatology blended with his observations of the ways in which Burmese men and women utilize and adapt those elements of Buddhist epistemology that fill their needs in a modern society. He points out that the esoteric strand of Theravada Buddhism requires that in order for the individual to gain salvation, he must eliminate all desire for sensate pleasure. This state of non-feeling or non-desire produces non-suffering which is also referred to as *nirvana*. However in this state, the soul or the ego no longer exists.

Spiro claims that contemporary Burmese (along with other Theravada Buddhists) do not find this doctrine particularly functional and have altered the soteriology in favor of a more pragmatic Buddhism which is built on the laws of *karma* and *samsara*. In this tradition, the state of *nirvana* is the equivalent of Buddhist heaven where the enlightened ego or *deva* exists in a place of sensate happiness, comfort, and luxury. True suffering by contrast is represented by eight Buddhist hells, each of which is 80,000 years in duration and which one must endure each in its turn.[5]

> To be rich, to enjoy good food, to attend a festival, these are *thoukka* (pleasure) not *dukka* (suffering). If the life of a rich man or of a *deva* entails suffering then there are degrees of suffering. The rich suffer less than the poor.... Some forms [of life] involve so much pleasure as to render the suffering insignificant.[6]

The experience of the Burmese is quite comparable to that of Theravada Buddhists from Cambodia. For most Khmer, as with the Burmese, the objective is not to seek a state of non-existence, but to acquire the best rebirth possible. In order to do that, she or he must remain on the great wheel of birth and rebirth in which the progress toward heaven or hell is determined by an individual's actions in the world. The accumulation of good actions or bad actions is called *karma*, and it is *karma* that determines the quality of the next life.

> The moral universe is governed by the law of *karma*. Every volitional act (*karma*) if instigated by desire produces an appropriate consequence, desirable or undesirable for the actor. There are two types of volitional acts: the morally good and the morally bad.... If the act is morally good it produces merit for the actor; if morally bad, it produces demerit for him/her.... In either case these *karmic* consequences cannot work themselves out within the compass of one life, they must be worked out in successive lives and in cases of exceptionally meritorious or demeritorious action, it may require many lives before 'the fruit of action is ripened.' In short so long as action bears fruit there will be rebirth and since desire is the cause of fruit-bearing action, it is the cause of rebirth.[7]

In this pragmatic interpretation of Buddhism, the individual has no idea whether she has accumulated an abundance of good *karma* in past lives or bad. If in this present life she is happy, her family is secure and prospering, and she has enough resources to share with others, she can surmise that she entered this life with good deeds to her credit. The individual is, thus, motivated to add to her store of *karma* by first living according to the Buddhist precepts of loving-kindness.

The second means by which she can transform her *karma* is to acquire merit. Merit is acquired by actions that the individual undertakes without expecting present rewards, and these actions include morality, giving, and meditation.

> Every action is viewed from the standpoint of its merit potential. No opportunity for acquiring merit is rejected. The

unpleasantness of an act may be redeemed by discovering
some merit potential inherent in it.... Merit obtained from
giving and morality leads to a better *samsaric* existence;
morality leads to a long life; giving leads to wealth or
devahood.[8]

Giving is still the most common and most significant means for
acquiring merit. The primary reason is that giving in the form of time,
wealth, resources, or possessions can be *measured*, and the greater the
amount of the gift, the greater the quantity of merit. The ramifications
of this practice, Spiro points out, are that many Burmese turn giving
into a mechanical, self-interested act which, theoretically, does *not*
transfer merit to the giver. The monks continually instruct the people
in the punishments for those who are "tightfisted as well as those who
give with conditions, and the rewards for those who give
openhanded."[9] On the other hand, the act of giving, in itself, has
something of a sacrificial quality where the more you give, the more
you sacrifice. For those who are very wealthy as for those who are
very poor, the generosity of the gift implies a reduction in one's
comfort.

> To give to others is to give up something of one's own; the
> more one gives, the more one gives up.... The inordinate
> amount of wealth that is offered represents an important,
> sometimes extreme diminution in present comforts and
> pleasures. It is the act of self-deprivation that is the most
> conducive to the acquisition of merit.[10]

While the transformation of one's *karma* is considered a primary
motivation for actions that confer merit, a secondary motivation is the
honor and prestige that attaches to the individual who acts in this way.
One of the most prestigious actions that a young man can perform for
himself, but even more important for his parents, is to apprentice
himself to a temple for a period of time. Traditionally, all young
Cambodian men would spend from one to three years as a novice
monk. Today, the novitiate may last from one to three months.
Nonetheless, this action confers extraordinary merit upon the family,
particularly if they participate willingly in his decision.

> The Buddhist initiation ceremony by which a young boy is
> inducted into the Buddhist novitiate is the most important
> event in the boy's life. It is almost the necessary qualification
> for his becoming a truly human being.[11]

As mentioned above, the violent revolution and equally violent displacement of millions of Cambodians has had an impact on the ways in which many Khmer now interpret the laws of *karma* and *samsara*. Carol Mortland in her essay on Khmer Buddhists in the United states (1995), finds that many, if not all, Cambodian refugees have come to question Buddhist epistemology as it relates to their lives. For example, some Khmer have challenged the concept of *karma*. "*Karmic* law dictates that good action results in good *bon* or merit…the acquisition of merit yields success—ability, money, good fortune—in other words, conditions and possessions that decrease suffering and increase contentment."[12] Clearly, for some, the laws of *karma* do not explain the stupefying number of people who were methodically killed and starved by the Khmer Rouge implying that *all* of them must have been victims of bad actions in past lives.

Another aspect of *karma* implies that the acts of a single person can bring suffering and dishonor to the entire family, which in turns brings suffering to the village, the region, and ultimately the nation. "The high can bring suffering to the low, but the low can bring suffering to the high through acts of disrespect, betrayal or deception."[13] Many Khmer have come to question the logic that the excesses of the Khmer Rouge were the result of the bad karma of *an entire nation*.

Other Khmer explain the fact of the Pol Pot years and their subsequent exile to Western nations by reviewing the ancient Buddhist prophecies that Khmer have followed since the days of Angkor Wat. The prophecies are translations of Pali scriptures (ancient Indian Sanskrit) and have long predicted supernatural signs of catastrophe that include the downfall of Buddhism, the destruction of Cambodian culture, the symbols of doom in Khmer cosmology, and the prophecy that the salvation of the Khmer people will come from the West when peace reigns and a new era begins.[14]

Mortland concludes by observing that for Cambodians, questioning the law of *karma* is equivalent to calling into question the epistemological core of their beliefs. She does not believe that the Khmer, as a whole, have rejected this part of their faith and refers to Clifford Geertz's insights that "people who undergo a progressive increase in doubt, question their belief... its strength, its hold on them—*not its validity*. The question shifts for individuals from *what* shall I believe to *how* shall I believe what I believe."[15]

It is possible that some Cambodians in Forest City no longer believe in *karma* or reincarnation. Yet among the eighteen people I interviewed and with whom I spent time, the values they espoused, the rationales they offered for their actions, and their personal aspirations all were consistent with a Theravada Buddhist worldview and a cultural epistemology rooted in Cambodian village society. While the women in particular struggle against what they perceive as old-fashioned traditions that severely restrict their freedom, men and women both describe Buddhism as the most important Cambodian tradition.

From my perspective, the experience of liminality—living in between two different realities—is the greatest test of a cultural epistemology. In order to remain viable, a cosmology must be able to reconcile the paradoxes that exist in daily life as well as explain phenomena that occur in times of crisis. Coherence may be less important than whether or not an individual's explanations to her children or her peers still make common sense.

SUMMARY

No doubt it is apparent to many readers that Cambodian values as expressed in Buddhist philosophy are compatible with some of the more expressive American norms. The idea that the individual is responsible for her own actions and that the consequences of one's actions determine one's future life path is a familiar tenet of Puritan ideology. Max Weber (1904/1958) in his discussion of capitalism and the protestant ethic reminds us that the Puritan covenant with God required each individual to live by a similar maxim: "[T]he man of the Reformation was forced to follow his path alone to meet a destiny which had been decreed for him from eternity."[16]

Most Cambodians accept the concept of *karma* which is the accumulation of one's actions—good and bad over many lifetimes. Thus, the most direct way to build up good *karma* is through generosity and compassion to others. The individual who acquires a fine education which leads to a lucrative career may be thought to have good *karma*, but if he does not spend time giving back to his family, friends, and community, he is assured that his next life will be one of ignorance and poverty. As MP, one of the adolescent participants in this study, says,

> I believe in reincarnation. I believe that if you do good, then
> this is what is guaranteed, not given, but this is what you will
> be able to get. But it is what you do with it that kind of brings
> about what your next life is going to be. Say in this life, all of
> a sudden I am hit with at $20 million lottery. That was
> probably because of my last life, but what I do with this
> money will determine what is going to happen in my next life.

Though some Buddhist precepts square nicely with American norms, others do not. In contrast with the Khmer philosophy of living in the present moment—to avoid the pressure of modern life by "eating time," the Puritan ideology influenced a cultural model that has become a distinctive part of the American character:

> [It] is not leisure and enjoyment but activity which serves to
> increase the glory of God according to the divine
> manifestations of his will – Waste of time is thus the first and
> in principle, the deadliest of sins…loss of time through
> sociability, idle talk, luxury, more sleep than necessary for
> health is worthy of absolute moral condemnation.[17]

Ideas of competition, striving, achieving, aspiring are all common American cultural models. Andrew Carnegie was one of America's wealthiest and most powerful men at the turn of the century. His views on competition are taken for granted as characterizing an American model of success.

> The law of competition may be hard for the individual, but it
> is best for the race because it insures the survival of the fittest
> in every department…. Individualism, private property, the
> law of accumulation of wealth, the law of competition are the

highest results of human experience, the soil in which society, so far, has produced the best fruits.[18]

Competition and effort exist for Cambodians as well, but as Buddha points out, the successful individual only competes against herself. As Srey, another of my adolescent informants, says in her college essay,

> I set high goals for myself and each year I assume I will reach new goals. I compete against myself. I do not like to compete with others because everyone is different. When I compare myself with others, it leads me nowhere, and I lose self-confidence and self-esteem. The best way to learn is from my own mistakes and I try to grow from them.

Prior to 1975, Cambodian society was non-industrial. The Cambodian royalty supported the development of scholars, artists, and philosophers instead of industries and modern technology. The Buddhist theocracy preached a life of balance and emotional fulfillment. Today, Pirun comments on a central Cambodian belief that when a path becomes too difficult or too stressful, it must be the wrong path. The successful person is one who finds the path ahead to be smooth and free from struggle.

In Cambodian culture, the second stage of life is centered on the family. While Cambodians prize highly the right to be free and self-reliant, there is no freedom from one's responsibility to care for the family and to help every family member succeed. One of the households in my study is headed by Rath, and Kusal is her oldest son. As he has gotten older, he has begun to voluntarily limit his freedom in order to help his family get ahead.

> I got to help the family out 'cause we have no older person in the family or my dad or my mom [a] husband or boyfriend. Most of the time I help out a lot, just like the old fashioned way, like the oldest help out in the family.

Even though Americans have a deep expressive attachment to the idea of family, the pursuit of one's self interest is a far more potent cultural norm, something de Tocqueville observed here as early as the 18th century:

> It is strange to see with what feverish ardour the Americans pursue their own welfare and to watch the vague dred that constantly torments them lest they should not have chosen the shortest path which may lead to it. A native of the U.S. clings to this world's goods as if he were certain never to die and he is so hasty in grasping at all within his reach that one would suppose he was constantly afraid of not living long enough to enjoy them.[19]

I seek to describe and understand what being successful means to the eighteen members of these Cambodian families. In order to accomplish this task, I have had first to understand the cosmology and epistemology that transcends their daily words and actions. There is no other way to gauge whether the members of Pirun's, Rath's or Chinda's families are successful Cambodians and Americans without learning more about how they perceive these two cultural realities.

The words of my informants reveal the patterns of Cambodian culture. Some words call forth the signs and symbols of ancient folk traditions found in dreams. Other words refer to the ever-evolving wheel of life and death which spins out one's *karmic* destiny from one life to the next. What seems to be consistent among all these accounts, regardless of generation, is the belief that success is possible if one can manage to live a life balanced between the two cultures.

NOTES TO CHAPTER 4

1. Maha Ghosananda, *Step by Step*, (Berkeley, CA: Parallax Press, 1992), pp. 30 & 41.

2. Ebihara (1968), op. cit., p. 428.

3. Mabbett and Chandler, op. cit. (footnote), p. 114.

4. John R. Hinnells, *A Handbook of Living Religions*, (London: Penguin Books, 1984), p. 279.

5. Melford E. Spiro, *Buddhism and Society: A Great Tradition and Its Burmese Vicissitudes*, second ed. (Berkeley, Los Angeles and London: University of California Press, 1970/1982), p. 121.

6. Ibid., p. 74.

7. Ibid., pp. 41-43.

8. Ibid., pp. 111 and 98

9. Ibid., p. 104.

10. Ibid., p. 107.

11. Ibid., p. 105.

12. Mortland, op. cit., p. 79.

13. Ibid., p. 81.

14. Ibid., p. 82.

15. Ibid. (Geertz), p. 86.

16. Max Weber, *The Protestant Ethic and the Spirit of Capitalism*, translated by Talcott Parsons, (New York: Charles Scribner's Sons, 1958), p. 104.

17. Ibid., p. 157.

18. Andrew Carnegie, "The Gospel of Wealth" qtd. in W. H. Werkmeister, *A History of Philosophical Ideas in America*, (New York: The Ronald Press Company, 1949), p. 248.

19. Michael McGiffert, ed. *The Character of Americans: A Book of Readings*, (Homewood, Ill: The Dorsey Press, 1970), p. 67.

CHAPTER 5

Research Design and Methods of Data Analysis

The questions you ask bring ideas to myself. [They] help me know what I want to do in life and give me a better understanding and clear view in my mind.

—*Srey*

FIELD STUDY I AND II

This book is the final product of nearly ten years of research in one community; it is preceded by two field studies. The first field study was conducted from 1992 to 1994 and was initiated and funded by the Pluralism Project, founded by Dr. Diana Eck, Chairperson of Harvard's Committee on the Study of Religion. The research included both a descriptive survey of the religious landscape of Forest City and a more detailed study of the Cambodian Buddhist community.

A primary purpose of the second field study was to describe and analyze cultural meanings of success and schooling for Cambodian refugees in Forest City. A rationale for this research came from observing that Cambodians in Forest City as well as nationally were not achieving at the same levels as their Vietnamese peers. Consequently teachers were beginning to lower their academic expectations for students even though they admitted to liking the students personally. The idea for the yearlong pilot study was an attempt to identify Khmer approaches to success both in traditional Cambodian culture and now as Americans with the adults of seven families in both public and private settings.[1]

RESEARCH DESIGN

The pilot studies uncovered concepts of success from the perspective of the parents, but it did not describe how their children conceptualized success, nor how the children interpreted and responded to their parents' expectations for them. It seemed appropriate to extend the research to include not only the parents from three families, but their teenage children and the grandparents when they were an ongoing presence in the life of the family.

As a result, the research questions for this study emerged as follows:

1. What does being successful mean to Cambodian refugee parents and children in this group?

2. In what ways do these parents connect their perceptions of success to cultural models represented by Theravada Buddhist beliefs, Cambodian institutions, and/or American institutions?

3. In what ways do these children connect their perceptions of success to cultural models represented by their parents, Theravada Buddhist beliefs, and/or American institutions?

The primary tool I used to describe and analyze the ways in which these three families approach these questions is the case study (Becker, 1990; Erickson, 1995; Stake, 1995; Wolcott, 1994; Miles and Huberman, 1994). The case study is a powerful qualitative technique which requires the researcher to document the multiple realities of the different and even disconfirming views of what is going on and what that means to the participants.[2] The result is a detailed study which provides context along with interpretation that, in this case, fills out the existing research on Cambodian social and academic mobility. The interpretive objective of the case study is toward particularity, not universal generalizability and thus the case highlights patterns that distinguish Cambodians within the "family" of ethnic groups labeled Southeast Asians or Asians.

The Sample

I selected the families for the three case studies according to the following criteria:

1. The families were a part of the pilot study and were willing to participate in at least two structured interviews, numerous semi-structured interviews, and review an individual profile constructed for each of them from interview transcripts. The members of each family had to be willing to interact with me through the period of data gathering and analysis for up to three years.

2. The parents must have resided in the United States for more than 10 years. First of all I wanted to interview and observe children who were born in Cambodia as well as the United States. Families from the first wave (1978-1981) had had more time to learn English and thus were more likely to be bilingual; they also had had more time to experience and adapt to American culture. I predicted that the individuals born in Cambodian and individuals born in America might have different explanations for what it meant to be successful.

3. The families could be either dual-parent or single-parent. Approximately one of every four adult Cambodian females is a widow, and in a sample of Cambodian students approximately half live in single-parent households (Rumbaut and Ima, 1988). Census records for Forest City suggest that slightly more Asian families are in dual-parent families, but there is a high percentage of households that are headed by single mothers with children under the age of 18. My key informant confirmed that the majority of the families in Forest City consist of widowed or divorced women with children.

4. The families would include three generations living together or nearby. As in criteria #2, I predicted that the three generations might have different explanations for what it

meant to be successful and I wanted to observe how these family models were being passed down.

5. Parents and children must be bilingual. Regrettably I do not speak Khmer, so it was necessary to work with families who were primarily bilingual or who had a number of family members willing to translate the meaning of my questions and the response to my questions.

6. It was important that both adults and children had had some experience in American schools (public schools, Adult Basic Language Education, GED classes, citizenship classes). Traditional Cambodians brought with them a reverence for education and a deep respect of teachers. For most parents, schooling, as a practical strategy, is the first step on the ladder of success; education, on the other hand, involves more than commonplace academic subjects as it primarily includes studying the norms of the culture, i.e., the tenets of Buddhism. I was therefore interested in each individual's experience of American schools as students and parents of students.

7. The family members would be insightful analysts of their own experiences and their culture and would be willing to share their comments publicly. (As Sarah Lawrence Lightfoot states, "You choose people with whom you will have good conversations.")

The families in this sample meet these criteria in the following ways:

- All three families have been a part of my research since 1995 and agreed to continue as participants in my research.

- All three families have been in this country for fifteen years; six of the children were born in Cambodia and five were born in the United States.

- One family is a dual-parent family; two are headed by single mothers.

- Three of the parents are bilingual, and one is primarily monolingual; all three grandparents are monolingual.

- Although the grandparents speak only Khmer, two grandparents have attended American citizenship classes, three parents have attended adult ESL programs, one parent has nursing degrees from Cambodia and the U.S., and another parent is working on her associates degree at a local university. Three of the nine children were not attending school at the time of data collection: one adolescent dropped out of school in the fall of 1998, one adolescent missed three weeks of classes due to illness and had a leave of absence for the fall semester, and one son is married and working full time.

Data Collection—Interviews

The first source of data collection was the structured interview. Each *adult* in these three families was interviewed according to a protocol that consisted of twenty-three open-ended questions in three parts. Part I included questions about personal aspirations and aspirations held for their children, Part II included questions that compared Cambodian and American ways of life, Part III included questions about Buddhism. Since this protocol was designed specifically to answer the research questions, adults who had been interviewed for the pilot study were re-interviewed with this new protocol. I conducted the interviews myself. One parent was interviewed in his office; the other parents and grandparents were interviewed in their homes. Each interview lasted approximately two hours, and sessions were audiotaped. I transcribed each interview myself, and the transcripts range from twenty-five to thirty-five pages.

Seven of the eight adolescents were interviewed according to a specific protocol consisting of thirty open-ended questions organized into three parts. Part I asked questions about personal qualities, Part II asked questions comparing American and Cambodian culture, and Part III asked questions about Buddhism. I interviewed the first adolescent in his home using a draft of the adolescent protocol. After reviewing the transcript, I revised the protocol and used the revised version for all subsequent interviews. One adolescent, after numerous attempts over a ten month period, refused to be interviewed.

The structured interview with the adolescents lasted for two hours and in all but two cases was conducted in my apartment. One adolescent preferred to be interviewed at school during her study hall.

In spite of good intentions and a willingness to participate, adolescents seem to lead greatly over-scheduled lives and I learned not to make appointments for interviews too far in advance because that frequently resulted in no-shows. I transcribed each interview myself and produced transcripts that ranged from six to thirty-five pages. In all instances I listened to each audiotape twice.

Data Collection—Observations

Formal participant observations began in August 1996 and again in January 1997 when I began to assist Pirun with citizenship classes. Fearing the loss of their SSI benefits resulting from a change in the welfare law, a large group of Cambodian elders began attending citizenship classes which were taught at the Multilingual Center. I went most Monday mornings for two and a half hours to give mock tests and eventually worked with a group of women who were trying to pass the test. Recognizing that none of the women could read or write Khmer, I spent my time teaching them to read standard INS forms and applications that required some knowledge of English to complete them.

In October 1997 I began to tutor Srey, the teenage daughter of one of the families. She had started attending a highly competitive, college preparatory school as a junior and discovered that she was unprepared for the pace and the intensity of the work. Her greatest struggle was with English grammar and composition, and I began to help her with her writing twice a week. Our tutoring sessions continued throughout her senior year, the 1998/99 school year. In April 1998 I also began tutoring Chinda, the mother of one of the families. She was enrolled as a part-time student at the local university and she also needed help with her English grammar and composition.

I spent a day shadowing each of the adolescents in their respective high schools. I arrived at school alone, met the student who introduced me to his or her teachers and who then tried to ignore my presence as I watched, listened, and took notes during the classroom sessions. In all but one of the visits, I ate lunch with the adolescents accompanied by their friends.

I continued to attend cultural festivals as well as some public performances of the Cambodian dancers. I attended fundraising events at the Cambodian Buddhist Center and participated in the annual New

Year events as usual. In May 1997 I was invited to attend the wedding of Rath's oldest son. I was not able to attend the Cambodian wedding ceremony so I viewed the three-day ceremony on videotape at Rath's house over the summer. In November, 1998 I was invited to attend a traditional Buddhist service for Rath's father who is dying of old age. All of the couple's children and grandchildren were present for the service which included four monks from a neighboring state to chant the ceremony that clears the way for Rath's father to die. All of the events were captured by detailed, descriptive field notes, first by hand and then transferred to the computer.

Data Collection—Documents
I continually refer to Maha Ghosananda's book of wisdom, *Step by Step* to guide my thinking about and interpretations of the ways in which my informants approach the concept of success. The Cambodian "Readers" that were compiled by the Forest City Multilingual program are also invaluable sources of folk stories that model cultural norms. There are excellent contemporary novels and autobiographies that discuss the experience of the Cambodian holocaust and the experience of living in a new and very different culture (Crew, 1989; Nguyen-Hong-Nhiem, 1989; Yathay, 1987; Sheeny, 1986). The news media and the internet were also sources of contemporary stories about Cambodians in American society.

Additional sources of data were the students' essays and poems written for classroom assignments, college applications, or scholarship awards. These documents provided an expressive insight into the ways in which some of these adolescents interpreted themselves and their goals for an American audience of their teachers and their peers.

DATA ANALYSIS

The data analysis follows the inductive, interpretive method favored by grounded theorists (Strauss and Corbin, 1994; Erickson, 1986; Maxwell, 1996; Wolcott, 1994). Glaser and Strauss first articulated this inductive, interpretive process of data analysis in 1967. The central premise of the method is first that the researcher's interpretations must include the "perspectives and voices of the people she is studying."[3] The interpretation is an analysis of what people say, what they mean, and what they do. According to the Strauss and Corbin, grounded theory is specifically structured to develop theory of

> great conceptual density and with considerable meaningful
> variation. Conceptual Density refers to richness of concept
> development and relationships which rest on great familiarity
> with associated data and are checked out systematically with
> these data.[4]

The objective of my data analysis, therefore, is to describe the concepts of success that are articulated by the people in these three families and to interpret their responses to my research questions by utilizing a categorical and contextual analysis (Maxwell, 1996) of my informants' words and their actions.

Contextualization

Contextualization strategies, according to Maxwell, are based on elements of contiguity where the researcher is interested in maintaining the context of an informant's narrative. Miles and Huberman (1994) describe this as a way of "restorying" the text, pulling out the instances where the informant answered a research question, and crafting a narrative representation based on their words. Variations of contextualization strategies include case studies (Stake, 1995, Mischler, 1986), crafted profiles (Seidman, 1991), voice-centered method (Brown & Gilligan, 1992), and ethnographic microanalysis (Erickson, 1992).

> What all of these strategies have in common is that they do not
> focus primarily on relationships of similarity that can be used
> to sort data into categories independently of context, but
> instead look for relationships that connect statements and
> events within a context into a coherent whole.[5]

Data Analysis—The Crafted Profile

Working with the first interview transcript, I crafted a profile for each individual. I began with an analytic question, e.g., "What are all the ways this individual talks about success in relationship to his or her family?" I read the transcript and, using different colored pens, I underlined sections of text where the speaker talked about qualities of being successful, people who they thought were successful, family expectations for success, and so on. Each color related to one of the categories embedded in my research questions: success for the individual (highlighted in red), the family (highlighted in black), the Cambodian culture/religion (highlighted in green), American culture (highlighted in blue), and schooling (highlighted in brown).

I re-read each transcript selecting all the text where the informant made biographical statements (highlighted in yellow). I transposed his or her exact words as they related to this category, bracketing my own words when it was necessary to complete the meaning of the sentence. Care was taken to maintain the natural syntax of the individual's speech, including their English diction and their unique use of English metaphor, homilies, and clichés.

The final profile was crafted according to four analytic questions: 1. biographical statements, 2. success for the individual , 3. success within the context of the family, and 4. success as a Cambodian and an American. In a few cases I included a fifth question: success in the context of school. One profile ran four pages, another twenty-seven pages. The completed profile was given back to each individual to keep and to comment on during the second structured interview.

I then re-read each profile, looking for missing information, noting places where there were apparent contradictions, and marking instances where I was confused about the meaning. I crafted a second interview protocol of questions related specifically to the profile. I included some questions related to the informant's experience of the interview, i.e., What was your experience reading the profile? How were the questions meaningful to you? What did you learn about yourself from this process? How have these interviews influenced you? The purpose of these latter questions was to account for the issue of reflexivity between the informant and myself.

I conducted a second interview at my apartment. The interview lasted between an hour and an hour and a half; it was audiotaped. I transcribed the interview myself and crafted a second profile based on the same categories as the first. In all but two cases, I merged the two profiles, indicating in the margin whether the selection of text came from the first or second interview.

Categorization

Categorization is perhaps the most common technique of qualitative data analysis in the way it reduces quantities of data by coding, sorting, and displaying to reveal patterns and themes. It allows one, as Maxwell states, the ability to "develop a more general theory of what's going on. The two strategies (contextualization and categorization) need one another to provide a well-rounded account."[6]

Data Analysis—Open Coding

Working from my crafted profiles, I used my word processing program to reformat the text into paragraphs that were four inches wide. Each paragraph was identified with the speaker's initials, the transcript number, and the page where the quotation appeared in the transcript. For the first stage of open coding (Miles & Huberman, 1994; Strauss & Corbin, 1990), I assembled five-by-eight-inch index cards in three color groups to represent each of the families. I then cut out each paragraph or series of paragraphs and glued them to the index cards, writing in pencil the category under which they had appeared in the profile (individual, family, Cambodian, American, schooling), and including words or phrases that captured the essence of the quotation. I repeated the process with the entire set of field notes for each family, keeping the same color designations, and writing in pencil the categories to which they related.

For the second stage of open coding, I worked within one family, re-reading each quotation, combining the words and phrases used by the speaker to talk about different dimensions of success. I grouped cards with similar words and phrases together into the following clusters: Individual—Goals, Expectations, Role Model, Buddhism, Self-Reliance, Money and Wealth, Leaders and Followers, Helping Others, Between Two Worlds; Family—Expectations, Norms, Self-Reliance, Closeness, Trust; Cambodian/American—Customs, Getting Ahead, Identity, Buddhism, and Education. I repeated the process for each family.

Data Analysis—Thematic Narrative Summaries

Working with the tentative themes, I crafted a narrative summary for each individual. The final product includes a discussion of what it means to be successful as an individual, within the context of the family, and as a Cambodian and American, and it is illustrated with the individual's words. I created a matrix for each individual to compare and contrast the themes.

Data Analysis—Triangulation

After establishing a set of themes inductively derived from the interview and field note data, I related my interpretation to the findings from the pilot study, noting the similarities and contradictions. At each stage of the analysis process, I asked three colleagues to read and comment on my interpretation. Each of these individuals is conducting research on immigrants and the immigrant's adaptation to American social and educational institutions. My colleagues' insights from their personal experience, as well as their extensive knowledge of the immigrant literature, were invaluable in challenging those claims that could not be verified by the data.

VALIDITY ISSUES AND GENERALIZABILITY

Language

As mentioned above, one limitation posed by this research is the fact that I do not speak Khmer. While this was rarely a problem when interviewing the seven adolescents, it presented a challenge when interviewing the monolingual grandmothers. I chose my sample specifically because the majority of the family members were fully bilingual, and in the case of the older adolescents, their level of sophistication with the English language as well as with the nuances of their own language was impressive.

There are two specific advantages of the longitudinal study with regard to this issue of language validity. First, by the time I conducted the interview with one of the grandmothers, I had been interacting with her and the other members of her family for over two years. I had completed both interviews and the crafted profiles with the adolescents so they were very familiar with my questions, and they had their own interpretation of what the questions meant in the Cambodian context. Srey, in particular, was very helpful in translating my interview questions for her grandmother and in explaining her answers.

The second advantage is that over time I became very familiar with the way each speaker used English and was able to shift into his or her pattern of diction. When I was unsure of a response during the interview, I asked the speaker to repeat the phrase, or I repeated the phrase and asked for confirmation. Thus, after listening to the audiotape twice, as noted above, I believe that I captured their full responses. Occasionally, my tape recorder malfunctioned, and in those instances, I took sections of transcript back to the speaker and asked him or her to fill in the missing information.

Researcher Reflexivity

> Understanding context is important for intelligibility and comprehension. The significance of context for interpretation and understanding and the inevitability of reflexivity for all sense making, offers ethnography an additional resource for its authority. Field workers place themselves in the contexts of experience in order to permit the reflexivity process to work. Experienced ethnographers, then do not avoid reflexivity; they embrace it.[7]

I do not see the issue of reflexivity as a limitation given the rich and complex data I have collected over the past five years. Without a thorough grounding in the context of the Cambodian community in Forest City—both geographical and epistemological—the claims I might make in regard to my research questions would be superficial at best. More specifically, since the purpose of my research is to understand what it means to be successful to the members of these three families *in connection with their cultural and religious beliefs*, I can think of no other way to approach this level of understanding without becoming a trusted friend.

I made a conscious decision to relocate my residence in order to interact consistently with the three families in this study. I had found unsatisfactory on a number of levels the method by which I had completed the pilot studies: commuting to Forest City, conducting one or two interviews, and then leaving. First, the relationship felt subtlely manipulative in which the Cambodians were required to provide me with information while I gave nothing back in return. The concepts of generosity and caring are extremely strong cultural models for the Cambodians; they were very generous of their time, their insights, and their hospitality. I felt it was important to reciprocate in some way with the members of these three families; offering tutoring sessions, helping with the immigration agency, filling out college applications, and typing resumes and letters seemed appropriate.

Given my status as a white, well-educated American, I am fully cognizant that by normative American standards, I hold a privileged status position vis-à-vis these families, and this was made evident as I began to ask questions about role models or respected people within the American community. In spite of years of public schooling, only one of the adolescents knew an American whom they considered a role model. Two of them named me as their role model, I suspect because of the time I spent listening to and respecting their ideas. Another possibility is that I am the same age as their parents and all Khmer adolescents are socialized to honor and respect elders, especially those with high education. All but one of the adolescents confided that they had trusted me with information they had not shared even with their peers. I concluded that when a relationship of mutual respect and reciprocity is established, and confidences are not betrayed, the issue of power—either from education, age, economic status, or cultural status—was mitigated.

Ethical Issues

Historically, ethnographers have gone to great lengths to disguise the individuals and the setting in which they conduct their research. Feminist researchers have challenged this practice, stating that informants should be allowed a say in how they are represented in qualitative research.

> A feminist methodologist, for example rejects the belief that
> one can separate the "subjectivity" of the researcher from the
> "object" of her research, and in fact, creates research practices
> that close the inevitable distance between the researcher and
> the participants in the research.[8]

I explained to each person I interviewed that their words would become a part of my book, and I asked them to mark any passages that they did not want me to include. I explained that I intended to disguise the name of the city, each of the schools they attended, and other distinctive local features, but I wanted each of them to choose the name I would use in the manuscript. I gave my respondents a release form in which they gave me permission to use either a real first name or a fictional first name that they created.

I asked the parents and the children to sign consent forms that explained the purpose of my study and described the conditions of anonymity, use of recorded material, and potential publication goals. I also asked the parents and children to sign release forms giving me permission to spend one day with each of the children in school. This form was given to an administrator at each of the high schools I visited. I had one adolescent and her parent sign a release form giving me permission to request an English essay from one of her teachers. I requested permission verbally and in writing from the other adolescents to use samples of their written work for English classes and their essays for college admission.

Generalizability
The generalizability of this study is limited to the particular context of the three cases. However, the depth of the ethnographic methods and the length of the research study provides significant insight into an issue that has not been fully explored by some of the prior research on Southeast Asian families—that being the influence of cultural epistemology on expressive and pragmatic concepts of success. Case studies in particular are of value in refining theory and suggesting complexities for further investigation as well as helping to establish the limits of generalizability.

> Feminists write case studies…to explain the process of
> development over time, to show the limits of generalizations,
> to explore uncharted issues by starting with a limited case and
> to pose provocative questions. For example a carefully chosen
> case can illustrate that a generalization is invalid and suggest
> new research directions.[9]

Connections between these cases and other Cambodian families may be made by readers who discover in the findings analogous experiences of their own. Given the attention paid to the range of data, the variety of methods used to triangulate the data, and the way in which I accounted for validity issues, I feel confident that the perspectives and the interpretation in the following chapters authentically represent both my own position as researcher and the position of the members of these Cambodian families. It is in that regard, that I believe the findings are important for practice and for theory generation.

NOTES TO CHAPTER 5

1. See Appendices A and B.

2. Robert Stake, *The Art of Case Study Research*, (Thousand Oaks: Sage Publications, 1995), p. 12, and Frederick Erickson, "Transformation and School Success: The Politics and Culture of Educational Achievement," in *Anthroplogy and Education Quarterly*, Vol. 18, No. 4, December 1987, p. 130-131.

3. Anselm Strauss and Juliet Corbin, *Basics of Qualitative Research: Grounded Theory, Procedures and Techniques*, (Newbury Park: Sage Publications, 1990), p. 274.

4. Ibid.

5. Joseph Maxwell, *Qualitative Research Design: An Interactive Approach*, (Thousand Oaks: Sage Publications, 1996), p. 63.

6. Ibid., p. 63.

7. David Altheide and John Johnson, "Criteria for Assessing Interpretive Validity in Qualitative Research," in N.C. Denzin and Yvonna Lincoln,eds., *Handbook of Qualitative Research*, (Thousand Oaks: Sage Publications, 1994), p. 496.

8. Annie Rogers, "Voice, Play and a Practice of Ordinary Courage in Girls' and Womens' Lives," in *Harvard Educational Review*, Vol. 63, No. 3, Fall, 1993, p. 266.

9. Shulamit Reinharz, *Feminist Methods in Social Research*, (New York and Oxford: Oxford University Press, 1992), p. 167.

CHAPTER 6

Research Setting

I kind of keep those two worlds sort of different, like there is the life of the minority side and the life of the middle class side; it is pretty tricky. If you don't enjoy it you will drive yourself crazy.

—Touch

INTRODUCTION

A front-page story in the January 3, 1983 Forest City *Press-Herald* read as follows: "A seven pound, ten ounce girl was born at 12:01 a.m. to a Cambodian refugee couple who came to America penniless a year ago. She is the state's first baby of 1983. The baby was born at W. Hospital to Ran Mao, 34, and her husband San Mao."

While to many appearances Forest City is a traditional East Coast city with a predominantly white population, more than fifteen years of refugee resettlement has profoundly changed the physical and cultural landscape of this small city. In 1999, baby Mao—by then a teenager—attended high school with children from Cambodia, Ethiopia, Somalia, Sudan, Afghanistan, Vietnam, Laos, India, Mexico, Bolivia, Russia, Poland, the Czech Republic, Bulgaria, Romania, and the former Yugoslavia. That same year the Cambodian community in

Forest City comprised over 220 families, part of a state-wide Khmer community topping 1300 families.

The background of Forest City reveals a long history of immigrant settlement beginning in the eighteenth century. In fact, Forest City takes great pride in this history and examples of ethnic solidarity are evident in the distinctive character of city neighborhoods where families have lived in the same houses for generations.

FOREST CITY—HISTORY AND DEMOGRAPHICS

Forest City stands on a narrow peninsula that is surrounded by a deep water harbor which serves as one of eight principal ports on the east coast of the United States and accommodates naval and commercial shipping vessels. The City was incorporated as a town July 4, 1786 and as a city in 1833.

Early immigration records indicate that the first ethnic groups were English, Scots, and Welsh. French Protestants arrived in 1686, followed by the Irish in 1718 and the Italians in the 1830s. The 1880 census recorded the following demographics for Forest City: Irish, 2,627; English, 188; Scots, 84; Germans, 36. West Indian and African immigrants also came to Forest City as workers on trade vessels.

Forest City's religious history followed the traditions of the early British settlers. By 1720 the first church parishes were Presbyterian, Episcopalian, Congregationalist, Anglican, and Quaker. Steady immigration from Irish Catholics persuaded the regional diocese to establish Forest City's first Catholic church and parish in 1827. The West Indians and Africans founded the Abyssinian Congregational Church and Society in 1830 and created a school for their children. (Black children began attending integrated schools starting in 1857). By the end of the nineteenth century, there were also two Jewish synagogues and a Korean Presbyterian church.

REFUGEE RESETTLEMENT IN FOREST CITY

Forest City's long history with immigrants notwithstanding, large-scale refugee resettlement is a phenomenon of the 1980s. From the beginning, United States State Department policy has specified that refugees from a single ethnic group be dispersed around the country in order to avoid the establishment of ethnic enclaves in predominantly urban areas. Individual states have no control over the number or provenance of the refugees resettled within their borders.

For Southeast Asians, the application and resettlement process begins with the refugee locating a sponsor in the host country, usually through the services of the American Red Cross or a voluntary agency such as Catholic Charities, National Jewish Federation, or Lutheran Immigrant Services. Refugees fly to Hawaii or the Philippines where they spend a few months undergoing health check-ups and learning rudimentary English before they fly to their designated city. Each refugee is responsible for paying his or her own airfare from Hawaii or the Philippines to the final destination.

The Office of Refugee Resettlement in Washington, DC allocates money for cash assistance, medical assistance, and a formula grant, 100 percent of which goes to the voluntary agencies (VOLAGS) to pay case workers. The VOLAGS provide a job placement service which recruits employers to employ refugees. Refugees unable to find jobs upon arrival are eligible for cash assistance for up to eight months through the VOLAG. Families with single parents also qualify for Aid for Families with Dependent Children (AFDC), which is 60 percent federally funded and 40 percent state funded. Once the refugees are settled in an apartment, they are assigned a caseworker and a public health nurse who takes them to a local clinic for a health screening.

In 1975 the Roman Catholic Diocese of Forest City and the United States Catholic Conference underwrote the foundation of a small non-profit organization in Forest City called the Refugee Resettlement Program. By 1976 the first Vietnamese refugees began arriving, followed by the Khmer, Laotians, Africans, and Eastern Europeans.

The Khmer presence in Forest City is attributed primarily to Anchina Bugden, a Khmer woman who emigrated to the United States during the 1960s. After undertaking the successful reunification of her extended family beginning in 1979, she took the lead in sponsoring and settling other Khmer families around her city and state. During 1983-84 alone, over 180 Khmer were served through the Refugee Resettlement Program. While most of the Khmer stayed in the metropolitan area, a number of families moved to nearby cities in search of job opportunities and housing.

In 1982 the Forest City public schools offered the first classes in English for Speakers of Other Languages (ESOL). The classes were offered primarily in one elementary, one middle, and one high school in the inner city. All refugee children were bused to one of these three schools where they attended ESOL classes containing, at times, speakers of up to nineteen different languages. When the students were ready for mainstream classes, they were allowed to attend the schools in their own neighborhoods. By 1999, with the continuing influx of refugees from Africa and the Eastern European republics, all elementary schools in Forest City had implemented ESOL programs, and at least one ESOL classroom may be found at each of the public middle and high schools. (There are no ESOL programs in the city's three private high schools).

The superintendent's office funds a small staff to operate the Forest City Multilingual Program. This program provides all of the family intake services for incoming refugee children, placing them in appropriate schools and locating tutoring or GED programs for older children and adults. Part of the staff includes liaisons from each of the ethnic communities; my key informant is a member of this staff. Another part of the staff research and write grants to support staff development and inservice programs that assist mainstream teachers with instructional practices designed for a multilingual classroom population.

The Forest City Adult Language program provides GED classes for refugee adults on an ongoing basis, and a number of city and Federally sponsored programs support at least two learning centers that are located in the city housing projects. Native-language tutors spend between one and five hours a day providing academic assistance to any student who walks in the door.

The Refugee Resettlement Center continues to provide assistance for newly arrived refugees, particularly with welfare benefits, cash assistance, housing, and job placement. There are a number of non-profit organizations that work with the refugee population, some of which have been started by refugees themselves. For example, SPIRAL Arts, a community-based, non-profit arts organization working in low-income Forest City neighborhoods, has had a long-term relationship with the Cambodian community. SPIRAL Arts provides space, instruction, and supplies for a variety of Cambodian arts activities including traditional dance, Khmer language classes, cooking classes, and citizenship classes.

THE CAMBODIAN COMMUNITY IN FOREST CITY—HISTORY AND CURRENT STATUS

> North America is a melting pot. We Cambodians have been here for just one generation. In recent years, we have also resettled in Europe, Australia and throughout Asia. As we rebuild our lives in new lands, as we become part of new societies, it is important for us also to preserve our cultural identity. Without our culture, we will become lost and confused like a fish out of water.... When we are in the river, we flow with the river, zigzag. But we cannot forget our boat, which is our tradition.[1]

In 1979 the first wave of Cambodians arrived in Forest City. A small group formed a Mutual Assistance Association called Union Cambodia, and the group held meetings which were designed to educate Forest City residents about Cambodia and Cambodian culture. In 1985 a second association formed around a group of Cambodian elders and called itself Watt Samaki or "United Temple." The elders comprised the governing board and began to raise money to recruit and house a monk to live in Forest City. In March 1988 Venerable Lok Ta So was installed as the community's first spiritual leader.

In the meantime, the Watt Samaki elders continued the search for a building and a piece of land on which they could rebuild their Buddhist temple. In 1989 the elders located an abandoned, 167-foot-long, three-story chicken barn on a little over five acres of land twenty miles to the west of Forest City. The property was located in a modest neighborhood in a rural town of around 7,000. The town was equidistant from the communities in which the majority of Khmer families had settled after arriving in the state.

The Cambodians intuitively knew that communicating about their religion with members of this small rural community would be critical to their acceptance, so Venerable Lok Ta So and the Board of Watt Samaki arranged to discuss their plans with the Protestant and Catholic leadership in the town. The Director of the State Council of Churches presided over four meetings between church leaders, parishioners, and representatives from Watt Samaki. At the end both groups believed that they had succeeded in dispelling whatever apprehension might have existed at the prospect of a Buddhist religious center locating in their town.

However, at the public hearing on the Cambodian's application for a variance to turn the chicken barn into a religious center, the hearing room was inundated with over sixty-five local residents. The leader of the local residents' group submitted a petition to the chair of the Planning Board stating that, "the proposed use does not serve the current interests of the neighborhood, nor will it *favorably* impact the neighborhood." After lengthy exchanges between a lawyer who had been retained by the petitioners and the lawyer for the Watt Samaki Board of Elders, the application for variance was tabled pending submission of further information. The Planning Board subsequently required that the Cambodians provide architectural drawings and soil studies before they would consider the application. Within weeks the individuals and the issue became the subject of intense media scrutiny throughout the region, eventually making the national news.

The Cambodian elders and the monk, distraught over the publicity and ensuing conflict, withdrew their application and forfeited their $1,500 deposit on the property. The reaction of the townspeople had brought back memories of distrust and hostility from the four years under the Khmer Rouge. It was with great courage and persistence that the Cambodian elders continued to search for a home for their Buddhist center. Six months later in January 1990, they purchased a small two-story house in an outer suburb of Forest City. In support of their efforts, donations amounting to $800 arrived from Protestant and Catholic churches throughout the state.

In seeking to maintain their privacy and anonymity in this working-class suburb, the Cambodians did nothing to distinguish the small house as a religious center. Unable to maintain a monk in full-time residence, the monthly ceremonies were conducted by local religious leaders (*achaa*) which were attended by no more than thirty to forty individuals. Between religious ceremonies, the building stood empty.

In the summer of 1993, vandals broke into the unoccupied building, attacked the interior with hatchets, and painted hate slogans on the walls. They removed most of the contents and scattered them around the yard. Remarkably, nothing on the altar was touched, though all of the electronic equipment beside it was stolen. No one was ever prosecuted for the crime.

The incident shattered this peaceful community, and the elders began to question whether the Center would ever become a viable religious home without the presence of a full-time senior monk. Finally in September 1996, the Watt Samaki Board of Elders succeeded in bringing a senior monk from Cambodia via Thailand to spend a year as the community's spiritual leader. Venerable Lok Ta Ros's first task was to heal the wounds caused by a previous monk who had abused his position. That monk had spent the Center's funds without permission from the Board of Elders and had subsequently been asked to leave the community.

For the year in which his visa was active, Venerable Lok Ta Ros brought great security and stability to the Cambodian community. For a short time he was able to restore many of the traditional practices including the initiation and teaching of novice monks, family counseling, weekly teachings of the Buddhist *dharma*, monthly religious observances, and family ceremonies for weddings, births, and funerals. In 1997 he returned to Cambodia to take up the restoration of a new temple. The Watt Samaki Buddhist Center is once again without a monk in residence.

The high point of the Khmer ceremonial year is the New Year celebration in April. In Forest City this ritual brings Khmer from around the state, so leaders of Watt Samaki must rent a large function hall in order to accommodate all the participants. Four monks are brought from a Cambodian Buddhist temple in a neighboring state, and three days are devoted to a constellation of traditional and new events.

In Cambodia it is customary to celebrate the New Year with both cultural and religious events. Because the arts have always been at the center of Cambodian society, music and dance are integrated into every celebration. In the mid 1980s, one of the first public presentations sponsored by the Cambodian community was a performance by the Royal Cambodian Dancers. Inspired by this ancient and exacting art form, a small number of women began to study traditional dancing. In 1996 the Watt Samaki Board and the city's arts council sponsored a month-long residency with Royal Cambodian dancer Chan Moly Sam and her husband Sam Ang Sam, Ph.D., a specialist in Khmer music.

For three consecutive years, these consummate artists have patiently built a small dance company comprised of young girls age seven to twelve and teenagers age fifteen to nineteen who perform the difficult and highly stylized traditional dances, along with a corps of young men and women who perform the folk dances. The central performance occurs on the first day of Cambodian New Year in April; additional performances have been scheduled at the high school and for international festivals in and around Forest City. A professional music ensemble made up of six adult men who play traditional instruments accompanies the dancers.

Cambodians have settled primarily in four locations around the center city. Many of them continue to live in the housing projects, and these ethnic neighborhoods operate as micro-villages where extended family members watch out for youngsters while parents work. Backyards have been converted into elaborate gardens, providing native produce for Cambodian dishes.

Cambodian weddings are combined with an American wedding ceremony for many couples; intermarriage appears to be limited for this community. Health and healing is accommodated both at the International Clinic, part of the city hospital, as well as by local folk healers who live in the community and in neighboring cities. The traditional ceremony that surrounds the death of an individual, like the weddings, incorporates both native Cambodian customs with American touches. When a monk is in residence, the customary induction as a novice monk has also become an opportunity for young teenage men.

In lieu of a large Buddhist temple which serves as the social and religious center of the community, the Khmer in Forest City stay in touch with community activities through a weekly one-hour Khmer language program on a local community radio station. It is customary for the resident monk to host a call-in program where he can respond to individuals who live within listening distance.

A number of Khmer in Forest City have been back to visit family in Cambodia; it is common practice to arrange a group charter flight and plan a two-week stay. The ones who travel are usually those individuals who have acquired American citizenship which ensures their safe and uncomplicated return to the United States. Most return with videos of temples, homes, and family visits that they share among family members and friends in Forest City along with paintings and posters of Angkor Wat, representations of the Buddha, and portraits of Royal Cambodian dancers.

SUMMARY

This is the setting in which I have conducted my research since 1993. The history of Forest City is, among other things, a story of immigrants. These new immigrants display many of the same qualities that characterize the older, long-established immigrant groups—they maintain close, extended families, they retain religious beliefs and practices, and they adhere to cultural models of success that often include both an expressive attachment to cultural identity along with pragmatic strategies for getting ahead in society. Distrust, racial bias, and poverty are persistent themes among the new immigrants, particularly those of color, as are themes of ethnic solidarity, academic achievement, and a rich bicultural identity.

Forest City has come to terms with its pluralistic identity over the past five years, compelled in large part by its religious, health and educational institutions, all of which interact with the immigrant community on a daily basis. Because the city is small, the ethnic communities are small and members are well known to one another. This facade of security and stability has increasingly drawn families from larger, more violent, and more impoverished cities to resettle in Forest City. My informants consistently commented that they "do not know" these new Cambodians, that they are not "members of the community." And as a result, they do not know whether to trust them and draw them into the circle.

The Cambodian community in Forest City, which is approaching its twentieth anniversary, appears on the outside like a small village with physical and metaphysical boundaries; a local epistemology that explains the way things are done in this setting; and the recognition that there are outsiders who may or may not be welcome. On the inside, the setting is infinitely more complex in the ways individuals and individual families negotiate the expectations both of the Cambodian community and the larger American society. Inside, this process of negotiation about what it means to be successful is constructed again and again.

NOTES TO CHAPTER 6

1. Ghosananda, op. cit., p. 72, 73.

CHAPTER 7

Case Studies

We change a lot now, I feel like we want everything. We don't care about whether we poor, so we happy family. We support children, go to school, grow up good life.

•   *Rath*

INTRODUCTION

I met Pirun's and Chinda's families in 1992 when I began my first field study of the Cambodian community in Forest City. Pirun became my key informant, translator, resident philosopher, storyteller, and friend; he was known statewide for his work on behalf of the Cambodian community. Chinda was not as well known in the wider Forest City community, but within her own community and in the university community, she has made her reputation as a skillful translator, one of the Khmer radio personalities, and a dedicated student.

I met Rath's family in 1996 just before moving to Forest City. During the three years of data collection and writing, I became very close to this family, sharing birthdays, weddings, funerals, graduations, college decisions, and numerous daily interactions. Rath and her mother were known in the Cambodian community for their generosity and religious devotion. But Rath was equally well known among the Cambodian elders for the good reputation of her five children.

Each family arrived in Forest City in 1981 and they have remained a part of the Cambodian community the entire time. Their stories share many similarities and differences and form the heart of this case study.

PIRUN'S FAMILY

Biography

Pirun, his wife Rany, his mother-in-law Yeang, and his four children live in a modest neighborhood, about a mile from downtown Forest City. Pirun's sister-in-law and the five members of her family, recently arrived from France, now live with them as well. Their home is a small, three-story, duplex building, cedar shingled, with a "city-sized" front yard. The back yard has a small patch of ground which is used for growing vegetables. The rest of the space is taken up by a garage and three automobiles parked in the narrow driveway.

The preferred entrance to the house is the back door which leads into a kitchen that opens up into a dining room and then into a living room; the rooms are small and worn. As is typical of so many Cambodian homes, the living room is dominated by an impressive entertainment center comprising a large-screen television, VCR, stereo system and speakers, and quantities of videotapes and CDs. Against one wall is a couch, against the other is a small hammock where the youngest member of the family naps; bedrooms and bathroom are up a narrow set of carpeted stairs. There are pictures of Angkor Wat, Cambodian calendars, and photographs on the walls; a small shrine with a Buddha and incense holder sits on the top of a bookcase in the dining room.

Grandmother Yeang lives with the family; her husband died in 1977. She watches over her youngest grandson as young people run in and out of the rooms, up and down the stairs. The telephone rings constantly, and conversations in English and Khmer rise and fall with predictability. When he is home, Pirun can generally be found either on the telephone or out in the garage sanding and patching rust spots on his orange 1983 Mercedes Benz sedan.

Pirun is a handsome man of average height and slight build. His face, which resembles the statues that surround the temple of Angkor Wat, has full lips, dark eyes and black hair that shows no signs of gray. He was born in 1952 and grew up in Kok-Pouch village in Kampong Chnang province, Cambodia. Kok Pouch was typical of rural villages in the 1950s, comprising rice fields and private dwellings. His mother was his father's second wife, and he was their only child; Pirun has a number of stepbrothers and stepsisters. Pirun's father died when he was very young, and they moved in with his maternal grandmother. Pirun's adolescence was largely spent working in his family's rice fields with his mother. She died when he was twelve, and he continued to live with his grandmother Young Nay and her youngest daughter Kong Sith.

Pirun attended the public school in his village for three years and after much persuasion, Young Nay allowed him to continue his schooling at the temple school for three more years. The temple, which consisted then of 50 monks, was supported by nine villages, of which Kok Pouch was one. The actual pagoda was located about five miles from Pirun's home. At age fourteen he was formally accepted into the temple school as a novice monk and moved away from home. From then on, the course of study included Pali language, Buddhist texts and doctrine, and standard academic subjects.

Around this time, Pirun's uncle, his mother's youngest brother, informed Pirun that unbeknownst to anyone in the family, he had formally adopted Pirun at birth and registered the adoption with the Cambodian government. This was a common custom for people who worked as civil servants in Cambodia. Salaries of government employees increased with every child. Pirun's uncle, who was single for a long time, believed he could increase his income as well as provide for his nephew's education. When Pirun passed his examinations to enter high school, the uncle, who had married by this time, came forward with enough money to pay for his schooling. To this day Pirun speaks of his uncle and aunt as his parents and keeps photographs of them in his office.

Pirun completed four years at the Buddhist high school in Phnom Penh and received a diploma along with the status of Buddhist monk. Upon graduation, he was accepted into nursing school and received his nursing degree in 1974. He worked in Phnom Penh until the Khmer

Rouge captured the city and forced everyone into the countryside. Pirun eventually ended up in a small town outside of Battambang province where he met a friend of his father's who worked on the railroad. This man introduced Pirun to Rany, and they were married in 1977; the Khmer Rouge subsequently transferred them to Battambang city. Pirun, his wife, and their oldest son escaped from Cambodia in 1978 and spent two years in the refugee camps before coming to the United States in 1981. When asked about his marriage and his new life in Forest City, Pirun's answer reveals a central Buddhist belief—the concept that one's *karma* foreshadows one's destiny in this life.

> The winds blew in the right way and brought us together. But we don't know if we will be together all of our lives because if the wind blows another way at some point then we may separate, we may divorce, we may go our way. One of us may die. We may have more than one partner. There is no way to know what fate has in store for us. If we are supposed to have more than one wife, we will. If we are supposed to have more than one husband, we will. If we are supposed to leave Forest City to live in California, then it will happen. According to the law of *karma*, I lived in Forest City 1000 years ago; it is part of our belief that every 1000 years you will go back and re-live your life in an area where you were before. It may be the same, it may not be the same.

Pirun and his family arrived with the first wave of refugees to Forest City. The U.S. Catholic Charities sponsored them, along with 100 other families. Because of his facility in English, Pirun soon became a liaison between his community and the Americans, demystifying complex policies in the area of health, education, social services, and immigration policies for the new Khmer refugees.

Pirun's first job was working on a farm four miles from Forest City. He purchased a bicycle and rode into the city every day to complete a nursing certification program. He worked as a home care nurse from 1983 until 1989. He later stated that nursing would be his preferred career, but it required too much travel and time away from his family.

Pirun became a citizen in 1986 and began working for the Forest City public school system where he has been instrumental in developing many programs to benefit all multi-lingual children. He collaborates on publishing Cambodian/English instructional materials and assists staff members with grant proposals. Pirun is a member of the state refugee board, Forest City's Bias Task Force, and the Parent Advisory group. In 1996-1997 changes in the welfare law threatened to cut off SSI benefits and food stamps to legal resident aliens who had not acquired citizenship. Pirun began a weekly citizenship class and has guided numerous Khmer through the testing and interview process.

Aside from his liaison responsibilities, Pirun is far more revered in the Cambodian community because of his determination to establish a Buddhist center in Forest City. Because of his Buddhist training in Cambodia, Pirun is frequently expected to take on the duties of the *achaa* in the absence of a senior monk. He officiates at fundraising ceremonies for the temple, at weddings and funerals, at the annual New Year celebration, and at various Buddhist holidays throughout the year. He pioneered the Khmer radio program, and he designed the programs which are a combination of music, news of Cambodia, and events connected with the Buddhist center. An avid student of Buddhist history and philosophy, Pirun frequently instructs his listeners in the complex epistemology of their culture.

Family, work, and religious duties define Pirun's responsibilities, but he thinks of himself, first, as a musician. Over ten years has Pirun studied and performed traditional Cambodian music—he plays at least three instruments and also sings. In 1988, he formed the Samaki Ensemble, a classical Cambodian music group that performs at traditional festivals, and in cultural events throughout the state and regionally. Pirun was invited to study and perform with other Khmer artists who attended Jacob's Pillow in 1991. He is the primary musician for the locally based group of Cambodian dancers, and he assists with their rehearsals and performances.

Rany was born in 1960 in Battambang Province. She is an attractive woman the same height as her husband but slightly heavier. Her features are plain, her eyes dark, and her hair is worn short. Rany attended public school in her village for seven years but has not continued formal schooling in the United States. At the time of the interviews, Rany was not an American citizen, and she spoke English cautiously. She was participating in an ESL program sponsored by the company in which she worked and Avy, her oldest daughter, was volunteering to help her mother improve her spoken and written English:

> My mom is not as skilled as my dad. She is not as educated as
> him 'cause he, I think he graduated high school, but my mom
> didn't. I don't think she ever went to school until now.
> Where she work, she is going to school cause my dad wants
> her. I help her too. It is so funny, she is like starting out in the
> second or third grade level. It's funny because she is an adult,
> and I am helping her.

Rany has three sisters and two younger brothers. The oldest sister and her husband live in New Hampshire with their four children. The youngest sister still lives in Cambodia. In September 1998, Rany's middle sister and her family emigrated from France with their four children to live in Forest City. One of Rany's brothers lives in Forest City with his four children and her youngest brother Veaseth is completing college also in Forest City. Veaseth is 30 years old and has maintained a close relationship with his sister and his nieces and nephews according to Avy.

> My uncle, he was accepted to Bentley, like a business school,
> but he didn't go. It was back in the 80s. He went to Phillips
> Business School [in Forest City] because he needed to stay
> close to my grandma. She was alone, and he just stayed here
> because he didn't want to leave [his mother] 'cause he was,
> like, her last son that's not married and still isn't.

Rany owned and operated an Asian food store in downtown Forest City for four years; in 1996 she sold the store to her two brothers and went to work in one of the local industries. This allows her to be at home with her youngest son and her mother during the day while Pirun is at work; while she works the evening shift, Pirun takes care of family responsibilities. Their oldest daughter, Avy, describes their household their household and the rituals that bond this extended family to one another:

In the morning [my mom] stays home and my dad goes to
work. When she goes to work my dad comes home. Almost
every Sunday we get together at my uncle's house. He makes
[a] big dinner, a special kind of dinner. We go around 4:00 or
5:00 and come home around 10:00. We usually sit and we
talk and we would just laugh all sitting around the table
watching TV. He has this karaoke thing, the Cambodian
music, and we are all singing around the microphone. It is
how my family is; we just get together and have dinner and
stuff.

MP is Pirun and Rany's oldest son; he was born in 1979 and spent two
years in the displacement camps on the Thai border before coming to
the United States with his parents. MP is the same height as his father,
slender with similar features in a strikingly handsome face. He wears
his hair just below his ears and dresses casually in carpenter's pants, t-
shirt, jacket, and heavy lugg-soled shoes. MP was a high school senior
at the time of the interviews, an honor student who worked 20 hours a
week at a local sporting goods store and still had time to hang out with
his friends. MP spent very little time in an ESL classroom as an
elementary student and quickly found himself mainstreamed in middle
school. Although his behavior is consistent with most American
adolescents, he clearly recognizes that he is perceived as a minority by
the larger society. High school has been something of a cultural
watershed for him since Forest City High School is the most diverse
school in the city.

I am like American-Cambodian, speak like American-
Cambodian. I speak more American than Cambodian, [but] I
can't say I am an American. I am pretty Americanized to a
certain extent, but if I walk down the street you don't think I
am an American, you are going to think I am Asian. I grew up
in the American system, white American system. I went to
Wadsworth Elementary school—98 percent white, Grant
Middle School—79 percent white. Then I go to Forest City
High school and all of a sudden culture shock!

Forest City High school is located in the center of the downtown. Approximately one-third of the students are from refugee families compared to around five percent at Stevens High School, Forest City's other public high school. The fall semester of his senior year, MP was taking honors English, accounting, physics, calculus, and advanced Spanish. He did not belong to any school clubs, conserving his time for his schoolwork, his job, and his friends. After spending a day shadowing him in school, I observed that MP was always serious in class, answering questions posed by the teachers, volunteering occasionally. Possibly because all of his classes were small, honors classes, the students were friendly with one another, but not inclined to fool around. When asked to describe himself, MP stated,

> I am like a very shy person. If I don't know you, I don't have anything against you, but I can't just walk up to you and go, "Hey, how's it going?" I am the person who kind of sits back, takes everything in, speak when spoken to, do a little bit. I can't just open my mouth. I can't just go off and keep going and going about nothing. It's not there. I am usually that person in the group who takes a step back and checks out everything, just kind of sits there. If you ask me my opinion, I hesitate before giving you an answer, but after I give it to you, I go to the background and not say anything.
>
> If you are my friend, if I feel close to you, then I am all different. I am cracking jokes all the time. I make noise, whatever. I am usually the one who says, "All right, let's go here. We're going there. All right, let's go get something to eat. Let's go dancing. Let's go to the ball game."

When asked to describe the people he usually hung around with, MP describes four Khmer friend he has known all his life.

> There are like four [Cambodians in my group]. We are a tight group. We are all going to be seniors this year. Only two of us, we are kind of separated in school. I go to Forest City High School, B. goes to Stevens High School, and Touch goes to Danforth Academy. Touch and I have been friends since we came here when we were three or four years old. We used

to live on the street with the Boys Club. [At age] four we moved away, [and I] don't see him again until eighth grade. I was 13. That is when we started talking again. The first time we talked it was like we had never been separated. I don't know when it came about; it might have been at a football game. Nothing had changed. Same old person. We clicked like we used to.

MP was accepted to Tufts University in the fall of 1998. He spoke earnestly about his desire to attend a "good" college, one in which the graduates could anticipate finding prestigious jobs. He was planning to declare computer science as his major, but admitted that he thought of college as an opportunity to expand his knowledge and hoped to enroll in a variety of liberal arts courses.

I think I might stick with computer science [as a major] but there [are] so many things that I want to do. I am really into philosophy. I want to learn the thoughts about people. It is really interesting to me. More than likely I will take three or four [philosophy] courses throughout my college career because I think it is so interesting about the way people think in general and how you can use that in your own thinking. And astronomy, I find that interesting just studying different galaxies and stars. There is a whole world out there, [a] universe that we can't even tap into, so many unknown things. There is just so much to discover. There is a lot of things like psychology studying the way the brain works that is interesting [to me]. Things like that I want to take just cause I want to learn it, that would be fun.

But I will probably get into computer science. I mean the whole computer system, the world wide web, the internet and all that is really interesting. It just kind of fascinates me how you can reach all these sites and everything, so I think it would be kind of fun. [When I grow up I want to be] something along the lines of business or maybe an engineer. I don't know, I am contemplating just those two.

Avy is Pirun and Rany's oldest daughter. Avy was born in 1980 in the displacement camp. She arrived in the United States at one year old.

> When I was born [my grandmother] names me and Avy is my
> short name. My name means I was born on Wednesday and
> she said that Wednesday is a real lucky day to be born on.
> [My birthday is] November 19, 1980. I came to America
> when I was one year old.

She is very slender, about five feet tall with shoulder length hair, which at the time of the interview was streaked light brown. She has a heart-shaped face, dark eyes, and full lips like her father and brother. She wears jeans, a pullover sweater, and Doc Marten style shoes. Avy describes herself as more private than her popular and gregarious brother, "I am not outspoken at all. I am wicked quiet unless someone says something that offends me. I am not active [in school]; I don't like to join sports or anything. I am not an athletic person, but I join clubs."

Avy is a junior at Forest City high school, and while not as academically competitive as MP, she nevertheless, maintains As and Bs in her classes. Avy's classes include algebra II, chemistry lab, English, honors U.S. history, pottery, and Latin II; she does not have a study hall.

During the day I spent with her in school, I noticed that Avy tends to gravitate toward the other Asian students in her classes. One of her best friends in her pottery class is Vietnamese, and they shared stories throughout the class and on the way to and from their other classes. Avy speaks openly about the level of prejudice from teachers and students that she feels as a Cambodian-American in Forest City high school.

> When [the teachers] look at us [Asians], I don't know, they all
> have [stereotypes] like [the] gangster type and when they see
> somebody, they assume we are all like that because some of
> the [Asians] are rude. Some of us aren't. Some teachers act
> differently toward me than they act toward other students. I
> don't know what it is. At the beginning of my sophomore

year, I had switched to this English class. It was really full
and we switched over to this other English teacher cause we
had to get split up. And she gave me this attitude the whole
time I was there. She didn't really know me and she thought I
was rude and stuff. I never act like that to my teacher. I told
other teachers about it. Well, after a while she changed; I
guess she was nicer to me.

One of her outlets has been to join the International Club in Diversity.
Primarily refugee students from a variety of different countries attend
this organization; no American students are members.

[The club is for] different groups of races to come together
and they do activities and talk about like racial issues. I deal
with a lot of prejudice every day. I like to talk about it with a
bunch of other people from different races, and see how they
deal with it.

But in spite of the racism, Avy is engaged in school and clearly prefers
some teaching approaches to others. Even though she has mixed
emotions about her teachers, she knows that she must maintain her
grades if she wants to attend college next year.

I used to love to write. During my freshman year I had this
English class. There was a new teacher and when I look back
he taught really well. He taught me how to learn stuff. We
used to write every day and I used to love writing in his class.
But in my sophomore and junior year, [the teachers] don't
even compare.
My history class is horrible. Whenever we get into class
all we do is take notes; like all [the teacher] does is talk and
we take notes. She usually does straight lecture, either that or
going over our homework giving us more notes and giving us
tests. I think it is boring. I don't look forward to that class.
I can't do math. Well I can do science. I guess I can sort
of do science, but I can't do the math. I am not good in that
area. I just stink in math. I will stay away from the careers
that involve a lot of math.

Avy, like her brother, has her sights set on college and a career after she graduates. But Avy is also pulled by the traditional path toward marriage and family.

> I have always told myself that I want to get married when I am like 20 or something cause Asian girls they [are] getting married like my age right now or even younger. But since I have to go to college, I don't know if I want to get married after or before college. If I wait until after college, then I will be 30 years old. I [would like to have] three or four kids. My parents have four kids and my aunt in France, she has four kids. My other aunt in New Hampshire she had four kids, but one of them died, and my uncle had four kids. They all had four kids.

When asked if she will return to Forest City to work, she surprised me by stating that she prefers the pace of a small town to living in the City.

> [When I am old] I don't want to live in Forest City. So many people move here, the Asian community, they are like, all bad. It is starting to get dangerous here. [But] I wouldn't want to live in a large city, maybe to go to college, but not to raise a family because it is wicked hectic there. There is a lot of noise.
> I wouldn't want to live in Cambodia [though]. I really want to visit there, but I wouldn't want to live there cause I think it is wicked hard. There is not a steady government there. I think it is much easier here [in America] when I think about it.

As for careers, Avy has a vague idea about running a business, but after more discussion, admits that because she is not strong in math, perhaps running a business is not for her. Avy is drawn to this career because it is a family tradition and she has in some ways grown up helping her mother with her business.

> My whole family is in business. Businesses ran in my family. [All the rice fields and businesses in Cambodia] were owned

by my grandfather, but [my grandmother] was in charge of it.
She just stayed home and my grandma she took care of the
products coming in and out for the business.

My uncle, he owns a grocery store in downtown Forest
City. And my uncle and my aunt in New Hampshire, they are
in business. They own a company and I have worked for
them. I would rather work in a family owned business so I
could help the family. It seem like fun working with people.

I want to be in business, but I sort of don't. It is just when
people ask me, I just say I want to be in business, but
somehow I don't really want to. My uncle he wants me to be
a doctor or something and my dad wants me to be a pilot. I
have always liked a lot of traveling.

Pirun and Rany's second daughter Alyana was born in 1984. She
is a strikingly beautiful young woman, slender and medium height,
with long black hair, a perfectly oval face, and intense dark eyes. Her
smile is both shy and mischievous. Alyana is outspoken in the manner
of young adolescents and dresses in the fashion of most
teenagers—jeans, sweaters, and jackets. Her natural friendliness and
apparent comfort in social situations contradicts her own self-
assessment. "People look at me and they think that, 'Oh, she is
outgoing,' but really I am quiet because I like to be by myself."

Alyana attends Grant Middle School, as did her brother and sister.
In our interviews, she did not devote much of her conversation to a
discussion of school, indicating that it is tolerable, but not the center of
her life. Alyana was more reflective than her siblings when asked
about her future. She is very close to her father and has clearly been
influenced by his choice of careers and his values around service to the
elders in the community.

When I was really small my dad was working as a nurse and I
got really interested. I was always with my father and
sometimes I would go with him and see how it is. That got me
to thinking what do I want to be when I grow up. My family
has been telling me [that I] should stay in Forest City [to be a
doctor]. I don't want to go too far because I want to stay close

to my family. I will probably work in a hospital or clinic; I
like to work with kids and probably elderly people.

But school, nonetheless, is a part of her long-range future:

I want to go to college and probably get all my degrees, but if
I can't reach all of the [degrees] I want to probably go up to
either the bachelor's or master's [and a possible Ph.D.]. I
want to be a doctor, [but] not surgery. When I was seven or
eight years old I got interested [in being a doctor.]

Alyana combines her ambitious goals with an equally large
commitment to classical Cambodian dance. Three years prior, Alyana
decided to attend a lecture demonstration given at the high school by
Chan Moly Sam. Alyana fell in love with the dance and quickly
became a featured performer with the local company. She stated that
she had never been able to listen to her father's music, that it made her
too sad, but once she was able to combine the movement with the
music, she grew to love performing this most difficult and demanding
classical dance style.

As for her personal goals, Alyana stated that she will probably
marry a Cambodian man, but not through an arranged marriage, and
she will raise her children to be comfortable in both a Cambodian and
an American world.

I don't want to have [just one] child, you are going to spoil
them [and] I don't like that. I probably want two or three,
probably even four. I would like [my children] to speak both
Khmer and English. There is no point of your being that
religion and not knowing how to speak your language.

Pirun and Rany's youngest son was born in 1994 and is just
approaching school age. He is adored by every member of the family
and clearly has developed a self-reliance fostered by the attention of
three generations of his family.

Pirun indicated that he is raising his children differently from the
way he was raised. While Pirun is strict with his family and sets

explicit rules, he also maintains open lines of communication with each child, encouraging them to express themselves and their opinions.

> When I grew up my father was so strict, I was not free to talk back to him. I talked more to my mother. I remember being the closest to my mother's mother and my great-grandmother. It was a competition between them as to who would love me more. They treated me like a diamond. But being silent and respectful to my father, it is a Cambodian norm. I have been different with my children. I talk with MP, and he likes the back and forth debate. So does Avy. I noticed that they were oppressing Alyana and making her be silent. I made them stop.

Throughout the five years that I met with Pirun and members of his family, I was struck by the powerful attachment they had for one another. While family loyalty is considered characteristic of Asian cultures, I was unprepared for the degree to which it was the physical and spiritual foundation on which Pirun, Rany, and their children built their relationships with each other. According to Pirun,

> Our family unit is so very, very close. My brothers-in-law and my sisters-in-law, we never have anybody fighting among our member. We always have a good time and travel back and forth, back and froth since we have been in the United States Not one of my family has gone through divorce. And the one in France, it is first-time marriage. We stick together and try to raise our children. That's who I admire the most, the whole family unit.

Interpretations of Success: Findings
As a Buddhist scholar and former monk, Pirun believes the successful individual may take one of two paths on his or her journey to become a "full human being"—into a spiritual life or into the day-to-day life of the worldly and human. The person who takes the first path accepts the ultimate goal of Buddhism which is to not be reborn.

> The ultimate goal of Buddhism is you don't want to be reborn
> because when you are reborn you have to run through all kinds
> of pain, suffering, and death. So you have to become like a
> diamond, so your soul never have to suffer again. That is the
> goal.

Buddha is the exemplar for this kind of life. The process begins
when a person stops "creating material things to the mind" and "trains
the mind with meditation." The competition to achieve is with oneself
insofar as the individual brings himself to the "top of the human
being," "the top of the mind," or "the top of the ego."

> Buddha, he doesn't compete with somebody. He try to bring
> himself to the top of the human being so that is competing
> with himself. Buddha he is among a lazy hand, lazy feet, lazy
> eye, lazy mind. These are the cause of failures that remain in
> everyone human. He competes with these internal enemies, so
> finally he got it. Those kind of things you have to fight
> internally all the time, day or night.

The second path the individual may take is to "turn around into the
world again" and become a full human being. The second path is also
concerned with training the mind, and in this case, the body is led by
the mind through the three stages of life. Each stage is a preparation
for the next ending with the "retire" stage [sic], which is a preparation
for the next life. The emphasis is not on thinking about or living in the
future, but caring about this life and living in the present.

> The Cambodians classify life as school age, productive age,
> and retire age; no mixing, no mingling. The middle period is
> working, productive life. You do the best you can while you
> are in the powerful knowledge and physical stage. Then you
> pass that stage, and you retire; no schooling, no working, you
> just there.

School age is the first stage for the successful individual. This first
period is finite, usually ending when the person is between 22 and 25.
It is the period when the individual must make room in his mind for

education and knowledge. Some of the knowledge is academic in nature, but the most important knowledge in Pirun's perspective is training the mind to "operate within the frame of the culture."

> The whole body one man or one women is led by the mind. If the mind operate within the frame of the culture then the whole understanding, the whole thought is going in the right direction.

The culture in this instance means the Buddhist Eight-Fold Path. It also means the norms and customs of Cambodian society. If this knowledge "sticks good in the mind," Pirun states, then the individual is ready to begin the productive stage.

Productive age or the middle period covers the time during which the individual begins working, marries, and raises a family. The individual does not have time to do much else but provide for his or her family. People are "tied up surviving." But the successful person in this middle period is someone who maintains her mind in the norm of the culture and resists the pull of the media, gangs, enemies, or unfaithful friends who try to change her direction.

> If the mind has been brainwashed by enemy, media, unfaithful friend, or gang, then that thought can lead the whole body to do something not within the norm of the culture.

She is a person who stays away from trouble, cares about her body (stays healthy), and tries to do well financially. All of this prepares her for the next stage of life.

Pirun's role model for the true person, the full human being, is the person in the retire period. The third stage of life is one of contentment, a time to be silent and look at one's past deed.

> The third stage is the period that people enjoy the fruit of good deeds. They can become a monk. You can leave your family, be silent, and look at what you have done from when you were born and become good.
>
> [The retired group] have the most wonderful time for the

society. [They] have more time to do things thankfully,
honestly. They give everything they have.

He specifically refers to the critical role the retire people play in
sustaining the most important Cambodian community institution.

The retired are very strong and powerful community
supporters. They give thousands and thousands of dollars [to
the temple]. Every temple costs thousands and thousands of
dollars. If [the retired] would not exist, [the temples would
not exist].

However, if the individual has not provided for this time of retirement
by building up financial security, the retire period is a time of suffering.

The [person] that do fine from the previous two [stages] have
time to help people and join more of the temple. If people
lack from previous education or working, [they] will have a
rough time or rough mind.

Pirun is especially eloquent as he describes the most important
institution in the Cambodian universe—the family. For him, the goals
and expectations of the individual must always be in harmony with
family goals and expectations. The highest ideal is the "beautiful
family," which Pirun describes as the ways in which parents and
children operate within the community.

If you are looking at what is done well in the family, it is
beautiful in the family. They are good friends in the
community. You look at how the family operates, parent and
children very nice. The children go to school and are loved by
associates, friends, teachers, adults and peers. Then [children]
get out of school come out to do the community piece of work.
They will get along very well and have respect by employers
and coworkers.

The Cambodian family is the basic foundation for everything;
problems and issues are worked out within the family rather than with

outsiders such as teachers or social service personnel. Pirun equates the family with the "frame of the culture" and this frame incorporates the guidelines for raising the children to be full human beings.

> Cambodian life is set up by a culture frame which is the norms and values of a good child of the family. You have to respect the family, take advice seriously so the family won't lose face among community members. It is a frame which leads the people to become the best person now.

Once the parents have done their job teaching their children, they step back and allow the school to take over. Parents refer to the school as a second parent and they expect the school to train the child in moral behavior, good attitude and provide opportunities for the child to have success. Everyone in the extended family shares the student's good experiences and honor which bring great merit to the family among the Cambodian community.

Pirun is very specific when describing the duties of the Cambodian parent. "Parents must pass along to the children the Cambodian Way, the way we dress, the way we eat, the way we play." Parents must take the middle way with their children—not too strict, not too loose. The appropriate guidelines are to lead the child into the peaceful way and bring them up with right understanding, right thought, right effort, right look, and right attention (the directions of the Buddhist Eight-Fold Path).

> Parents pass along to children the Cambodian way. They have to be not too strict, not too loose. If you stick so hard to the point, most of the time you won't get the point; the youngster will not follow the rules very good. If you are too loose they become unorganized and they go in a different way. They want to do anything; they may do harm to other people, not save other people.
>
> The parents still have to be the best model for the family, for the children. The children have to take any kind of instruction from us in terms of which [Cambodian tradition] is too strict for them to follow in this society.

When describing a child's potential, Pirun describes a common Cambodian cultural model which embodies the concept of destiny. Buddhism says that a child's future is predetermined and although a parent may be able to determine the child's life path, the parent has neither the power to change nor judge that path. "Cambodian parents know if their children are going to be somebody or not; they will be either in-between, on the top, or zero." Thus Pirun states that the parents observe the performance of the child in school and at play; they scrutinize their child's friends, particularly their best friends. Even if they do not know how the children will succeed, the parents keep pushing the child to follow the guidelines of the family and of the culture.

> Even though they cannot read their own stories to their
> children, Cambodian parents believe their children can do
> anything with their life. Even if they don't know how their
> child will succeed, they know how to push their children. "I
> don't know where you go, but I keep pushing you."

Pirun observes that in the United States with access to higher education and good careers, some parents push their children into careers that have high status within American society—doctors, lawyers, computer scientists. He firmly believes that this attitude is against Cambodian norms and is not the behavior of a responsible parent. The parent should neither choose nor control the child's career, since it may be against the destiny of the child. Moreover, careers which encourage service to others such as teaching, medicine, and social service, are more highly valued from the point of view of status within the community as well as ensuring merit for one's next life.

Pirun does not expect his children to "raise him" when he and his wife are old. The productive stage of life is seen as the time to provide for one's children and spouse. If this stage is managed successfully, then the parents have provided sufficiently for their retirement years and it is not the child's duty to support them. Pirun believes that the son who takes on this duty along with the responsibilities to his own family may cause harm to his spouse's future harmony.

You cannot sit up there and demand, "I am [your] parent so
your duty have to raise me when I am old." That is not a good
parent in terms of Buddhist religion, not a good parent. You
cannot put yourself in a higher position so that you lower your
children's position. That may cause harm to his or her future
in terms of a wife who [won't] mate with him because he have
his responsibility to raise two families, two parents, plus his
wife and their children.

This particular family concept is one place where Cambodian
Buddhists diverge from Chinese, Japanese, and Vietnamese culture.
The Cambodian family, while extremely close and interdependent,
nonetheless exists as a relatively autonomous unit with regard to
extended family members. As a rule each family has their own
dwelling, and only in the case of death or divorce do elder family
members live with one of the children. In spite of centuries of close
association with Vietnam, the Khmer culture has not adopted the strict
hierarchical pattern of filial duty common to Confucian-based
Buddhists.

Pirun makes a special point of discussing the qualities of the
successful mother. He states that the mother, and even more directly
the grandmother, has the greatest responsibilities within the Cambodian
family. If they want to earn the respect of the Cambodian community,
mothers must be strong mentally, physically, and financially.

In America there is no security anywhere in the country for the
males to feel comfortable enough to let their spouse stay
home. [The woman] has to be strong physically, mentally,
financially so she can help her spouse, her children, the
community, and the country. That is the traditional way. If
you are not in this way, nobody can respect you.

Pirun refers to the mother's "job" as preparing the child to be self-
reliant and not dependent on the parents, to have good character in
school and with friends so the child does not shame her in the
community. This cultural model of the mother's responsibility is
deeply internalized in Cambodian culture even though the majority of
mothers now work part- or full-time in the United States. It is why

many agencies have observed that Khmer mothers remain on welfare until their children are attending school full-time. The stigma for single mothers of accepting welfare in American culture does not appear to be an issue for many Cambodian women—it is appropriate to accept help from the government so they, in turn, can help their families.

Children have equally important responsibilities to the family, the most important being respect for parents and grandparents. The concept of respect is such an essential cultural model that it is instilled in infants beginning with guidelines set up in the family and reinforced by the Buddhist monks. The underlying foundation of respect for parents prepares the child to obey the parent's rules and take advice seriously. All of the young people in this study describe this process as "the lectures." Nonetheless, the degree to which the children demonstrate the parents' teaching is directly tied to the status of the parents within the Cambodian community. The standard "lecture" in Pirun's home as well as the others is to make sure the son or daughter chooses friends whose minds operate within the norm of the culture. There is also the sense that becoming too Americanized is also a danger.

> Each family has to be careful of other children. What kind of friend my child associate with [in school]. If my child associate with teacher, excellent; best friend, excellent, but if he associate with somebody whose mind operates outside the norm of Cambodian culture or being a true American, [then parents] are afraid.

One gets the sense that not even wealth brings as much merit to the family as the child who follows Cambodian norms, has good character, succeeds in school, is loved by friends and teachers, and is generous with his resources. This is why the child is under great pressure to prevent his family from losing face in the community; Pirun describes it as the child being in the parents' debt and thus must save face for his parents.

> [How well the child does in school reflects] on the family, the community. For example, if I make one mistake [in school],

fail in one course, for me it is OK because it is a learning
process. But I feel bad for my parents because I am in their
debt. [Being in my parent's debt] puts so much pressure on
me to do the best I can to save their face. [Saving face for
one's parents] is a pressure on children, but the children have
to understand that anything they do, someone around them
shares that good experience and honor.

Once the child is out of school, Pirun states, the "best knowledge
person" will usually take off from the family. While this is difficult for
the family, Pirun counsels that the parent must let the child go to find
her own way. The more successful she is in society, the more she is
able to save other people.

The oldest child, according to Pirun, has particular responsibilities
to his siblings and to his or her mother. If both parents pass away, the
oldest child must develop the "strong character, strong mind to bring
his siblings to the right direction." Without a deep cultural foundation
and family guidelines, the oldest child is frequently incapable of
handling the responsibility, states Pirun. This is particularly true in
families which have divorced. In one family, the older son may
withdraw from the family to spend time with his peer group. In
another family, the older son may become the partner to his mother and
help to raise the younger children providing both income and security.

In the old culture, as indicated, parents' responsibilities were to
provide shelter, love, understanding, and inspiration to do well in
school, as well as to instill the norms of the culture. Families which
have been fractured by divorce, or emotional or financial instability
may not be able to meet their responsibilities to their children. Pirun
states that the Cambodian culture provides a guideline for the child
whose parents neglect her and do not take care of her needs. She is
encouraged to find someone else who has the quality of the parent.

If the parent neglected them, doesn't take care of them,
doesn't care much about anything, the quality of being a
[good] parent is not there. So the children may find someone
else, a relative with the quality of the parent so the children
can speak to that family.

A dilemma that has significantly affected the Cambodian family is both a consequence of the war and of resettlement in the United States. The Khmer Rouge methodically destroyed this fine balance of respect and trust between parents and children by pressuring family members to betray one another in order to survive. The seeds of distrust sown during their four year reign of terror continue to grow in American culture.

In American society, Cambodian children learn that they have the right to report their parents to the legal authorities if they believe their parent's discipline is too harsh or restrictive. Respect between parents and children is further eroded when the parents who may be illiterate in their own language must depend on their children to interpret for them thus subverting their authority. If respect is not intergenerational, young people are unsure who is in charge. In the village, young people know that the monks, elders and grandparents as well as the parents were to be listened to and obeyed. To many Cambodians, American youth have more respect for their peers than for religious people, elders, teachers, or parents. This conflict of cultural norms is significant for most Cambodian parents and their teenage children.

Pirun frequently cites the different expectations Cambodians and Americans have for women. In Cambodia, he states, it is very difficult for a woman to be a top professional because of the intense prejudice and peer pressure from her male colleagues. The norm in Cambodia is for the woman to become the "best country woman who is hunted by the best male in the country." In America, Pirun encourages Cambodian women to maintain their tradition while they also become self-reliant through education and careers. He comments that Cambodian girls must be pushed for education because the cost of living in America requires that both spouses work in order to support their family.

There is obvious inequity in the Cambodian educational system from the girls' perspective. Girls do not attend the temple school past the third grade, and it is rare for a girl to attend public school past the sixth grade. However in the United States, girls can go as high in education as they want. The Khmer believe that boys and girls should have equal access to education, but Cambodian tradition is very protective of the girl's reputation in the community. The longer she stays in school, the more Americanized she becomes and the more difficult it is for parents to negotiate issues of dating and going out with friends, especially since these activities are perceived to compromise her good reputation.

Pirun further describes an important contrast between Cambodian and American pedagogy. In Cambodia the child in the public schools must pass the subjects as opposed to being promoted by his or her age. The most successful student is one who has learned each of his subjects in such depth that when he graduates, he needs no further schooling.

> In Cambodia in the high school it may take more than 13 years 14 years until they pass every subject. Sometimes the parent would not let their child go to the next grade because they did not feel like the child got it. The subjects must be passed, [the schools do not pass students] by the age. And then when they graduate they do not need more school. But they are getting a little bit old, so they can get a job right there. If they marry they have to get a job and take care of the family.

Pirun observes that Cambodian students who complete high school in the United States usually take the opportunity in their junior and senior years to conduct research into who they are and where they come from. This exploration of their ethnic identity, Pirun believes, gives them an appreciation of their culture and may bring them back to traditional ways. The student who drops out of high school, however, has no opportunity to become reflective of the value of the culture and why he should hold on to it. I believe that from Pirun's perspective, the best educated student and the most successful student has assimilated academic knowledge along with the knowledge of what it means to be Cambodian.

Pirun approaches the concept of "getting ahead" by contrasting his perception of social status in the Cambodian and American experience. Social status in Cambodia, as indicated before by property and education, is commonly explained by *karma*. Pirun states that he has "earned" middle class status for this life, but he cannot move up to the King class in this life. He must do the best he can in this life to get a better life next time.

> Middle class, that is what we earn [that] is what we get from
> now. But [a person] cannot move himself to be in the King
> class for this life. The [middle class, lower class] person can
> try to do the best he can for this life if he want to reach that
> better life, but not this time.

As a way of compensation, Pirun observes that each class has its own
karma—some poor people have good lives and some suffer just as
some rich people have wonderful lives and others have tragic lives.

> If people look at *karma* they say that every class has their own
> *karma*. Your *karma* leads you to be in that class whether you
> suffer, have a good time or whatever. If you look at [*karma* it
> says] you are in this class only, you cannot move. Then the
> mind gets stuck there.

However, Cambodian folklore introduces an alternative
explanation for social mobility and class status. Like folk stories in
virtually every culture, Cambodian folk tales include examples of the
poor young man who through luck and talent is discovered by a King
and is able to "cross all the classes." The belief that you may be poor
or lazy now, but next year you may become rich, a Cambodian
variation on the rags-to-riches story, is as potent in the culture as the
acceptance of one's fate by virtue of one's *karma*.

Pirun believes that their rags-to-riches story is nourished by the
American cultural model which implies that there are no classes in
America. Cambodians say that in America they are not able to detect
the person of higher status by the way they dress, their speech, or their
behavior. Thus everyone appears to be equal. "America doesn't put us
in classes," which means that Cambodians may be poor now, but with
education and hard work, they or their children may someday cross all
the classes and be very successful.

Finally, Pirun offered his own definition of the phrase "getting
ahead." He believes that in America, getting ahead means to compete
or race with others to get to a better position in a job, school, or life. In
Khmer, "getting ahead" means to improve your own life in order to
ensure a bright future.

Listening to Pirun, one is tempted to take his perception of success as referring to the ideal; as describing a person who has internalized the highest moral and social standards of the culture. The reality is that Pirun is the living example of his beliefs, and he meets these exacting standards every day as noted by his children and others with whom I have talked over the past five years.

MP connects success, first of all, to the concept of *karma*. A person's good fortune—wealth, talent, comfort, success is a reward from past lives during which the person did good things. The only way to guarantee this full human life is to not sin and to do good to others. The successful person doesn't stray, meaning that the person sets limits on his actions to prevent him from sinning.

> *Karma* is very important and keeps me from doing bad things.
> If I do [bad things] my *karma* it will come back. That is what
> my mother says. So there is so much drilled in my head that I
> can't.... You gotta be good, you can't just go out violent.
> What's going to happen the next time when you catch another
> life. You are going to be the person asking for food.... It is so
> instilled in me that I can never do something really bad. There
> is a limit and I am not going to go past that limit because I
> know what is going to happen to me. I'll sin. You can't have
> that. That's one strike against you.

The critical piece here is that a person ultimately must take responsibility for his own action. It is a solitary process because no one intervenes on your behalf—not family, not friends, not teachers, not even the monks.

Personal success is connected to fulfillment of certain goals that happen in certain stages. For MP, the first stage is to get accepted to a good college and complete his degree in four years. The next stage is to get a good job. But this is not enough to keep one fulfilled. The next stage or goal includes having a family and becoming a role model for his children.

> Fulfillment right now would just be doing good in college then
> getting a good job. But then when I get to that point, that's

not going to be enough fulfillment for me, so then I have to look farther. I have to look about family, my parents, about money. So that's a different part that I have to fulfill. So it is kind of like goals.

The point of working through these stages is to better himself. MP is motivated in this regard by stories of the self-made.

I respect the person who had nothing, kind of rags-to-riches story, had nothing and made something of himself. Do what he had to do. [I respect the person who] bettered himself in some way to make his life better, to make society a little bit better, that kind of person.

MP's role model is the person who sets a standard which he defines as striving to improve one's current status—better education, better finances, better reputation.

A role model is someone who kind of sets standards, [a] person who does good, a person who doesn't stray too much. Human nature you are going to stray a little, but as long as you know what was wrong, you can make it better.

MP has a strong inner drive, self-motivation, and self-reliance that support his goals. MP believes he must provide his own "safety net" because his parents aren't wealthy enough to provide one for him.

[Striving] is important, it keeps you heading toward that next step. If you don't want anything and you are happy with where you are, then [you can't] improve [yourself and society]. It's just an inner drive. I am self-motivated. I don't need people. I can do it myself if I have to.
       Where am I going to go if I don't achieve. That's what I like about the rags-to-riches story. People, they have that self-drive because they lack the safety net. They can't fall back on their parents because their parents aren't wealthy. They can't fall back on their father because their father left them. Who

else can they turn to but themselves. They have got to do it by themselves.

Ironically, MP describes the person who is *not* going to get ahead with metaphors of contentment, staying in place, being stuck, slacking off, falling back. This person is the opposite of MP because he lacks ambition, hunger, motivation, and drive. Graduating from high school, getting a job and getting married, staying in the same place you grew up are the pitfalls of contentment and making do.

> If I am dead broke and I don't have a job. I didn't go to a
> good school, just got through high school, but had to stay here.
> I didn't better myself. I lived my whole life here and so how
> did I make myself better? How do I give back. You don't
> want to do better; you are content with this.

In an American context, this drive to achieve could be equated with the entrepreneurial spirit. Paradoxically, MP prefers working *with* a group, not *leading* a group, although he recognizes that he is something of a role model for other Cambodian youth. MP describes himself as just another person in the world, not someone to command attention.

> I don't believe I am a leader. I am just another person in this
> world. I don't need to be that limelight-type person. I don't
> need power. I just see myself as another person in [the]
> corporate world; a person in the work force, another person
> just trying to make it.

MP doesn't want to stick out in a crowd, but he is highly motivated to help others. He prefers to be the one that helps everybody, rather than the one everyone turns to for leadership.

> I think I can help others and still be part of a group instead of
> being the head of a group. I don't want to be a leader. I can
> be like the person in the group that helps everybody, but I
> don't want to be the one that everybody turns to for help. I
> don't want that pressure cause that's a little bit too much. I

don't want people looking towards me, but that doesn't mean
that I won't help them.

Leadership for MP represents too much pressure and brings out the bad
side of people who want to back stab, talk-behind-your-back, or target
you.

> I don't want to stick out in a crowd; I just want to be another
> person in the crowd. If you have too much power, if I am the
> leader..., then you see a different side of people. You see the
> kind of backstabbing side, the talk-behind-your-back side.

Once MP has mastered his personal goals of bettering himself,
taking care of his family and being a role model to his children, he
turns his attention to society. MP sees the point of his education and
his wealth to improve society and to give back to others. In spite of his
goal-directed intensity, MP struggles with the need to live in the
present. He states that it is important to know where you want to go,
but it is not good to look too far into the future.

> I don't really look that deep into the future. The farthest I
> look is just maybe right after college, but you shouldn't really
> look too far into it because then you lose sight of what is going
> on right now. You can't really plan too far ahead but you
> need to know where you want to go.

Reminiscent of an American norm, MP states that his life is
"dominated by time;" he is "time-oriented," "time runs his life," he sets
a "timetable." The pressure to make good time comes from the goals
mentioned above and the expectations he places on himself. This is
emphasized by his belief that Americans are driven by time and by the
need to conquer and compete.

> I am so time-oriented. American culture is so time-oriented.
> Everything is based on time. You have to be at a certain place
> at a certain time. Time runs my life. I set a certain timetable
> for everything like I have to fulfill that goal. I kind of
> structure everything around the concept of time. I have to

graduate from high school in June and then I graduate from college in four or five years, but then I get a job. [The family and the money] aspect is ten years away after I graduate from college, so that is kind of a timetable. [Even if I were in Cambodia] I would have to go to the temple and serve my time.

This particular discussion of time occurred in the fall of MP's senior year in high school. When I asked him one year later what he thought about his first semester at college, he immediately responded with "I have so much time. I have time to study and to just take time for myself. It is kind of amazing!"

Success and wealth are not always correlated for these Khmer families. MP has a great deal to say about rich people. The rich person MP respects is someone who shares his wealth; someone who is not conceited, "me first," or greedy.

The rich people that give back those are the ones that I respect more because it shows that they care and they are not just out for their own sake. I hate rich people [who just keep their money to themselves]. There are certain qualities across the board that people should have. Rich people who are greedy then what's the purpose of having that amount of money if you are going to be greedy. [You] kind of have to share your wealth.

MP believes that he has an obligation to use his education to give back to society. Along the same lines, MP admires the wealthy person who uses his or her money for good.

If I am rich, if I do bad things with my money, if I rob and steal, or if I just throw it away kind of gamble, buy alcohol, drugs. You know what is going to happen when you get good things? Next life, you are not getting them because you didn't do good. What was the purpose of all that money? Someone else could have gotten it and done something good with it.

But the observation that brings MP closest to his Buddhist roots is his conviction that money and material things are not fulfilling in themselves. Fulfillment, then, has a greater value, is more representative of success than wealth.

> Money can take you certain places, but it's what is inside of you that will bring you to another plateau. I think we have to conquer ourselves first. Kind of like Americans are constantly going out but they are not looking within. Material things can bring a certain amount of fulfillment, but it is just not going to bring you complete fulfillment. It fulfills you for the first couple of months.... Then it is just going to be normal; it is just part of your life. You are not going to be content.

The meaning of success for MP in relationship to his family is connected to his religion and to his age. The successful Cambodian male follows certain cultural guidelines which ensure an abundance of merit to his family as well as prepare a smooth path for his parents' eventual rebirth. This goal or expectation for the son is another aspect of bettering oneself, in MP's perception—it is a goal of making good for the family. As he indicates, if he were living in Cambodia, he would spend three months or more as a novice monk in a Buddhist temple. This action brings significant merit to the family and makes them spiritually better off in the next life. The action is enhanced if the parents honor the son by fulfilling certain Cambodian customs such as shaving their own heads and supporting his novitiate.

Paradoxically, this discussion brings up conflicts in MP's narrative as he describes a young American man who serves his time at the Cambodian temple and brings great merit to his family. MP wonders why this American can embrace Buddhism, but he can't.

> If I was back in my homeland, I would be making good for the family. That's a way of getting lots of merit for the family. It makes them better off in the next life. I looked at [another kid trying to become a monk] for the first time. He had a shaved head. I said this kid is not Cambodian because the new monk was talking American to him. I was thinking an American kid can become a monk, but I can't. He comes to embrace this

religion; he is not brought up with this religion. He comes to
honor the religion. His whole family has shaved their head as
a way of honoring him. That is so much merit for his family,
especially since they are supporting him; they are not against
him.

MP admits that going to the temple is not his inclination; that his
parents have not made him attend the *wats* or trained him to pray with
the monks. These observations cause him to step back, to make him
wonder when or where he will find the time to reclaim the ways of his
culture.

> I'm not a going-to-the-temple-everyday type of person. My
> parents didn't make me go to the *wats*, they didn't make me
> pray, but they instilled in me certain religious values that are
> important values. Recently my parents had this celebration a
> few weeks ago. I asked my mother what it was, she said this
> is what you do for your dead parents. If you don't do this they
> don't catch up with life. They don't get reincarnated. They
> stay dead, the soul stays dead. I was thinking, I never knew
> this. What would happen when my parents are gone and I
> don't do this for them? They never come back to life. That
> part of my culture is to taken away from me that I kind of lose
> it.

MP acknowledges that most of Cambodian culture is the family
aspect which he has come to value as he gets older. Even at age 19,
MP comments that the family—his parents and grandmother—have
become more and more important to him as he begins to embark on the
period of his life which is destined to take him away from his home.

> I think Cambodian culture is more a family aspect. You are
> always surrounded by your family so you always have that
> kind of group around you. The older I get things that were a
> privilege before, they get a little bit more important. Your
> parents get more important, the religion.

Thus, he speculates that being successful as one gets older also means being surrounded by one's family.

> When I am older like my grandmother, I want to be around my family. I need that family just to keep me going because that is all that I got left when I am retired. What else am I going to do? I have to be around the younger children that will keep me, that will make me want to wake up every morning.

Avy's role models are the monks because they teach her how to honor her culture. The monks instruct her that the true person does not take life for granted and so dedicates her life to helping others, giving all she has.

> The monks give so much of themselves to the society and to the community. They guide you through your life. From the monks I have learned don't take life for granted. Don't think you are going to live forever. Someday your time will come and you just give everything you have. Don't be greedy or anything.

As a result, the most important Cambodian traditions for Avy are going to the temple and praying to lose her sins.

> Going to the temple and praying are the most important Cambodian traditions. I just believe in that so much. I just think that when I go to temple, I lose my sins when I pray. Every time we have to go to the temple, my grandma would always help me to go and just release all my sins. I like going there, I am honoring my culture.

A frequent topic in her discussion is her grandmother who has taught her to honor the Buddhist religion by being religious. While this has advantages in guaranteeing a future human life, it is primarily the inspiration for being generous in this life.

> My grandmother told me that if you are human in one life, then you should give all you have in your one life so that in

the next life you can become human. The people that don't give all they have, like they don't go to temple, they don't respect the culture, next life they are just not important in society. That is why my grandmother says you must be really thankful that you were born as a human in this life so you can help out other people and help all the things around you so you can become human in the next life.

The other role models in Avy's life are her father, brother, and grandmother. To her, Pirun is successful because he follows the teachings of the monks. He dedicates his life to helping others; he spends much of his time helping people in the community, often at the expense of ignoring his own family members.

A good role model is very helpful with others, understanding and taking the time to help them. I am describing my dad because I think he helps the community. He helps so many people no matter what time of day it is, they call him up and he will just go to help them. I don't think I would be able to do that cause it takes so much time. He dedicates his whole life to helping people. He never, *never* stays home.

Avy is particularly aware that her father is different from some of the elders of the community. She is grateful that he and Rany follow the practice of listening to their children and respecting their opinions. While her parents have consistent guidelines of behavior for their children which are in line with Cambodian tradition, they are willing to adapt some rules to American norms.

He is a very strong person. He thinks very in-depth; he is such a critical thinker. Like between him and other Cambodian old men that I know, he is wicked different from them. He helps so much in the community.

MP is a role model for Avy because he is such a hard working student. Because she equates school success with success in American society, MP's intelligence and commitment to achieving in school are things she admires.

I think that my brother works *really* hard in school. I look at Asian students that came from Forest City High; some of them don't really care about their education [but] my brother he is like a schoolaholic. I don't think that *I* work even as much as he does. He always stays in his room; he does his homework. He is just so *smart*; he is smart in every subject. I don't know how he gets so smart.

It is intriguing to me that for both Avy and MP, the concept of role model does not embody the concept of leadership. Like MP, Avy also prefers being a member of a group rather than being a leader.

I like to be a member of a group. I like to listen in the back, I don't like to lead. I am not that type of person. When I am with my friends, we just talk, but if I am around people I don't know, I don't like to be a leader.

Avy's grandmother Yeang is a role model because she is so highly respected by her family and by other members of the Cambodian community. Yeang is highly religious and has taught her grandchildren how to talk with the monks, how to pray, and how to respect the Buddhist tradition. (She also reads their fortunes from an old book of Cambodian prophecy). Avy recognizes that her grandmother is old fashioned and has not adapted to American ways. Nonetheless, Avy does not dispute her grandmother's wisdom and is more inclined to obey her grandmother than her parents when asked to be careful of her friends and of her reputation.

In describing her ideal of the successful person, Avy speaks almost exclusively of someone who has a college degree and a good career. This is something she wants for herself because she wants to prove to her family that she can make it on her own. She is highly motivated to prove that she has achieved according to American standards and that she has lived up to these more challenging expectations.

Success, in her mind, does not mean becoming wealthy and powerful. Avy states that some people get wealthy because they are lucky, but most people become wealthy because they have knowledge. The person who has the most knowledge and who works really hard, is the person who will be the most financially successful in her opinion.

Success doesn't mean wealthy. I mean if you work hard and
go to college and graduate with a degree, you can get wealthy
out of school from that knowledge. Some of those people that
don't go to college, the only reason that sometimes they get
wealthy is because they are lucky in life. I will be more
successful if I go to college and get more education for myself
in a field I am interested in.

It depends on how you look at life. If you [are] willing to
get something then you work really hard for it. Some people
work really hard to get where they are now and their life
change dramatically. If you strive to do whatever you want
then you can get there, if you are not willing to [do] whatever
it takes, then I don't think it is going to go.

During the course of our interviews, Avy became especially
reflective as she tried to make sense of success represented by a college
degree and a professional career and the success represented by having
a close family and being respected in the Cambodian community.
Because her extended family respects the educated person so highly,
Avy is highly motivated to attend college. She is also highly motivated
to remain close to her family, to have a large family herself, and to
raise her children in the Buddhist traditions.

Avy's narrative with regard to education focuses on her need to
prove to her family that she "can make it on her own."

I don't just want to work in a store; I want to have my own
degree and my own career. It will make me and my family
proud. I want to get a degree and prove to my uncle that I can
make it.

You have to prove to yourself that you can make it, with
maybe a little help from other people. But you have to prove
to yourself that you can make it on your own.

However, there is a subtle tension in the way Avy refers to "making it
on your own" and "being on your own." Avy wants a certain amount
of freedom after she graduates from high school, but this does not
mean that she intends to strike out on her own. She is choosing

colleges that are close enough to Forest City so that she can visit her family frequently.

> The farthest I want to go to college is in [a city two hours from home] so I can visit my family often. I wouldn't want to go off on my own cause I don't know if I can do it. I am so used to being with my family every night and stuff.

Tension is also evident in the way Avy describes having her own family and having a career. She would like to have four children since her own parents and all of her aunts and uncles have had four children. But Avy also expects to have a career—possibly working in a family owned business or something involving travel. For her, there is no point is going to college and getting a degree if you don't do anything with it. In other words, just getting married and having a family may not be sufficiently successful for her as an individual or as a parent.

> I think I would have to balance having a family and having a career. I am not going to have a family and not have a career cause what is the point of going to college if I am going to go to college and then knowing after I graduate, I get married and have kids and don't do anything afterward.

Avy does not articulate as clearly as MP her perception that one type of life path common to Cambodian culture, is less successful than the life path followed by Americans. However, she clearly recognizes that in American society, the person who graduates from high school, gets a job and gets married might be successful for now, but the person who followed American culture and went to college and received a degree, would be more successful in the future.

> If I was to follow the American culture, I think I would be more successful 'cause I would be able to go to college instead of after high school graduation just work or get married. I think I would be successful maybe right now, but in the future, I would not be as successful as the person who have a degree and go to college.

Avy's narrative is the most conflicted when it comes her identity a Cambodian woman of "high praise" in the community. In listening to the stories that frequently surface in the Khmer community, she is aware of how easy it is for a young woman to be judged on the basis of external behavior or innuendo.

> My [Cambodian] friend she wears oversized clothes [and] people talk about her. She did something in the past [and] everyone talks about it like they think she is a bad person. I have known her all my life [and] I don't think she is. It is just one thing she did [and] it ruined her reputation in Cambodian society.

Avy states that her parents don't want people to talk behind her back because someone in the community has seen her with a boyfriend, or because she is out late with her friends.

> I can really understand why my parents don't want me to be seen with guys because they don't want people to talk and say behind their back, 'Oh his daughter goes out so much with guys and she is partying.' Stuff that they assume in a bad way. I can understand it, I guess I would be like that if I was a parent. I would be more protective of my daughters because guys can't get pregnant and girls can.

She especially does not want to worry her grandmother with whom she is especially close. Avy is reluctant to challenge her grandmother's traditional beliefs about a girl's reputation, even though Avy argues that it is not good to be entirely stuck in Cambodian culture now that she is an American.

> It is because I am getting older, they are so worried I am going to get a bad reputation. I still go by the culture, but I think of the fact that I am in America. I shouldn't be like *so* stuck to the Cambodian culture since I am an American, you know.

As a compromise, Avy has voluntarily chosen to limit the time she spends going out with friends.

> During my freshman year I usually went out a lot. I went out
> really late. In my sophomore year I did too, but I set a limit
> for myself. I don't want my parents to worry about me. I talk
> to my friends about it all the time. When they go out now they
> set limits for themselves.

As she reflected on her parents' reasons for being over protective
with their daughters, Avy was surprised to discover that she would
probably raise her own daughter the same way. As much as she resents
the social labeling, she admits that she would protect her own daughter
from this kind of social judgment.

> I really didn't understand why my parents wouldn't let me go
> out, but now I know it is because I am a girl. I hated that, but
> now I understand because when I have kids I am going to be
> like that too. I don't want them to go out as much. I was
> thinking, if I was my parents, I wouldn't let me go out as late.

Avy clearly does not want her parents to arrange her marriage. On
the other hand, she knows that the married couple will be more
successful if the two sets of parents know one another and love each
other's family. She believes that it is the parents' duty to find out
everything about a potential husband to ensure that he does not have a
bad reputation in the community.

> It is good for a couple if the parents know each other because
> they probably love each other's family so they just want to
> keep it more through the kids. If I brought a guy home [that
> they didn't know] and they don't know the parents, they don't
> know if he has a bad reputation or how he was raised.

Finally, Avy emphasizes her belief that the successful parent
honors and follows Buddhism when she states that she will raise her
children to honor the religion. Her family's expectations for leading a
good Buddhist life are the expectations she carries with her as a future
parent. She wants her children to believe in the power of the monk
who can help you with life and guide the way to right living.

I would teach my children that even though we are living in American culture, we still have to honor our religion cause that is what we were brought up to be. That is our original religion. I would teach them if you ever have a chance to go to temple, just go pay your respect to the monk. I think it is good to honor religion so it can help you guide the way to right living.

Alyana is, from all appearances is a well-adjusted, highly motivated American teenager. Yet, she, like her sister Avy, connects her personal success to her family. Her role models are her father and her grandmother. They exemplify the qualities she most admires: honesty and trust. She describes her father as someone who doesn't judge people but accepts them as they are.

A role model for me would be someone like my grandmother, but like my father, like a mix. That is what I want to be like when I grow up. They have honesty, and I like the way they deal with family things, the way they deal with us. I respect my grandmother very much. Whatever she says is what goes for me because she is like the top in the family.

Alyana especially respects her grandmother who sets down rules for her to follow, teaches her about Buddhism, and interprets her dreams.

I don't think my grandmother would be highly respected by American standards because she doesn't speak English, so you know, there goes a comment and I don't like that. All her Cambodian friends respect her and she respects them, everybody who knows her.

I asked her if there was someone in literature whom she specially admired; she named Cinderella as a personal role model. The qualities she most admires in Cinderella are her willingness to work hard and ignore the abuse. In this example, Alyana makes a distinction between when it is appropriate to speak out against bad treatment and when it is not. Presumably it has something to do with the respect one owes one's parents or guardians. Nonetheless, Alyana admires the fact that

Cinderella stays truthful to herself and to her friends. The most important thing to Alyana is that Cinderella respects other people (even her abusive step family) and she treats other people kindly.

> I identify with Cinderella. She is hardworking, she puts up with the abuse. Even if she wants to say something, she knows that it is not right to say that. She is going to keep it to herself, but she tells her little friends. She is very truthful to herself and other people. She respects other people and treats other people kindly.

An important theme in Alyana's personal narrative of success is one of self-reliance. In contrast with Avy, Alyana frequently describes herself as independent, someone who likes to be by herself. In school, she does not want people to do things for her. She wants to work alone, solve her own problems, and think for herself.

> There are times when I like to be with other kids but most of the time I like to be working alone to know how I think for myself and how I am. I like to think for myself. I don't like other people to take over for me. Even if I am trying so hard and I can't get that, I don't want anybody else's help. I just want them to explain it, but I want to think for myself.

Self-reliance is a deeply internalized cultural model, and Alyana demonstrates a great deal of confidence in and acceptance of her abilities—in school and in her outside activities.

> I think it would be better if you rely on yourself cause you know what you are doing and what to expect. When you rely on others, sometimes, or all the time, you get a different answer and it is not always positive.

Alyana uses a Buddhist concept when she refers to personal goals. She does not compare herself to other students because she believes that she thinks differently from other people. She wants to be judged on the quality of her work, not in competition with others.

> Everything that I do, even if it is bad or good, I consider it as high quality because that is how far I can go. If I did a test and I got a really bad grade, like sure it is a bad grade, but I tried my best so I accepted it cause that was me. I don't care if other people have higher grades than me because if that is how they can do it, then that is them. That is the way they think. The way I think is different from other people. If that is the grade that I got, then that is the grade that I deserve because it was me.

Alyana says that unless family or work intervene to "mess up her thinking," she wants to go all the way to a medical doctorate. As stated earlier, Alyana's ambition is to be a medical doctor and she has some indication of the amount of schooling required to reach this goal. The status of the M.D. is not what seems to draw Alyana to the profession, rather it is the opportunity to help other people. In fact, status which sets a person apart from others does not seem successful to Alyana. Like her siblings, the Buddhist concept of the middle way seems more appropriate

> A prince, a queen or a king would not really be a [successful person] because it is just too much. I couldn't handle that. I just want to be an average person, not too high. If I am famous, just keep it right there, or maybe if I am just average, just keep it right there.

Alyana has a powerful relationship with her religion and her culture. It comprises her personal worldview in the way she describes going to the temple as the most important Cambodian tradition. When she was a little girl she "sat right up in front because she loved looking at the Buddha." As she gets older, she states, she "prefers to sit in the middle." The monks represent people she can trust because they listen to her with respect; they tell her to go the right way and to respect elderly people. She equates talking with the monks to talking with her grandparents.

CHINDA'S FAMILY

Biography

Chinda is a small, sturdy woman with short hair which has the remnants of a permanent. She wears glasses, and the fingernails on her slender hands are frequently painted dark red. Chinda dresses in layers, choosing slacks and sweaters or shorts and blouses depending on the season. Chinda was born in 1954 in Phnom Penh to an upper-class family. She recounted that her grandfather worked as a "law" clerk in a village in Suayring Province, helping people who could not read or write. Her father, who had to walk many miles to attend school, completed his education and joined the military.

Colonial French forces predominantly staffed the Cambodian military in the 1940s. Chinda's father spoke French, which made it possible for him to continue his education eventually rising to the rank of colonel in the army. According to Chinda, he became very wealthy and was appointed to the royal guard that protected King Sihanouk. Members of the military, particularly at this level, were among the first to be killed by the Khmer Rouge; this was the fate of Chinda's father.

Chinda's mother, also from Suayring Province, was a traditional wife who stayed at home taking care of her two sons and five daughters. As was common for Cambodian women of her generation, she did not attend school. Chinda recounts an interesting but perhaps typical story of her birth.

> When I was a baby my mother had a problem raising kids.
> Two of my sisters before me die at one or two years old.
> When I was born I was very sick. I got an eye infection, when
> I open my eyes [I had] all kind of blood coming out of my
> eyes.
>
> Then a fortune teller told [my mother] that [she] cannot
> raise me. She had to pay someone else to be a caregiver for a
> year and I [have] to live with that person. [The fortune teller
> told my mother] you have to let that child wear ragged clothes,
> not to put something pretty on her. That's how Cambodians
> think. If the child is really sick, they have to make the child
> look ugly [so] that the ghost won't like them [and] won't take
> them. I was two or three [when I came back home].

I think the caregivers [were] afraid of my parents because
my mother pay them money. They have to be gentle with me.
No matter how far away they [lived] from my parents, they
wouldn't do anything bad to me. They had to pay *extra*
attention to me. [So] I grow up with a high self-esteem, with a
lot of hope.

Chinda's first husband was also a military officer; their son Rithy
was born in 1971. Chinda's husband was killed by the Khmer Rouge
in 1975, leaving Chinda and Rithy to survive all four years of the
Khmer Rouge revolution. In 1978 Chinda met and married Seoun, her
second husband. At the end of the war, just after the Vietnamese
invasion, Chinda and her husband walked to the Thai refugee camps on
the Cambodian border. Anticipating that the journey would be very
dangerous, Chinda left Rithy with her mother.

Chinda's, second son Mam was born in the refugee camps in 1980.
She describes that experience:

After I got [to the displacement camps] it was like being a
prisoner. We could not get out of the camp, [but] the camp
was not safe. There was a lot of robbery, killing, and raping
of women in the camps. We stay like in a cage and cannot get
out, cooped up, cannot see anything. We [always] thinking
about getting out of the camp. We are desperate about getting
out. People just keep writing to the embassy, submitting the
applications. I didn't have any English, but people get the
model [of the application] from the American Red Cross. The
people have that model and they just wrote to the embassy.
We asked people who had good handwriting. My sponsor in
the United States was one of my Cambodian friends from the
camps. She had a relative living in Forest City. She had a
sister who was married to an American husband before the
war.

Mam was born in the camps during the starvation, the
Cambodian starvation in 1980. In the camps when I was
pregnant, we were surrounded by killing people and mean
people. We stayed with a very abusive family. The woman
also very abuse. She doesn't have children and she like to

have Mam all the time. This woman was very, very mean to
everyone else [but not to him].

Chinda, Soeun, and Mam arrived in Forest City in 1981, and her
daughter April was born two weeks later. After they were settled in the
U.S., Chinda's brother and sister-in-law, traveling with her five-year-
old son Rithy, made their way from Cambodia to the Thai border. All
three were eventually resettled in Australia. Chinda admits that the
first two years she was separated from Rithy, she cried every day for
him, but she states that they never talk any more. April, her daughter,
has struck up a friendship with her half-brother and dreams of going to
live with him one day. Chinda divorced Soeun in 1985 and he moved
to a nearby state; neither have remarried.

None of Chinda's extended family have followed her to Forest
City. Her mother is still living in Phnom Penh with her younger sister.
Chinda says that her younger sister is very close to her mother and has
followed a more traditional path than she has. She wants to bring one
of her sisters to live in Forest City, but she needs to have a full-time job
to act as a sponsor. Chinda intends to complete her associates degree
before she looks for full-time work, so her sister waits in Cambodia.
Chinda's closest friend is a Romanian woman, herself a refugee.

Chinda, Mam, and April live in one of the low-income housing
projects about five miles from downtown, not far from where Pirun and
his family live. Their duplex is at the end of the street and sits next to
an open field. The building is small and unpainted with a postage-
stamp front yard that is littered with toys, cans, and plastic bags. Next
to the driveway is a small piece of land where one of the residents
plants vegetables and flowers in the summertime. As you climb the
stairs to Chinda's second floor apartment, you come to a landing which
contains exercise equipment, plastic bags full of something, and pairs
of shoes. One must remove one's shoes to enter the living room which
contains a large, overstuffed sofa, coffee table, two chairs, and a large
entertainment center complete with television, stereo system, and VCR.
Statues of the Buddha adorn the top of the television set and the tops of
tables, and images of the Buddha and relatives cover the walls. The
kitchen is off the living room, and light streams in over a large kitchen
table and a counter piled with dishes, boxes of cereal, and snack food.
Three small bedrooms open to the right off the main hall with a single

bathroom on the left. Chinda recently purchased a new computer which is ensconced in April's room and is set up for late-night conversations over the internet.

Chinda became an American Citizen in 1987 and acquired her GED in 1988. She spent a year of intensive English study to prepare herself for college and simultaneously enrolled part-time at the local university. Taking two courses a semester, she has earned sixty credit hours toward her associate degree; she needs 120 credit hours to graduate. Chinda has supplemented her AFDC and housing benefits by working at a variety of part-time jobs over the past fifteen years, from housekeeping to welfare case work. She gravitates toward jobs in social services, specifically in the counseling field. Her major field of study is psychology and human development, with a focus on the status of minority women and children. In 1994, Chinda assisted the director of the nursing education program at the university as the interpreter on a yearlong research project to gather the stories of Cambodian women. The social science field speaks both to her intellectual interest and her own personal experience as a refugee.

Because of her expertise with English and Khmer, Chinda is frequently called on by members of the Cambodian community to translate, especially to help people interact with the welfare or health care system. Chinda does this willingly, without pay in most cases. She also served for three years as the primary Khmer radio announcer, taking over from Pirun in 1994. She kept the community informed on the political ups and downs of the Cambodian government, on the changes in the U.S. welfare laws, and about events at the Buddhist Center.

When Venerable Uch Ros was living at the Center from 1996 to 1997, Chinda began spending time at the temple, bringing food to the monks, discussing Buddhist philosophy with them, and helping with cleaning and errands. She attends the New Year ceremonies, but is not a regular at fundraising events. She is sensitive to the remarks by many community elders that she is far too independent and allows her daughter too much freedom, and so Chinda limits her attendance at large public ceremonies.

Chinda's second son, Mam is eighteen years old and a high school dropout. He is dark skinned with a closed, somewhat brooding face. Over the course of one year, after persistent attempts, I was unable to persuade him to be interviewed by or even talk with me. All of the information I have about Mam is anecdotal from his mother, sister, and one of his close friends. When I first met Chinda in 1993 and again in 1995, Mam was living with his father in another state. He was not attending school. Chinda describes Mam as a very angry, very mean person.

> Mam was very sick in the camps, very, very sick. When we got [to the United States] he had to be hospitalized about a week. He [was] coughing a lot, like pneumonia. Mam very, very mean [when he was little]. He scratch April. He is very jealous of her. I cannot hold April or he is going to get jealous. Mam was like my ex-husband, his father. His father doesn't have a life structure and I see in Mam the same thing, go the same [way]. He doesn't do any [planning] he just go.
>
> Mam is not too open, even with me. He doesn't like to talk about his problem. Same thing like my ex-husband, [he] doesn't like to talk about his problems. [He is] not open. I don't think Mam trusts many people. Mam respect his father, but his father talk with him. [His father] told him it is hard to work at a factory, so you need to study hard. I am thinking Mam suffer very emotionally from being separated from the father because the father tried to ignore him.

Mam returned to Forest City and enrolled as a junior at Stevens High School for the 1997/98 school year. According to his mother, Mam had a very troubled year and ended up flunking most of his classes. He returned to school in the fall of 1998 to repeat his junior year, but by November he had dropped out again.

> He was the student of the month and on the honor roll. After grade six he moved to Grant Middle School. The problem started then. Sometimes he complain about the teacher picking on him [because he was not white].

Chinda stated that Mam has recently passed the math portion of the GED with a nearly perfect score, but has not taken the English test.

[At Stevens High School] the teacher told me Mam very
polite. He just called me last month and said Mam very polite,
he very intelligent, but the problem [is] he doesn't do the
work. [In school,] he like math. He is also good at science; he
doesn't even study hard to pass the test.

Both his mother and sister report that Mam's personal life has
taken priority over school and work. According to Chinda, his
thirteen-year-old girlfriend recently became pregnant and would have
kept the baby had she not miscarried. She and Mam continue to see
one another, even though Chinda observes them fighting all the time.
Mam and April also fight. Chinda told me that the police were recently
sent to Stevens High School to stop a fight between Mam and his sister.

Mam can be found at home most days, sleeping or listening to
music. He has gone through a number of jobs and is currently working
at a local car wash. The money he earns goes to pay the lease on his
car and his late night excursions with his friends. Kusal, a one-time
friend, describes Mam:

Mam is a very smart kid. He is very smart, you know, 'cause
he grew up here when he was little. His English is very good.
But he keep a lot of stuff to himself, and sometime he get very
angry. The temper is very bad. When he don't get his way,
his own way, he slam things and smash things. He can be a
very nice person, but sometimes his violence, sometimes he
goes crazy. He is just kind of lost sometime, like sometimes
in his head.

He just don't care, he don't have respect for his family. I
went there one time. Him and April got in a fight and they
really fight, fist fight, punches and all that, yelling and
screaming. They don't have respect for each other. They
don't respect sister, brother, help each other out, like he only
care about himself. He care about himself a lot. I saw him a
few times, he is with the wrong crowd. All it takes in the
wrong crowd for anybody.

April is 17 and half way through her junior year at Stevens High
School. April is about five feet tall, with short black hair blunt cut just

at her jaw line. She has a round face, clear complexion and serious eyes. Her build gives the impression of an athlete, and she admits that she likes to play basketball, softball, and has a special passion for canoeing and kayaking. She describes herself as a poet and prefers writing poetry to talking. In fact, our first interview was relatively brief and unrevealing. I learned more about her by spending the day shadowing her at Stevens High School. April turned out to be popular with a wide variety of students—Asian and white, upperclassmen and her own peers. With her friends, she was talkative, opinionated, and appeared to be something of a leader. In the classroom, April chose a seat at the front of the class. She was prepared for each of her assignments, she participated in discussions, and she worked intently on work that was assigned in class. Her teachers consistently commented that April was one of the best students in the class and frequently made the honor roll.

My second interview with April was held at her home. Although she ignored two appointments for the interview before finally agreeing to meet with me at her apartment, April was more relaxed and almost eager to talk.

To facilitate our second conversation, I analyzed her first transcript using the Voice Centered Method created by Brown and Gilligan, 1992. I gave her three poems I had created from her words—one for the Self, one for the voice of We, and one for the voice of They. She was delighted when I showed them to her and read through them thoughtfully. She was intrigued that I was able to capture her personality from an interview done almost one year before. She went on to describe herself:

> I am just a regular teenager, that's all. [I don't talk to anyone
> about my feelings], I just write poems. I want to live in a city.
> [In the] city there is more stuff to do, different types of people
> and more activities to keep me busy. [I like living with] a
> variety of people. I will probably get married; I want two
> kids, no more than two.

April transferred from Forest City High School to Stevens High School at the beginning of her freshman year and lost a half-year of school, which she has made up by taking extra courses. She made the honor roll both terms in the 1997/98 school year. Her favorite subject is science, and in my first interview with her, she stated that she wanted to be a marine biologist. April started her junior year with great promise, but as a result of a serious illness in November, she had to drop out of school. She took a part-time evening job and spends time with her friends.

> I am barely ever home now; I am usually out with my friends. [I work from] 3:00 to 9:00. I am not usually home until like 3:00 in the morning. We go to Zoots [a local dance club], we go to the clubs. We find places to hang out.

In spite of missing the fall term, April is determined to complete her junior year and then leave Forest City for good. Every time I have met with April, she has spoken of wanting to live in Florida. Chinda recently informed me that April has contacted a former teacher and his wife who live in the Orlando area about living with them while she completes her senior year.

> I am going to live with my teacher and his wife [in Florida]. I was close to my teacher ever since sixth grade, we were close in sixth grade. He was a science and English teacher. He has one son, and his wife has three other kids. Their [kids] are old, they like in their 40s. In Florida, I am three minutes from the high school. I am going to leave in the beginning of August to check out the school and get to know the area. If I finish this year and take summer school, I will have exactly enough credits to move on as a senior.

Based on her past performance, there is every reason to believe that April will complete her school requirements and enroll as a senior in a new high school in Orlando, Florida. Her long-range goals are to attend Central Florida State which is also located in Orlando. She has been looking into their business programs and is intrigued with the possibility of learning how to scull.

> Central Florida University has been like my dream because it is in the city. I have been looking them up and they have a

good business program. It's in Orlando, plus they offer
sculling. It's fun. I want to get a college degree in business
management.

Chinda is very proud of April and she allows her much more
freedom than most Cambodian parents. As she put it, "If her grades
continue to be good, then there is no reason to restrict her fun time."
Nonetheless, Chinda expects April to respect her authority and to stay
away from bad influences. Chinda wishes that April would be more
responsible around the house, and at 17, April still does not know how
to cook. Unlike many other Cambodian adolescents, she does not have
younger brothers and sisters for whom she is responsible. Chinda
seems pleased that April is planning to move to Florida in August. She
states that it is time for her to learn how to be independent and live on
her own so that she doesn't come to depend on her mother the rest of
her life.

Interpretations of Success: Findings
From our earliest conversations in 1993, Chinda has stated that being
successful is being independent. She has found evidence within her
Cambodian traditions that women have historically had equal power
alongside Cambodian men. In early Cambodian history, she states,
"The women were more powerful than the men. But when the woman
who ruled Cambodia met and married the Hindu prince, then women
became the subjects of men. The women fought against the Hindu
Way for a long time." In Cambodia, Chinda fought against her
parents' restrictions and a culture which made it difficult to have a
college education and a career. In America, Chinda has reclaimed her
ancient right to be equal with men. Thus, the strong, well-educated
woman who is free to follow her own choices and ambition is, in
Chinda's mind, both a Cambodian and an American concept.

I kept wondering if I would become an educated woman or a
professional and have a career on my own. I thought it would
be wonderful to have all the freedom I want in my life. But I
always wondered how long will my freedom last? Could I
find a way out of the prison of my parents' expectations for
me. I was wondering why my parents had very different

expectations about freedom from me. I would cry for my freedom all the time. I kept dreaming about freedom and finally got my freedom in the United States. I hope some day that I will accomplish my education and become an educated Cambodian woman.

Freedom is a major theme in Chinda's narrative of success. She wants to be free to express her feelings, her desires; she wants equal power and access to opportunities with men; she instills ideas of independence and freedom in her daughter, and occasionally she exerts her right to challenge authority and voice her own opinion.

I am too 'Americanized' because I am going out and talking about my feelings. My culture suppresses women, everything about their feeling, about their sexual desire. We are supposed to say nothing about that. You keep feelings inside, you don't talk about them, it make you sick mentally, make you feel lonely, depressed. I want to change what is bad about my culture, so I have to keep talking about my feelings.

I give my children more freedom, especially the girls, than the way it supposed to be. I like the Americanized way because the girl can choose her own life to live. As her mother, I can tell April what is right or what is wrong, but it is up to her to decide; it is her choice. I wouldn't force her to get married to someone or choose her husband for her.

The freedom to control your life, to choose your friends is commonly given to men in Cambodian culture. Chinda argues that women deserve the same freedom and should not end up penalized by the community which equates freedom for women with a bad reputation.

The men have more power [than the women]. The men can decide if they want to do something, meet their friend, or go out somewhere. They don't have to ask their wives. If a woman wants to go to a friend's house, you are going to have trouble if you get a very strict husband. My brother have much more freedom. When he had different ideas, he went

out and did them. They didn't give him a lot of advice
because he is a boy.

Women have power over men in the way they have to
raise the children and how they should be in the world, but in
terms of freedom, no. The girl doesn't have as much freedom
as the boy. Cambodians value the girl's virginity; they are
considered a good girl. The [good girl] can get an arranged
marriage with whomever the parent want.

Chinda believes she has realized her dream of success in the
United States. She is proceeding with her college education; she
accepts some public assistance and works part-time to support her
children; and she volunteers a significant amount of time helping
people in her community. From an American perspective, Chinda
would probably be considered a successful, self-reliant single mother.
In the abstract, she should also be considered "high praise" in the
Cambodian community. The fact that she is not has a lot to do with
cultural ideology around women's freedom which has been passed
along for generations and which is resistant to change—at least among
Cambodians of her generation.

Another perception of individual success has to do with being a
good Buddhist. Chinda is a thoughtful student and practitioner of
Buddhism. While not as erudite as Pirun, Chinda has spent a lot of
time in the temple talking with the monks about Buddhist philosophy
and practice. She states emphatically that Buddhism does not suppress
women, condemn them to abusive marriages, or restrict their education.
It is the Cambodian culture that does this to women, and so Chinda
finds no inconsistency between her Buddhist beliefs and her personal
stand on women's independence.

Buddhism doesn't believe that you stay with the bad people.
If the husband is very abusive, Buddhism says stay away from
those people and go find a master to guide you. The *culture*
do that, the Cambodian culture. The Cambodian culture make
the woman believe they have to stay married in order to have
the good reputation for your daughter. Buddhism say you
don't have to stay with the perpetrator.

Chinda's interpretation of the Buddhist Way compliments her personal philosophy. For her, the concept of *karma* justifies her self-reliance and makes her responsible for her own actions. Chinda follows the Buddhist precepts without feeling compelled to attend Buddhist ceremonies or spend time in the temple.

> Buddhism you don't need to go to temple to worship God to prove that you are a Buddhist as long as you know the five precepts like refrain from killing or right action, right speech. If I consider that I am doing something good for my life and I worship the Buddha, I don't need to go to prayer. I just don't lie. I don't hurt anybody. If I can't love them at least I don't hurt anybody.
>
> The Buddha say we should not say something that break up a friendship between two people, like say something that is not true. If I do that action, I am going to get the same action in some form in my life. I got to get it back, it reflect to me no matter where I go.

Chinda's chosen major at the university and her career ambitions are consistent with the Buddhist belief that helping others brings great merit to an individual. Chinda is drawn to the service professions, and so she has chosen courses in human development and psychology, social welfare, and philosophy. Her course work has supported her community work, but her experience of working in the Forest City Cambodian community exemplifies the conflict that exists between a Buddhist ideal and the cultural reality. Chinda believes that she is judged by her traditional Khmer peers for being a "liberated" woman. Yet these peers expect her help with the very skills she acquired through her independence. She believes they expect her to help with translation skills in a variety of circumstances—welfare services, physical and mental health care, education, and immigration. Because of this hypocrisy, Chinda limits the time she spends with them. She insists on setting up boundaries and tries to avoid expectations, dependency, and people who take advantage of her.

> My community say to me why are you going to school, you are too old for school. I don't buy what they say. I have to

live for my life now, I don't live for their life. I don't care
what they think about my family because that is not my
problem. If they hate me, that is not my problem. I cannot
make them like me.

I am very involved with my community but I had to set up
boundaries with my work. I don't make friends when I do the
translation. I don't get involved with their personal feelings.
Sometimes in my culture if a Cambodian invite me for lunch,
or to do something, I avoid that because they expect me to do
more for them. I don't want that person to be dependent on
me all the time. Some people take advantage.

Chinda is quick to state that when people treat her the way she wants to
be treated (respectfully, as an equal), she gives, as Buddha instructs,
from her heart with all that she has. "Some people, if they treat me the
way I want to be treated. I give them more. I respond to them
spontaneously without them asking me what to do."

Based on the story of her childhood, Chinda has a perspective on
what it is like to be rich and poor. In Cambodia, she states, the poor
have few opportunities to be successful because they are confined to
their social class by a power structure that denies them resources and
education. In Chinda's mind the ancient Cambodian (Hindu) concept
of the social caste defines the individual and is perpetuated in a modern
ideology of social determinism. The poor are blamed for being poor,
lazy, and dumb; the rich, by contrast, can do what they want, even if it
flouts cultural norms. She believes that the rich judge the poor by
external standards instead of considering all the circumstances which
contribute to their poverty.

The upper class [in Cambodia] never had the experience of the
lower class. They don't know what it is like to be in poverty,
how the people have to struggle. And they judge the people as
poor, dumb, or lazy. They stereotype them. I don't like to
judge people that way. You have to judge from the inside, get
close to look at how they came to be that way.

The high social class who get divorced and the poor who
get divorced, the poor get blamed more. The high social class
wouldn't get blamed because everything in the high social

class is good for them. They just tend to blame on the poor
people. They get divorced all the time, nobody say anything.
It is just to the lower classes that they say, "Don't get
divorced."

In America, Chinda believes that the lines between rich and poor
are much less absolute. With hard work and persistence, the poor can
get ahead in America because they are not confined within an
immutable condition of poverty.

In Cambodia the bias is between the rich and the poor. That
bias carry over from generation to generation, but in the U.S.
we get less bias against the rich and poor. It is not as bad as in
Cambodia.
    In the Third World there are people starving. In the U.S.
you have all kind of stuff, the government give you a lot of
stuff. You can cross the line even though we are poor, if you
just work hard. You have a brain if you just work. In the
Third World, when you are poor, you are poor. You cannot
cross the line at all.

Chinda believes that success and making money are not
necessarily the same thing. Families who spend all of their time
making money, she states, tend to lose their children.

I don't think it is easy for Cambodian kids to succeed. Very
few of them go to college. They got the impression from their
parent that school is not important, it is the money, money.
They have to go make money. Some people have two jobs
and they leave the kid out.

For her, having to make money sometimes gets in the way of achieving
the academic success she so desires. And in her opinion, the person
who is extremely wealthy, more often than not, has more misfortune
than a person who has a good life but is in a lower social class.

You can see people who have million, million, multimillion.
If they cannot be happy they commit suicide, they on drugs.

This is not based on their social class. The poor people think,
"Oh, they have a lot of money, they must be happy. They can
do everything they want." But it is not true, they are worse
than the poor people.

Chinda's personal philosophy of financial success is strongly
connected to her personal philosophy about education. Having enough
money to continue her education is the motivation behind making
money. "Sometimes making money gets in your way of success. I
need money to stay in school, in order to buy books, to support my
family. If I don't solve this problem of making money, I cannot
concentrate on my studies."

Chinda echoes many other Khmer when she states that education is
the most important asset—with an education you can make the money
you need. Thus education will bring you out of poverty; it will help
you cross class lines, and education will help you raise a beautiful
family. Money brings you certain status, but education is much more
highly valued.

Even though Chinda came from a wealthy family, she had limited
access to education in Cambodia because she is female. Temple
schools were off limits; public schools were expensive, and it was
difficult to advance to the high school level. Even if a woman passed
the examinations to attend high school, she was frequently pressured
by her family to abandon her goals.

When I was in junior high school, I passed the exam for high
school. I could leave home and stay at my friend's house in
the city of Koh Kong. This was my first experience that I can
be on my own. Every morning we went to school and made
different friends, and we had different teachers for different
subjects.

Most of my teachers in school encouraged me to become
independent. This meant self-reliance, become an educated
woman, have a good career. That way the woman would feel
happier by living independently. But my sister took the
opposite direction. She was really submissive to my parents.
Whatever my parents said, she obeyed. She remained like the
traditional Cambodian woman.

As noted before, continuing education for adults was not a Cambodian norm. However, Chinda's education takes precedence over finding a full-time job or being a more traditional stay-at-home mother. Because of her passion for education and the self-reliance it fosters, Chinda continually pushes her children to do well in school telling them that success in life is "part high skill and part strong will."

Education is Chinda's pathway to achieve individual success. It provides her with a marketable skill which ensures her freedom and independence. Her career is focused on helping people of lower social status which ensures merit according to the precepts of Buddhism. Her goal is not to make a lot of money, but to balance her life between her Cambodian and American identities.

Chinda's narrative is a dramatic example of the epistemological conflicts she personally experiences in balancing a Cambodian and American identity. When asked to discuss strategies for achieving this balance, Chinda speaks about the importance of family. In spite of the confrontational relationship she had with her own family, Chinda believes that a successful individual is the product of a close, open-minded family.

Following from her belief that the modern, industrial state perpetuates social inequality for the individual, Chinda also believes the obsession with competition and making money is toxic to the family structure. The most successful families, she believes, are found in societies, like Cambodia, where the norm is based on an agricultural, non-industrialized economy.

> In Cambodia we are very close in terms of the family. We live close together, but the country is not industrialized. It doesn't have social services because we don't need them. My opinion is that you can't have success in the family and also have an industrial economy. In an industrial economy, the family tends to fall apart from lack of communication and commitment. Everyone tends to pour all their energy into work instead of taking care of the family. It seems inhuman to me.
>
> Conversely, I find that in an unindustrialized country like Cambodia, the children tend to be much more respectful and loving and make more of a commitment to their own people,

especially when we get older. Those kids have a very strong commitment to take care of their parents and devote themselves to taking care of them.

The family, Chinda states, is the best place for the child to learn respect for elders, good Cambodian norms, and a strong sense of identity. Without this combination, the child is pulled between two cultures and often gets lost.

For the kid, being Cambodian is confusing; they don't know their identity. They get pulled between the two cultures. You have to respect yourself, who you are. No matter if you are from the third world, you are still Cambodian, you can't deny that.
 Cambodian kids don't have a role model because they aren't sure about their identity. They are not Cambodian and not American, they are pulled between the two cultures. In order to grow up and become a strong person, they have to have a role model at home. The girl can see the mother and the boy can see the father. That does not exist in this community, which is why we have all our problems.

While the family is the primary institution for teaching the cultural norms of discipline, respect, and obedience, the Cambodian community has similar responsibilities to teach and support children. According to Chinda, Cambodian public radio instructs children that they must take responsibility for learning how to live in a right way. If the parents cannot do this, then the child must seek counsel from teachers, relatives, good friends or the Buddhist master.

Discipline between the parent and children has got to be learned. I remember that they teach me about the discipline for the children on the public radio in Cambodia. They say that you don't need to rely on your parents for everything to teach you, to discipline you in a good way. You can learn from yourself, from the environment, from the teacher or good friend, or go to the master. In Cambodia there are teachers, friends, and masters who can support an individual.

Chinda bases her theory about families on the cultural model of "not too strict and not too loose." Families who are able to set appropriate boundaries for their children and encourage their children to express their own opinions and desires will perpetuate the Khmer ideal of closeness. They will "conquer the mind between the two cultures" in finding a way to support their children's development of a Cambodian-American identity.

Families who are too strict with their daughters, who don't trust their children or who are so strict they physically punish their children, will cause the family to fall apart just as in a family which is too loose with its children.

> Some Cambodian families are very, very strict. I think the more they control their kids, the reverse they get. They check the teenager and question their friends. The more they do this, the kid try to stay away from them. We have to conquer the mind between the two cultures. I don't say that we have to forget our culture, but we have to compromise between parents and children.
>
> Cambodian parents don't let their girls have any freedom, but the parents go to work and leave them home all the time. The more the parents control the girls, the more they try to sneak out, they try to lie. The girl is hungry for freedom, and if you put the bird in the cage, they want to fly out. If you give them enough freedom, they don't think about leaving.

Parents who find a middle way—between Cambodian norms as well as between Cambodian and American culture—will maintain respect and harmony in the family. The children who are trusted to handle a certain amount of freedom along with a certain amount of family responsibility will be less likely to break family bonds by running away.

> The most important thing you have to do with the kid is teach the kid to obey. You have to build your trust between the child and the parent. If you don't trust your child, if you question her all the time, accusing the girl of going to meet the boy somewhere, you are going to end up with a real problem.

> I look at April. If she study hard, if she get good grades, that
> mean a good sign for me to trust her. The bad kid that
> associate with the wrong crowd, doing drugs, they are not
> going to school, that a sign for me not to trust them.
>   Not trusting your children is worse than setting
> boundaries. They won't follow the parent's rules and end up
> running away from home. Cambodian run away from home
> because the parents are too strict and from lack of trust. If you
> are too strict it is not going to work. Too lenient doesn't work
> either. You have to find something in the middle.

At this point we are left with two, apparently contradictory concepts of success. In Chinda's narrative, the most successful *individual* is free to choose her goals in life—education, a profession, and a husband. The most successful *family*, however, is the traditional one in which children are obedient and respectful and are committed to care for their parents in times of distress or old age. The child is also encouraged to turn to relatives, teachers, friends, or the Buddhist master for guidance and support. As much as Chinda believes in the idea of freedom, she seems even more committed to the idea of closeness and reciprocity that is possible within a family which communicates openly and respectfully in an atmosphere of trust.

Chinda's reality is far from this ideal. Chinda's ex-husband lives in another state and has very little to do with his children. Chinda's extended family live in Cambodia, and they communicate infrequently. Her son, Mam, is a high school dropout. He is involved with a bad crowd; he has an underage girlfriend and a quick temper. Chinda regrets that her younger son does not trust her. In fact, she does not have a close relationship with either of her sons.

April and Mam are not supportive of one another and in fact are quite hostile. Partially as a result, April is moving to Florida to live with a former teacher and his wife where she hopes to finish her high school education.

Chinda's children have few Cambodian friends, and they no longer speak the language, nor do they visit the temple or attend Buddhist festivals and events.

It is hard for my daughter to socialize with the Cambodian
kids. They think I give too much freedom to my kids. The
other parents make the girls stay home all the time, so it is
hard for my daughter to do things with the Cambodian girls.
My children won't go to the temple or see the monk. It is
not for them. I would take my son if he believed, but he just
don't believe. He would say, "I am not a Buddhist."
[I tell April] you have to respect yourself, who you are.
You are still Cambodian, you can't deny that. April deny that.
She refuse to talk Cambodian. She might feel sorry along the
road. As he grows older, Mam start to talk more about
Cambodia, but April still deny.

Chinda concedes that her family is beset with problems, but
believes that her children are responsible for their own actions. The
more she intervenes, she states, the more she believes she loses them.

I feel bad about my son, but I tend to let him go. I must let
him experience that experience. Maybe later in life, he might
learn from the hard way. Even though I try to pull him, he
wouldn't listen to me. The more I try to control him, he loose
again. Maybe someday he come back to me and say, 'Mom, I
was wrong.'

Chinda's narrative is particularly complex and full of
contradictions. In order to rationalize her belief in freedom for women,
she draws clear distinctions between Buddhism and Cambodian
culture. If an individual follows the Buddhist rule and does no harm to
others, but gives to others with a free heart, she will accumulate good
merit for a future life. In this instance, it is consistent for Chinda to
spend time serving the monks at the temple, attending religious
ceremonies, and studying Buddhist philosophy. It is also consistent for
her to ignore Cambodian customs which impose strict sanctions on her
freedom, especially when it comes to remaining in an abusive
relationship.
Chinda puts her own education above all other goals and sacrifices
a certain quality of life to continue her studies. She rejects the cultural
norm which restricts schooling to the first stage of life. She believes

that education will help her change what is bad about Cambodian culture and replace what is bad with more modern ideas.

Chinda seems confident that she can construct a dual identity which will be successful in both Cambodian and American culture. If she is a good Buddhist, she, in effect, is a good Cambodian. If she is well educated and finds a good career, she becomes a good American. She regrets that her children do not have a strong Cambodian identity, but hopes that they come back to their culture on their own. Consistent with her commitment to the middle way, she does not try to control them or push them to adopt her beliefs.

When I ask April what being successful means, she mentions being independent, getting a college education, and a vague plan about having her own business. However, when I ask her about success in a Cambodian context, she criticizes adults who think success means spending all their time working and making money instead of developing a close family relationship with their children. This dichotomy persists throughout April's narrative and in many ways mirrors her mother's dissonance between her Cambodian and American identities.

> A really successful person is someone who has been through
> high school and college. That's basically it. I just want to
> graduate from college and open my own business, and then
> play it from there.
>   Success to Cambodians means they just want to work; all
> they do is work, work, work. My friends' parents usually
> don't put time into their families. They concentrate more on
> work because getting the money is what they really want.

Communication is a major theme in April's perception of success. The people she admires the most are those to whom she can tell anything without feeling "iffy" about their reaction.

> I look up to this person in the music industry. He has helped
> me a lot; he is trying to keep me on track. I don't like going to
> a counselor; I don't like talking to anybody, but he convinced
> me to go.

> [My former] teacher was wicked down-to-earth. He is,
> like, 65 years old, and we could tell him anything in class. I
> feel more comfortable talking with my teacher than with my
> mom. I can tell him everything.

On the other hand, April states that she doesn't like to talk, that she prefers to write her thoughts and ideas.

> I don't like to talk too much. I just like to write. Usually
> when I end my poems, I write, 'anonymous' because the
> poems are always about my life, and it is very private.

She finds it hard to talk with her father and her mother. She communicates with her brother by fighting with him.

> I want to be able to talk to my parents. My dad is not good in
> English. He has never been around me so it is kind of hard to
> communicate. We never have that father-daughter
> relationship. My dad and I don't talk about anything.
>   My mom is not the person I run to when I need to talk.
> We don't talk that much anymore. I want to be able to talk to
> her, but it is kind of hard talking to her.

April resents what she sees as Cambodian elders gossiping about her behind her back

> Where I live, these Cambodians gossip a lot. They say stuff
> and they are not nice people. Every time I go [to the temple]
> they talk about me so I don't like going there. I don't know
> what they say because they speak Cambodian and I can't
> understand them. Even when I am not there, they talk about
> me.

Nonetheless, April values highly those instances where she can talk freely about herself, her goals, her plans, and even metaphysical ideas like *karma* and reincarnation. In these instances, April usually talks with her friends. "I talk to my friends. They tell me I have a future, and I should not throw it away. These little problems I have, I can overcome them."

Clearly, one dimension of communicating that is difficult for April is speaking Khmer. Chinda frequently speaks to her in Khmer, but April replies exclusively in English. My experience is that April's Cambodian friends who live in her neighborhood are bilingual, and virtually all of the Cambodian elders speak Khmer. Because she does not understand what they are saying, she believes that their gossip is derogatory toward her. Regrettably, the Khmer language is a barrier between April and her culture which prevents her from integrating and understanding its deeper epistemology. Without that communication, that link, April's identity as Cambodian has a shaky foundation.

Being able to talk with someone means being able to trust them, so in April's narrative, trust, authenticity, and respect are strongly connected. The kind of person she tries to be and the kind of person with whom she is willing to form a relationship is someone who is genuine and trustworthy. April's criteria for success includes someone who doesn't try to impress others, someone who is down to earth, someone who is true to oneself and to other people.

> Genuine is somebody who is true to themselves and to other
> people or somebody who can be themselves and doesn't have
> to go out and impress anybody but themselves. A best friend
> has to be genuine and trustworthy.

April has grown up in a household where freedom of expression and freedom of action are taken for granted. Chinda expects April to respect and obey her, but at the same time, Chinda encourages April to dispute her opinions if she feels strongly about something. Consequently, April thinks of herself as a leader among her peer group because she has strong opinions and is willing to express them. Part of her self-confidence comes from knowing what is right and wrong for her and being willing to set rules for herself. As she indicated above, April stays out late on weekends with her (white) American friends. She knows some of them take drugs or drink too much; when they do this around her, April refuses to participate, and walks away.

I don't want to fall in the wrong crowd. It takes a long time to make friends and to trust them. I know a lot of kids who do drugs, but when they do them, I don't go around them. I try to be a leader because I don't want my friends to do bad stuff like smoke or drink. I try to stay away from that.

April's opinions about the ideal family are in many ways similar to her mother's. Relationship and bonding are words she uses to describe the perfect family. The family which has established an atmosphere of trust and non-judgment, which puts in time with their children instead of concentrating all their time on work, and the family which sets rules for their children is April's ideal family.

The perfect parent is someone you can go to and just tell them anything where you don't have to feel 'iffy' about telling them something. I think all parents should set rules on their kids so they don't take advantage of them.

April does *not* describe her family in these terms.

I don't have a good relationship with my mom, brother, or dad. I don't think I want one with my mother; it is just too late. My mom and me, we didn't have this bond. My brother and I, we don't get along. We don't have a good relationship 'cause we always fight.

Thus, April is seeking out her former teacher and his wife to be her surrogate family next year. They are older, retired from working, and have time to spend with her. They have rules about household responsibilities, school work, and about attending the Catholic church every Sunday. April seems willing to sacrifice some of her freedom to meet the expectations of her new "family."

[The teacher I am going to live with] used to be the best teacher in the whole darn school. He retired [to Florida] but then he went back to teaching part-time in an elementary school. [His wife] volunteers in a grandparent program for little kids. I will have to go to church every Sunday now with

them, some Catholic church. They help people out, they like
do food drives and they hand it out to the homeless people, so
I think that will be good for me; it will keep me busy.

April states that all parents should set rules for their children so
that the children don't take advantage of them. Chinda admits that she
does not expect April to help with housework or to cook, but I believe
that Chinda sets down rules about schoolwork.

My mom doesn't make me do the housework. When she tells
me to do the dishes, I will do it, but that's all I do. I don't
know how to cook. I tried once, but I almost burned the house
down.

Because April is a disciplined student who consistently makes the
honor role, she is allowed a great deal of freedom to go out with her
friends. April does not like rules that "keep her on a leash," something
she sees happening to her Cambodian friends who must follow strict
traditional rules.

The good things about having a lot of freedom, I can do
anything I want. I don't like being on a leash. I know most of
my friends are on a leash from their parents, but that's not my
life.

April is contemptuous of these old-fashioned rules that she believes are
no longer appropriate in American culture. Clearly for April, there is a
distinction between rules that parents should set for their kids and the
rules that Cambodian parents set for their daughters.

Cambodian way of life have less freedom. My American
friends can go outside, they can do anything, but when it is my
Cambodian friends, they can't come outside at all. In
Cambodia they didn't have that much freedom, but when they
are here, they treat their children the way they were treated in
Cambodia. My friends can't come out. They have to obey the
Cambodian rules.

Of the adolescents I interviewed from these three families, April is the only one convinced that maintaining her Cambodian identity is *not* a criteria for being successful. April considers herself to be an American; she grew up around white people, she speaks English, and her closest friends are American. April admits that she no longer knows how to speak or understand her language, nor does she know much about her culture. She intensely dislikes the Buddhist temple and does not believe in Buddhism. Her Cambodian heritage is not something she intends to pass along to her own children.

> I don't like the temple. I don't like church, and I don't like temples. I don't have a good relationship with the monk. Every time I go they talk about me, so I don't like going there. I don't know what they say because they speak Cambodian and I can't understand [them]. Even when I am not there, they talk about me.
>   I don't believe in reincarnation, in Buddhism. I don't believe that when I die I am going to become something else, become another person. I don't believe in *karma*. [My friends] talk about reincarnation [and] we joke about it. We make up an animal [and] we say that we were that animal before. [It is] nothing serious; none of us believe in it.
>   If I have kids, I will tell them about the culture, but I'll tell them that it is nothing I believed in. I don't believe in religion, period. I don't know much about Cambodian culture. I grew up around all white kids, I didn't grow up with many Asians. I don't think it's important to have a Cambodian identity, not really. No.

The poems I constructed with April's words according to Gilligan and Brown's voice-centered method (1992) bring into focus April's ambivalence about her Cambodian identity. It is beyond the scope of this study to speculate on April's psychological potential for leading a fulfilling and successful life, but perhaps the following examples shed some light on the personal tension she experiences as a Cambodian-American. April interpreted the voice of They as the Cambodian elders whom she perceives as highly critical of her.

Voice of 'They'
They smoke
They drink
Who they are
Not what they
They gossip a lot
They say stuff
They are not nice people
They don't
Where they lived
They didn't have that much freedom
They treat their children
The way they were treated
They were in Cambodia
They can't come out
They can't do anything
They have to obey the rules
They have to go home
They can't go outside
They can't go outside, period.
They can go outside
They can do anything
They can't come outside at all

They are
They talk about me
What they say
They speak Cambodian
What they say
They talk about me
They were making fun of me
They respect me
They don't
They don't like me

April acknowledged her own identity in the voice of the Self. And while she was unsure how to interpret the voice of We, I believe it reflects April's experience with her Khmer peers as they try to make sense of their Cambodian and American identities.

Voice of 'Self'
I don't like the temple
I don't know
I don't have a good relationship
Every time I go
I don't like going there
I don't know
I can't understand
When I am not there
I would marry
I don't want to marry
I never went to the temple
I don't believe
I don't like church
I don't like temples
I respect them

I don't know what you mean
I don't believe in it
I don't know
I don't believe it
When I die
I am going to become something else
If I heard a story
I didn't believe in that
I mean
I don't believe in that
Just what I know
I don't know
I don't know

Voice of 'We'
We do everything
We were supposed to go
We talk about reincarnation
We joke about it
We just say
We were
We just make up

We say
We were

We would talk about diversity
We had a culture

By one measure of success, academic achievement, April is doing well. She intends to finish high school and attend college in Florida. As a leader among her peers, April seems to have an internal sense of what is right and wrong, and she counsels her friends to stay away from smoking and drugs. April is self-reliant and independent, all of which make her successful by her mother's standards. She appears to be following a Cambodian custom of seeking out a family relationship that will nurture her. In contrast with the other adolescents in this study, April connects what it means to be successful to *American* models of independence, academic achievement, and leadership and not to an identity that is grounded in Cambodian culture and Theravada Buddhism.

RATH'S FAMILY

Biography
The head of Rath's family is unquestionably her mother Long. Long is a tiny, thin woman who dresses in layers of long flowing pants, tops, sweaters, and the occasional jacket. Her head is completely shaved, partially for respect to her religion, and partly because she is bothered with a type of eczema. Her eyes are full of delight when she speaks of her grandchildren, her gardens, and her life. Her teeth are stained dark red from chewing tobacco, but her smile is radiant, nonetheless. Her hands are the most expressive part of her as she clasps them together to greet a visitor, to pray at her small altar to the Buddha, or to prepare food for her extended family. This tiny, fragile-looking woman is the glue which holds this family together.
Long was born in the city of Phnom Penh. Her story has been captured by her grandson, Touch:

Long was a thin, small fragile girl in the growing country of Cambodia. She was born in 1925 and her mother Pin died five years later after she had given birth to her youngest son. Long's dad name was L. [He] was so devastated by his wife's death, he left his two children to the care of his wife's brother named Loy. L. quickly remarried [and] moved far away to start another life, though he did try to support his only two children. From there Long's life was a struggle. She had to grow up very quickly. She had very little schooling because she had to work and try to support her little brother, never truly establishing a childhood. This fragile girl was always on the move, working and cooking, trying to survive in the 1940s. Little that she know that these skills would pay off in the future. (English 10 essay, 1996)

Long goes on to fill out the story by relating that her younger brother stayed for a long time in the Temple where she studied to be a Buddhist monk and learned to speak, read, and write French.

I have one brother. When my mother died, I [was] young and my brother [was] younger. My brother stayed in the Buddha place to study and be a monk. He speak and write French. He [left the monkhood] and [became] a nurse in Cambodia until 1975. [Today] he [lives] in California with his family.

According to Long, her brother continues to practice traditional medicine within the Cambodian community along with his wife who is also skilled in Cambodian healing. For his work as a healer, he is considered high praise by his sister's family.

Long, as indicated above, was educated through the fifth grade by Cambodian monks, while her brother was able to attend college. "[When I was] a young child, [I wanted] education, but wealth and poverty intervened. [My parents] extended the education for my brother [so he could] go to college." She learned to read and write Khmer, something few women of her generation did. When she turned 28, her uncle arranged to marry her to Seoun, who was twelve years older. Touch continues the story of his grandparents' courtship and marriage:

Long was a woman of high praise in the community. She was a fine cook, a hard worker, and was thought to be an exceptional housewife. It was [the] tradition for the man to offer themselves. There were many men from all over the cities that came to ask for her hand in married. It was tradition to have the father chose the suitor, though Long whose father left her when she was young, had her uncle to decide which man would best accommodate her. Loy held many contests for Long's hand in married. He would have the suitors build houses, sell items at the markets, plow land. And the winner or the man that did the best job would have the right to wed Long, and would traditionally make a good husband.

Though only one man truly caught the eye of Long's uncle. He was a thin, clean cut young man and who was fairly educated from the temples in the mountains. A young man from Phnom Penh who was a monk of a temple. The man name was Seoun. Though he did not build the best, in fact the houses he built, just collapse. The mules used to plow the land ran off on him. The one thing that impressed Loy was Seoun's abilities to care. He took good care of Long and her brother while Loy was away. Seoun would help out any way he could, many times he would come running across the fields in the middle of the night half dress to care for sick mules. Loy thought that Seoun would make a wonderful husband. In 1953 Seoun and Long were married. They went on to have nine children, the oldest among them being my mother. (English 10 essay, 1996)

According to Long, her husband came from a very rich and successful family in Phnom Penh. After they married, he had a good job as a customs agent. Then, she states, he started to gamble and drink. He lost all his money and his job, and the family moved to Battambang City. Long ran a small store to help support the family.

Five of Long and Seoun's children survived the Khmer Rouge revolution and made their way to Forest city. In 1984 Long and Seoun were reunited with their children, and today live only a few blocks from Rath, their oldest daughter.

In the winter of 1997, Long decided she wanted to become an American citizen. Every Monday morning at 10:00 a.m., Long, along with a number of her elderly friends and her husband, walked to the Multilingual Center a few blocks from their homes to attend Pirun's citizenship classes. They arrived with copies of sample citizenship test questions, diagrams of the houses of congress, and photocopies of the state's legislators and senators. Long's neat Khmer script covered the pages and translated words like "legislative," "executive," and "judiciary," and attempted phonetic spellings for the difficult English words. The two-hour sessions were a mixture of jokes and laughter, questions, arguments, and responses to the questions Pirun would pose at the beginning and the end of each session.

In spite of her very limited English, Long stood out as one of the most dedicated and brightest students. She occasionally found herself arguing with Pirun over a question of American history or congressional structure. In February of 1998, Long took the written citizenship test and passed. Because she had been in the United States over five years and was over 70 years old, she was allowed a Khmer language interpreter at the obligatory interview with an INS examiner. Long answered all of the questions accurately, and took her oath of allegiance in June 1998. Seoun did not continue the classes and did not pursue citizenship for himself.

Besides her gifts as a cook and a gardener, Long's personal expertise is in needlework, and she produces extremely elegant, intricate banners that she gives to the local Buddhist center or sends to Cambodia to be used at Temple celebrations in her village. The banners are made from brightly colored silk panels; a central rectangular panel is attached to a wooden dowel, and the fabric is completely covered with embroidery, sequins, and beads. Long streamers of different colors are sewn to the bottom of the rectangle.

> When I was in Cambodia [I learned sewing and design] just
> from watching, just seeing the style and design at the
> Cambodian temples, [but] I never worked with [fabric] in
> Cambodia. The first time I worked with fabric and crafts
> [was] in the United States. I just played around with it and
> formed it into designs.

The banners are hung outside from the top of the Wat during a wedding, funeral, New Year, or some other special Buddhist holiday. I have seen Long's banners in a private home where a monk was leading a ceremony, and decorating the monk's platform during the New Year festival.

Long divides her time between her daughter's family, her husband, the obligations she accepts for the Buddhist center in Forest City, and a larger temple in a neighboring state. In spite of the gifts she sends to relatives and friends in Cambodia, Long has absolutely no question about where she wants to spend "her old age." "I want to stay here in America. I like America." Her granddaughter, Srey, attests to her grandmother's fondness for certain elements of American culture, "My grandmother loves the movie Anaconda and she owns a tape of Jurassic Park. She actually bought a copy and sent it to a friend in Cambodia. Now she wants to see Asteroid. She is addicted to ice cream and barbecue potato chips."

Rath was born in January, 1954. She is a striking woman of small stature, with black hair which curls around her face. Her face is round with the hint of freckles; her eyes are huge and full of compassion and affection for her family and her friends. When she smiles, her eyes light up her face, which often shows signs of great weariness. Like her mother, there is the impression of great calm and great strength.

As the oldest in the family, Rath was expected to assume responsibility for taking care of her brothers and helping her mother manage their household. Her brothers attended school, but there was never enough money for Rath to go to school.

> I feel like when I am younger, I want to grow up [reading]
> books, [being] good student, but the parent cannot afford. We
> are poor. My mom send me to school, but just the Buddha
> school. [It] is not a big school and I [want to go] to school.

By the time she turned 17, her father had arranged her marriage to Koeun, 20 years her senior.

> When I got married with [my husband,] I never talked with
> him at all. He [is] older than me, [I was 17 and] he was 36 or
> 37. I got married with Koeun and I never know him at all, he

live 100 miles from me. My mom feel like he always take
care of me, that is why.

Rath's first son was born in 1973 when she was 19. "I was only
nineteen, I didn't know anything about taking care of babies. He got
sick and we don't have medicine to help him; we don't have nothing."
The baby died in 1975, and her second son, Kusal, was born the same
year—the year the Khmer Rouge marched into Phnom Penh.

After the coup and forced exodus of the Cambodian population to
the country, the Khmer Rouge settled Rath's family near Battambang
with her parents located nearby. Rath's husband was sent to a work
camp 200 miles away and they saw very little of each other for the
duration of the war. In 1979 when the Vietnamese invaded Cambodia,
Rath, her husband and children joined her parents and four brothers and
the family walked for five days to reach the border. At one section, she
said the ground was full of so many land mines, each person had to
place his feet in the footprints of the person ahead of them. Rath's son
Touch and daughter Srey were born in the refugee camps where the
family spent two years waiting to locate a sponsor in the United States.
They finally arrived in Forest City in 1982. "It was like being a baby
in this country (America). Like being born all over again when I come
here. I didn't know the language, the customs. Everything was very
fast and sometimes very dangerous."

Rath considers herself still to be a traditional Cambodian woman,
but she broke tradition by ending her arranged marriage in 1984.

[My husband] beat me up, he beat me up a lot [with a piece of]
wood. He pushed me in the chest, beat me black and blue all
the time. I went to work two jobs. I work one at night time, I
clean three halls. Daytime, I clean at Hotel C. across from the
mall. [I] came home [and] clean the house, take care of three
children and he work only one job.

Around 1988 Rath met Cang. They married in a Cambodian
ceremony and Rath had two more children, a son and daughter. After
their daughter was born, he and Rath decided they would be married in
an official ceremony when he returned from a visit to Cambodia.
While Cang was in Cambodia, he fell in love with his cousin who was

20 years his junior. He married her and they returned to live in Forest City. Some time in 1997, he made an attempt to contact Rath and their two children. Their daughter J totally rejected him, but K, their son, has formed a tentative relationship and sees him now and then. Rath has no contact with Koeun, her first husband who has also remarried. Kusal, Touch, and Srey attempt to visit him on occasion, but his second wife is resentful of them, so they stay away.

Rath, her five children, and her daughter-in-law live in an apartment in downtown Forest City. At our first interview, the family was living in a large first floor apartment in an old Victorian house located near the Multilingual Center. During the winter of 1996/97, the roof began leaking and then the heat failed. The landlord was slow to solve the problems, and Rath finally found another apartment on the other side of town. Their apartment building is located in a low-income area where the buildings are run down, but the residents take fairly good care of the neighborhood. Rath's apartment is on the first floor at the end of a short hallway. A shoe rack and small bin for gloves and hats keeps order outside the front door.

One enters the apartment directly into the living room and must maneuver between sections of a large overstuffed gray couch. There is a dark green rug covering the floor. The windows look out onto the driveway beside the building where tenants park their cars. Frequently Long will have her mats, pillows, herbs, and sewing materials arranged underneath the windows.

Against one wall are the predictable wide-screen television, VCR, and stereo system with all the accouterments for fast-paced video games. A painting of Angkor Wat hangs on one wall, and a small Buddhist altar extends from the wall high above the television console. Long keeps the Buddha surrounded by fresh fruit and flowers. Glamour Shots© of son Kusal, daughter-in-law Sarem, and daughter Srey complete the wall decor.

Srey's room is off the living room and contains a pile of futons and blankets in one corner, a dressing table, a portable closet, her computer and her bed. Above the computer hangs a poster entitled "Success begins with ABC." A second small bedroom for Rath, J and K is also off the living room. The kitchen is quite large with space for a washing machine in one corner. A third bedroom off the kitchen is used by Kusal and Sarem.

In the summer, Rath and Long work at one of the local farms. They bring home discarded flats of flowers and vegetables which they immediately plant into a large flower bed that runs in front of the apartment building. The gravelly, weed choked back yard, undergoes a transformation as Long recycles cracked flower pots into a second garden full of flowers, sprays of lemon grass, and spindly tomatoes.

Rath works as a sea urchin processor during the fall and winter months. Until recently she did not want a full time job, preferring to be home with her younger children. Now that they are both in school, Rath takes them to school and picks them up in the afternoon. While the children are in school, Rath takes care of her ill father and chauffeurs her mother to the store and occasionally to the hospital. Her responsibilities toward her parents and children invariably mean that she must work the night shift beginning at 6:00 p.m. and finishing around 6:00 or 7:00 the following morning. She leaves her two youngest children with Kusal and her daughter-in-law or with Srey. Both Sarem and Srey are well versed in preparing food, cleaning the house, and handling any emergencies that arise.

Rath's spoken English is quite good, and she holds her own in most conversations. She understands more than she is able to articulate. Rath attended adult ESL when she first arrived, but abandoned school when she became the head of her household. I first met her in one of Pirun's citizenship classes. At the time, she wanted desperately to become an American citizen so that her three oldest children could automatically become citizens. Realizing that Touch and Srey would soon be applying to colleges, Rath believed that their college applications would be strengthened if they were American citizens. In spite of her crushing work schedule and her frail health, Rath attended classes for six months. She took the citizenship test four times but never passed. Kusal attended one of the examinations with his mother, and passed his citizenship test easily; he took the Oath of Allegiance in 1997.

Rath believes that when her youngest children are older, she will be able, finally, to return to school. She wants to learn to read and write, both in English and in Khmer. When asked where she wants to spend her old age, she states, "When I get older, I [want to] go live in Cambodia. I spend my retire in Cambodia. We just cook food or we stay in the Buddha place, be a nun. We [do good] for the next life or future. I get a good life."

Rath has never abandoned her belief in Buddhism and has raised all five of her children to honor and respect the Buddhist way of life. They attend temple celebrations both in Forest City and a neighboring state. She has made sure her daughters learn the proper respect for elders and has encouraged them to learn classical Cambodian dance. Srey studied and performed dance from fifth grade through her sophomore year in high school. It is now the youngest daughter's turn to begin learning this tradition.

Rath arranged the marriage between her son and Sarem who is a distant cousin of her mother's. With the help of her parents and brothers, she provided a lavish, traditional, three-day wedding for Kusal and his Cambodian bride. In late fall of 1998, she again, with her brothers' help, organized a major ceremony to honor her father and mother. With four monks presiding over the day-long celebration, the five children bought all of their father's favorite things as gifts for the monks to bless. The gifts will be kept in the temple until his death at which time it is believed he will take them on his journey to the next life.

Kusal is Rath's oldest son. He resembles his grandmother Long in face and stature. His handsome face is angular, and his features are sharply defined. He wears his hair cropped very short, and at times he sports a mustache and an earring. He dresses in jeans, sweatshirts and sturdy shoes.

Of all the young people in the study, Kusal is the only one who has memories of Cambodia as a child. Even though he was only four years old when his parents escaped the country, Kusal remembers their village, the rice fields, the Buddhist pagodas, the water buffalo, and how much he loved the warmth. It is, perhaps, why Kusal speaks so often of what it feels like in his mind to be both Cambodian and American.

> Half my mind is the Cambodian way another half is the
> American way. Right now I am studying to know myself
> better, who I am, who I really am and what I am going to do.
> Once I figure [out] what I want to do, this is me, this is my
> mind, this is my body, this is my heart [and] what does my

heart want, I will have to pick one goal, cause right now my mind is in both.

Though 23, Kusal gives the impression of a naive and trusting youth of 19 or 20. He is outgoing, with a ready smile and an easy conversational style. He describes himself as follows:

[The most important things about me are] my sense of humor.
I would say I am very generous and very straightforward; if I
like it or not like it, I will tell you. I am shy in a way. I like to
be on my own, independence. I like to be on my own out
there doing my own thing. I don't want to count on people,
and I love supporters, people who support and encourage me.

Kusal also thinks of his life as somewhat charmed. He speculates that he is being saved for some special destiny because of the number of accidents that he has survived during his short life,

I have a lot of accidents. I am surprised I am not dead yet.
When I was little, my dad, he beat me so bad I got the back of
my skull like crack. It was broken 'cause he threw me when I
was like four years old, he threw me to the ground and there
was a stem or a little rock on the ground [and] I hit my head. I
was unconscious for I think four or five days. I didn't wake
up. I didn't know who I was.
	[Another time] I was riding my bike down a steep hill,
very, very steep hill [and] the chain fell off. I did a 360 in the
air and land myself and knock myself [out] again. I am just
laying there for two hours and my friend went to get van.
When the ambulance came, I already woke up.
	When I was really young, I was like 17, I am with my
friends going fishing. On the highway the car had a flat tire. I
was going 75 miles per hour and we had a flat, so we flipped a
couple of times to the other side of the road. The fire truck
and the ambulance and this trooper pulled me out from the
seat. I look up to this fire guy [and] I wonder what the heck I
am doing here. The car is badly damaged, like windshield is
all crushed and everything just dented. I stuck out of the car,

the glass is all over my shirt. [We didn't have seat belts on,] we are teenagers, we are not really safe! [When] we step out [of the car], like everyone clapped. I walked to the cop car, not one scratch on me; no bruise, no nothing. They were surprised, shocked. I could have been dead right there.

Kusal was eight years old when he began school in the United States. Having had no education in the refugee camps, he entered the U.S. not speaking, reading, or writing English; Khmer was spoken exclusively in his home. "[When I first came to the U.S.,] I wasn't really interested in school because I was older." When school became especially difficult, Kusal withdrew into the safety of his Cambodian friends and any situation that offered less stress.

I was in ESL all my life, in grade school, middle and high school. In grade school there were like fifteen in a class, and we were in one big classroom [with] Vietnamese, one Chinese, and a few other ethnic. I was hanging out with the Cambodians all the time. We all speak Cambodian. We play games, fool around. I wasn't in the mainstream. I never had American friends, I was always with the Asian crowd. We didn't really go out and experience, out in the mainstream American. We [were] basically just trapped in one room, and [so] we study each other. We play more than we learn because we don't really *learn*, learn.

While Kusal did not excel in academics, he did excel in sports—track, soccer, basketball, and more recently playing pool! He was a state champion in the long jump. But eventually his difficulty with English and his willingness to be distracted by his friends, prompted his mother to transfer him to a different high school in a city 25 miles away. Kusal lived with his uncle, took care of his nephews, and tried to fit into his new high school. This, too, was a failure. He returned to Forest City and enrolled for a time at Stevens High School before dropping out for good in his sophomore year.

Kusal's failure in school precipitated a long period of rebellion that included drugs, fights, alcohol, and run-ins with the police:

I always got in trouble [in high school]. I don't cause the
trouble, the problem comes to me. Try to avoid, try to walk
away. I left my parents when I was 17. I got messed up and
stuff. I did listen to my family, it was just that I want to be on
my own. They can't understand that. So I left, just me and
my suitcase, just live with a friend; just try to be in the real
world. I did this for about four or five years. When I was 21
my mom asked me to come back. I was working so she asked
me to come home to babysit and help her with the brothers
and sisters.

Kusal has been living at home for the past three years, now with
his wife Sarem. After bouncing from job to job, he has finally been
offered full-time status at his current job in a food processing plant. He
works six days a week from 3:00 p.m. until midnight. It is very hard
work, but he is paid well, and now, for the first time, receives benefits.
Sarem works a similar schedule during the day at the sea urchin
processing plant, going to work at 6:00 a.m. and coming home often
after 10:00 p.m. Kusal says she does not work the whole time, but
remains at the plant through the different shifts in order to make as
much money as possible. They are saving, so they can get good credit
and eventually complete their educations.

I think that work has really made me responsible. I am doing
that work because I need enough money so that I can have
something of my own in the future. I can't go to the bank and
get a loan unless I get good credit or benefit. [They will] look
in my background to see where I work. I have to have a year
of working there steady. I used to do urchins before, but that
doesn't count. The bank isn't going to look at sea urchins,
they are just not.
    Right now I just want to work and save some money and
then once I saved enough money, I will try to open a shop or a
little restaurant or grocery store with a little restaurant. Once I
have got that opened up, I will just let Sarem work and I will
continue trying to go to school. If we both go to school, we
won't make money cause someone has to go to school and
someone has to work.

Sarem wants to have three children some day; Kusal wants "as many as God gives me." They intend to raise their children as Cambodian-Americans—"to have good attitudes [that] let them walk on a straight road, not a crooked road." Perhaps, it is the crooked road that has taught Kusal what he wants for his own son some day,

> [My son] he will be a lot better. He will go to college. [I will] make sure he has everything, make sure [he goes with] the right crowd, make sure he gets a lot of love. I am going to give him what I don't have, that's what I am going to do, what I don't have from family, father, or mistake I made. I will teach him. I will make sure he is really doing well, support him.

Touch is the second of Rath's sons. He is the image of her, a strikingly handsome young man of 19. He has a very round face, clear complexion, with deep-set eyes and black hair that frequently hangs in his face. He laments the fact that he stands about five feet, three inches tall, but he more than makes up for his slight stature with his magnetic personality. At times Touch can appear imperious or indifferent to people around him, but when he decides to give you his undivided attention, his smile and his intensity are compelling. Like Kusal, he is confused about his Cambodian and his American identity,

> I honestly can't really seriously tell you who I really am. I just sense I am a weird person. Like all teenagers, I do get confused over the question who I am. For me, I am born to a family that just survived the holocaust and [I] am just trying to establish myself in a new country; just trying to do something that is able to help better my family, and might benefit other people.
> Sometimes I talk about myself in the third person and it is kind of unhealthy. I look at myself and go, OK, that's weird. Some of the weird things I have done is more like the rebellious stage. I just realized I am not going to do [these things] when I am older, so I might as well do it now. It is a phase. Mom didn't totally understand. Once again it was the two societies clashing.

Touch spent elementary school in ESL classes, but by the time he attended Park Middle School, he was fully integrated into the mainstream. It was at Park that Touch started socializing with MP and two other Cambodians who became his closest friends. But he also formed friendships with Americans, especially those who seemed to be marginalized by the "popular cliques." Unlike Kusal, Touch has not "fallen in with the wrong crowd," and while he likes to socialize, he is not drawn to wild experiences.

> [Hanging out on the corner or drinking beer and playing pool] doesn't appeal to me. I have partied before but I am very light about all that stuff. I don't do it that much. It's a moral decision, you know. I would rather go home to sleep than go to Spot Shot to shoot pool for five hours. Some of my friends drink a lot more than I do. I don't really drink that much, but I just go with the flow.

Touch, more than other members of his family, has experienced the clash of two societies—one Cambodian, poor, and hard working, and the other American, rich and privileged. After successfully completing middle school, Touch made an inventory of the high schools in Forest City and decided he wanted to attend Danforth Academy. The Academy is located in an upscale suburb of Forest City. For his entire four years of high school, Touch was the only Cambodian student in the school, and one of only five students of color.

Touch received a full, four-year scholarship to attend Danforth Academy. The scholarship also provided Touch with his own tutor to help him master the increasingly difficult English reading and writing. Touch excelled at Danforth, becoming the senior class president and getting involved in a wide variety of courses, volunteer activities, and sports.

> I did a research [project] on the Cambodian bombing under Nixon in 1970 after the Kents Hill incident. Instead of an exam, [the teacher] gave us a topic and we could teach it, and that is what I did. It was a 40-minute presentation [where] I showed clips from *The Killing Fields*. By the end, people

were crying. They all evaluated me and gave me A's and
some A+'s.
     I am team captain of a JV team and it is a lot of
responsibility and training. You always have to motivate
people and encourage them. It is really weird, cause I didn't
even run for captain, the coach just said, "You run the team."

The drive to fit in with his Danforth friends and join in their
activities motivated Touch to begin earning his own money. From the
moment he turned sixteen, Touch worked during the summer. His first
job was with a telemarketing company in Forest City. He was soon
promoted to assistant manager where he was responsible for keeping
track of people's work and holiday schedules. He was so good that the
manager offered him a full-time job. In 1996, unbeknownst to his
mother, Touch got a job washing dishes at the prestigious Forest City
Country Club after school and on weekends. Within a few months, he
was supervising the rest of the dishwashing staff. The summer before
leaving for college, Touch worked three different jobs in order to raise
money for college, while not denying himself the opportunity to have
fun.

     I work at the Country Club. I am a dishwasher, and I think it
is fun. I am the number one person there—I am always in
charge; whatever I say, they do. I also work at supermarkets.
Here I am like working two or three jobs and even though I
am working a lot, I am able to provide for myself and help
support my family. A lot of people don't have that drive, you
know? A lot of my friends say I am a workaholic because I
put in, like, 82 or 60 hours a week. For me, I don't mind. I
just look at it like a game or sport. [The reward for working
that hard] is the option to do whatever I want with it, like save
it or go shopping or buy stuff for the family.

Touch graduated in June 1998 and was accepted to attend Clark
University. His college essay was an eloquent statement of a young
man caught between two cultural epistemologies:

I am going to write about becoming a citizen. I am writing
about taking rights for granted, like rights we have guaranteed.
I am not a citizen, so I wrote about how all my friends when
they turn 18 they can vote and do all these cool things. I
mentioned that when I turn 18, I probably can't do any of that;
I cannot slander someone's reputation or else I might be
deported from the country. I was researching [this] and found
out that if you are a resident alien you are guaranteed rights,
but limited rights. I am also saying how people in other
countries have gone through all these revolutions just to have
the right to vote and people here take it for granted; like half
don't even vote.

A month after Touch was accepted to Clark, he took the citizenship
examination and passed.

Touch's school ambitions extend beyond four years of college.
Although he is undecided about his major field of study, he dreams of
completing his master's and doctorate.

I want to go as far as I can [in school], getting a college
education and hopefully go on to get a master's and maybe a
Ph.D. My biggest fear [in finishing my education] is not
having the money and the resources to do that; it is not a
matter of emotional drive. It is kind of like saying, "You need
money to make money." It is how far my pockets can take
me, and then I will do what I can from there.

Touch's approach to religion is another example of "two worlds
clashing." He has been brought up a Buddhist and attended, up until
high school, religious ceremonies with his family. However, with four
years of science and Western philosophy, Touch has relegated religion
to the status of interesting historical phenomena. He no longer believes
in reincarnation, *karma*, or the power of the monks, nor does he believe
he will teach his children much about his religious heritage.

Religion has never appealed to me. I have taken classes in
world religions and we are studying all the major [religions]
like Buddhism, Hinduism, Catholic, Christianity, Judaism,

Taoism. They are just basically the same thing. I just study
the history.
      The last time I ever talked [to the monk], I was in middle
school. If I see him, I just bow down because it is nice and
that is about it. When I was in, like, second or third grade, I
was really small, and I am small now. I was like, 'Can you
make me taller?' He is like, 'Listen and be good to your mom
and drink....' I did everything he [said,] and it didn't work.
They [say] he can do miracles, and I did everything, and well,
I am just like, 'Why bother?'

Srey is one year younger than Touch; she was born June 1981.
Srey is about five feet four inches, slim, with shoulder-length black
hair. Her face is perfectly round with full cheeks and lips—she, too,
resembles her mother. Her eyes are large and very expressive; when
she laughs they become lost in the curve of her cheeks. When I first
met Srey, she had a severe case of adolescent acne, but over the past
two years it has subsided.
      Srey was born in the Thai refugee camps and came to the U.S. a
tiny baby. She dimly remembers the abuse her mother suffered from
her father but otherwise remembers little of her life before the divorce.
As the first girl in the family, and the daughter of Long's only
daughter, Srey quickly became the favorite of her grandmother and her
uncles.

      I remember I am always spoiled since I am little to now. My
      mom she says, "Everywhere you go, you always get
      everything you want; you always get to go to restaurants, you
      always get a lot of clothes and a lot of toys." At that time I
      was the only girl, [and] I was spoiled.

From the time she was six or seven years old, Srey had severe
allergies and asthma. Her mother, grandmother, and uncles took her to
Western doctors, but ultimately preferred to rely on Chinese healers
and traditional medicine to cure her. The family eventually found a
Vietnamese doctor in Chinatown who cured her asthma with two
injections.

Srey states that she always enjoyed school. Unlike Kusal, she, spent only two years in an ESL classroom, and entered mainstream classes while still in grade school. The experience was not without its stresses, particularly when it came to speaking and understanding English. Competing with herself became a common theme as she set and accepted her own standards for achievement.

> I did not learn to speak English until grade school. Back then I was the only one in class who struggled with pronouncing words. I was a very shy person. I was placed in a class with all Americans. I was the only girl who had black hair and tan colored skin. I remember the times when my classmates laughed at my accent. As a young child, I could not sing the ABC song. Other children laughed at my pronunciation and my different accent. I cried when I got home, though I told myself that those children were no better than I was. So I practiced singing the song. When the day finally came to have the contest to see who could sing the ABCs best, I sang it perfectly.

Srey told me that seventh grade at Park Middle School was her favorite year in school. However, it was at Park that she began to associate with a group of Cambodian and American girls who began testing the limits of authority—their parents' and the school's. Srey began to cut classes, hang out on corners with her friends, and affect a punk style of dress. Rath, frightened that she would head down the same path as Kusal, removed her from Park and sent her to live with her uncle in the southern part of the state. Srey lived with her uncle, babysat for his children, attended church every Sunday, and traveled to Forest City every other weekend to spend time with her family.

The change of schools and the stability of her uncle's household profoundly changed Srey's attitude. She skipped eighth grade and was enrolled as a ninth grade student in Berwick High School. Srey became a high achieving student in her sophomore year, making the honor roll and receiving academic and service achievement awards.

The summer before her junior year, Srey and her mother came to an agreement about her future schooling and her goals beyond graduation. Srey wanted to return to Forest City to live with the family; her mother wanted her to attend a strict, academically competitive high school where Srey would not be distracted from her studies. Srey applied to and was accepted at Elizabeth Seton, a private, Catholic girls school, considered to be one of the best college preparatory schools in the state. Srey, like her brother, requires full scholarship support in order to attend Elizabeth Seton, but the school does not have a large scholarship endowment. Rath's portion of Srey's tuition comes to $2500, and for two years, Rath's extended family has managed to raise this amount as well as help Touch with his college expenses.

Elizabeth Seton High School follows a strict, traditional classroom format which requires each student to work independently, and the school has not provided Srey with a tutor to assist her with English reading and writing. I volunteered to be Srey's tutor for both her junior and senior year, helping with research papers, grammar, composition, and sentence structure. In spite of the school's rigorous academic standards, Srey has opted to take a few honors courses in science and history where she maintains a B average. She has impressed her instructors with her discipline, her study habits, her willingness to ask questions (and to be "wrong" in her answers), and her consistently polite and respectful manner.

Although school consumes the majority of her time, Srey manages to balance her responsibilities to her family, a volunteer job tutoring refugee students, and her 15-hour-a-week job at the Forest City Country Club. Rath also depends heavily on Srey to keep the house running smoothly which means chauffeuring her younger brother and sister, running errands for her aunts and uncles, taking her grandmother shopping, or taking her grandfather out to eat. This allows Rath and Sarem to extend their work hours at the sea urchin plant. Following her brother's lead, Srey devotes the majority of her Saturdays and Sundays working as a waitress at the country club. She was promoted from salad prep to hostess to waitress within a six-month period, and comments that she now has customers who ask specifically for her. Srey is the only person of color on the wait staff, and she relates stories of customers who are both patronizing and rude as well as customers who ask about her goals and support her choice of challenging colleges and careers.

I first met Srey in September 1996 while she was a sophomore at Berwick High School. She was studying classical Cambodian dance, and I was helping Pirun rehearse the dancers for a Cambodian New Year performance. From September until April 1997, Srey traveled to Forest City every weekend to study dance technique, and she performed with a small group at the fall International Festival. Her technique improved along with her enthusiasm for performing. By the time of the New Year ceremony in April, Srey had all the poise of a seasoned classical dancer.

My conversations with her during this period revealed a young woman who was intent upon understanding her role as a Cambodian and an American teenager. She wrote frequently about her questions and insights into the experience of being a bi-cultural person. When I first met Srey, she was just beginning to articulate these differences—unsure of whether there was anything about being an "old-fashioned" Cambodian girl that was worth holding on to.

> As for being a Cambodian girl, it means no dating, doing chores, and being respectful to elders. I remembered one time one of my friends went on a date. Her parents didn't know she went on a date. Then someone told her parents. She got into big trouble because her parents don't believe in dating.
>
> Once in a while my mom makes a fuss on what I do. And on the other hand, I have my grandma who is old fashioned and believes that the way Cambodian girls are in Cambodia is the way they should act in this country. I told her no way!
>
> Cambodian parents are strict, especially toward daughters. Parents are very overprotective about girls. One big issue is a girl's reputation, Cambodians believe that their daughters should always have a good reputation. If their daughter has a bad reputation, the parents feel ashamed.
>
> Most Cambodian guys can do whatever they want. They have the right to do anything they wish such as stay out late, go places, and hang out. I tell my mom that is stupid.
>
> I would say being raised in American way would be better because the girls have more rights than in the Cambodian way. I like the American way in so many ways. American girls have more rights in dating than Cambodians do.

Basically being raised in two different way isn't that bad because I'm used to it. It's pretty cool though because I'm from another culture and I know another language besides English.

I do want someday to go to college to become a nurse or maybe a doctor. I want my mom to be proud of how well she has raised me in two different ways, and also, best of all, I want to be proud of myself and who I am. (Sophomore essay, 1996)

By the time Srey was ready to apply to college, she had had a number of opportunities to write about the advantages of being a bicultural person and made this theme the focal point of her college essay.

Being a Cambodian adolescent is very complex in American society. Many Americans may not see the different challenges that immigrant adolescents go through. When I am around my mother, grandparents, and relatives, I speak my native language. I follow the traditions of our culture, which includes no dating, earning a good reputation, and respecting our elders.

Yet when I am at school, I speak English. I try to fit in as an American student by speaking up in the classroom. But sometimes when I need an image for writing or analyzing a problem, I think of a Khmer image first. I feel a sense of pride and honor to be able to bring these two cultures together.

In my culture, women are not allowed to speak out. I am trying to prove to my mom that in America it is different; I can speak out and support my opinion. Although I don't want to give up being Cambodian, I also don't want to live in a Cambodian past which is not supportive for women. I know my college education will help me become a stronger Cambodian-American woman. (College essay, 1998)

Srey's ambitions beyond high school are large and complex. She intends to go to college, get a bachelor's degree and then go on for a nursing degree or possibly an M.D.

I want to attend [a] four-year college for just an education, like probably two years in medical school or four years if possible. If [I] can [only] do it for two or three years, probably be a nurse. If it seems like I am really interested in being a doctor, then I will continue for more years and be a successful doctor.

Once she has completed her schooling, Srey wants to spend some time in Cambodia working with people who do not have enough money to afford hospital care.

Someday I want to go to Cambodia and help cure the people that are sick, who don't have enough money to do for medicine or see a doctor for their health. [I want] to go there and to just help them. If I go [to Cambodia] I will work in a big hospital and can see bigger patients and charge them, because whoever goes to the hospital can afford it. But if there is a little refugee hospital, I want to go to that little clinic and I won't charge them, or I would go to their house in a small community. Seeing a doctor is so expensive, that is why I want to be that person.

As far as her personal goals, Srey also wants to have a family and live close to her relatives in Forest City.

I want to have a family and probably one or two children. [I] probably [want to retire] in Forest City because I was raised here and it is hard to go to a new place like in the city or the countryside. Like the old saying, 'nothing is like home.' I know everyone here; [in] this little city you know everything that is going on.

When it comes to describing the Cambodian traditions she holds most valuable and will pass on to her children, Srey shows no ambivalence about her cultural roots.

I believe in Buddha, and I attend the temples and I pray and worship. I pay respect to the monk. Nobody can change my religion, not even a teacher, not even a friend, not even my family. If my mom or grandma want to change to another way, that is *their* opinion of changing, but I was raised that way and I will continue in that way.

   I would let [my children] experience Buddhism starting when they were a child. [When] I go to temple, I will take them with me and let them see as they get older if they agree with that religion and if they want to follow that religion the same as I did. [If] I give them the opportunity to experience [Buddhism] when they are little, they [can] choose to continue with that religion or go with another religion. Whatever God [gives] them to believe in, they can go for it.

Rath's three oldest children, Kusal, Touch, and Srey, have had a painful relationship with their father Koeun. In May 1998 their father called them from the hospital. He intimated he was very sick and wanted to see them. Touch persuaded his brother and sister to go to the hospital, and they brought him gifts. Srey said that at the end of the visit, Koeun asked Touch what he planned to do now that he had graduated from high school. Touch replied that he had been accepted to college and wondered if his father would help him with some of his expenses. His father refused, stating that he had recently spent $3,000 on a new karaoke machine and $1,500 on a computer for his daughter; he had no money to give his son. Srey wept as she told me this story, describing the pain and rejection she saw in her brother's face. Months later, in October, Srey gathered her courage and called her father asking if he would fill out his portion of the financial aid forms that she needed to send with her college applications. His wife refused, stating that her husband had no money to contribute to Srey's college expenses.

Interpretations of Success: Findings
To Long, being successful is being able to do good and give to others who are less fortunate than she, so whenever she sees someone who is homeless she gives them as much as she can afford. She does not begrudge a kind deed or word to the people in her neighborhood who are frequently hanging around the street. Long constantly lectures her grandchildren on being open, warm-hearted, and generous people.

Such people earn the respect of the community and that respect is important to the family.

> It is important to know how to give to others who are
> unfortunate and not be greedy toward yourself. It is important
> to be an open-hearted person knowing who is unfortunate and
> to give them one or two, three bucks. It is important to the
> family.
>   I respect the good person, warm-hearted person. The
> person who is welcoming to the community. I like to do good
> for others when they are unwealthy, like sitting in the street,
> homeless. I cannot make a difference [in their lives] because I
> am just an elder person, but I dream if only I could help them
> out.

Long interprets the expectations for a devout Buddhist as giving and doing good. She listens closely to audiotapes of the monks' teachings which explain that the path to a comfortable next life is paved not with good intentions, but continuous deeds of generosity and caring.

> Buddhism is important to me because [the monks] make your
> bad sins go away, dust the bad sins away for your next life
> instead of living your next life with the same bad sins that you
> have acquired life after life. You need to learn from yourself
> and after learning you will give up the bad sins and try to do
> good for your next life. You are trying to do something good
> as possible to have a good life.

Life in America is "heaven" to Long who occasionally works with her daughter in order to send money to Cambodia. If she were still living in Cambodia she would not have what she considers luxuries—indoor bathrooms, income from part-time jobs, or the privilege of schools, books, and scholarships. Thus the *good* person finds a way to help the people in Cambodia who may never enjoy the material abundance of an economy like that of the United States.

> I am helping to rebuild the old temples and schools in
> Cambodia by sending $50, $30, $20 or $100. I would like to

> build schools in small poverty towns where students can't
> afford to go to Phnom Penh for education. I want to build a
> school and a portable bathroom for them.

Consistent with a majority of her peers, particularly women, Long reveres the freedom to attend school. Her "generosity work for her soul," therefore, is to send as much money as she can to help build schools in Cambodia.

> If I were in Cambodia, I would not have the privilege of
> schools, good temples or portable bathroom. When I am in the
> U.S., I have everything. Elders, young kids, anybody can go
> for an education in America. If I can just build it in
> Cambodia, then they can have it just the same as I, equally.
> American schools help Cambodians make it possible for
> everyone, including immigrants, to have a really good
> education for the future with books and scholarships to help
> out. Where we are living now is heaven where we can help
> others and rely on others to live happy together.

Long particularly admires the person who works hard to get ahead in life. In this regard, Long refers to her daughter, Rath, because she has always worked hard to raise her five children alone. Rath is the most dependable of Long's five children because she is always there to help both her parents with whatever they need. Long reciprocates by cooking and cleaning for her daughter when she is at work, and taking care of Rath's youngest children.

> I respect the person who works really hard to get where they
> are right now. I don't like a person who doesn't take
> advantage of that opportunity that they could get, but instead
> just gives up. I admire Rath the most. I can depend on her the
> most, ask for favors, and do things for me. She is the most
> dependable of all my children.

Long's ideal family is one in which the children have respect toward their parents, their elders, and their teachers. They must know good from bad, and they must obey and listen to their parents. A caring parent teaches her children the rule of "No and Yes." When the parent says, "No," the children must obey and not dispute or sneak out of the house in protest. But sometimes the good parent must also say, "Yes," and give the children what they want and need. Understanding how to balance No and Yes is the primary responsibility of the good parent.

> From old generation passed down to my grandchildren, I want my family to obey the parents, the elders, the relatives by listening to them and obeying them. When we say, "No," that mean, "No." That is a way of caring about my family. The children will not be sneaking out the window. But if they want to go somewhere, the parents must take the time and take them. That is important too. It is important not to break the rules of Yes or No.

Long has strong opinions about the Cambodian custom where the parents select the partners for their son or daughter. She is confident that the parent will always know who is right and wrong for the daughter, who in traditional Cambodian society is very shy and rarely goes outside.

> In Cambodia parents pick the husband for the daughters or pick the daughter for the husband. The parents will know who is right and who is wrong. Cambodian girls are really shy and hidden behind doors.

She expresses her disapproval of the American way of life where the children are raised to be very open, independent, and disrespectful of their elders. "I don't like American way of life when the children are raised with the doors wide open, where they have every privilege, every opportunity, and every freedom."

Rath's perceptions of success follow the expectations she carries as a daughter, as a mother, and finally as an individual. Beginning with her personal expectations of success, Rath states that she doesn't care for her own comfort if her sacrifices help her children to have a good life. Rath is a proud and strong individual, and she doesn't mind working hard to help her family get ahead. She also thinks of herself as a very strict person when it comes to raising her children the right way, so she lectures her children to respect and listen to the parents, obey their elders, and do well in school. "I work very hard; that is why the kid listen. He has to listen because I raise him to be the right way."

But she often comments on feeling ashamed that she cannot read or write, especially at those times when her son or daughter assume that she would not understand the content of a letter or a comment on television.

> I am not stupid, but my children treat me like I am stupid by opening mail, reading it, and then throwing it away without telling me what it says. I feel like I not have enough school. I am not a reading writing person, and I feel hurt very much when I don't know what is going on.

More recently, Rath has felt sad because she senses that Touch is ashamed to bring his wealthy American friends to their home.

> I don't care much for my own comfort or success. I want my children to have a good life, to complete college and get good jobs. I feel bad when Touch come home and tell me that his friends have parents who can just write a check to the college for full tuition. I feel ashamed because I think Touch is ashamed. When I ask why [his friends] don't come inside, he says he doesn't want them to see what a small, poor, ugly place he lives in. I say it is small, but it is clean and comfortable.

Remembering the trouble that followed Kusal in and out of school, Rath worries constantly about her younger children's safety, their reputations and the kinds of friends with whom they associate.

> Cambodian boy talk behind the girl's back. I explain to [Srey] that I am scared about that. They talk about her say, 'ugly send a picture to me.' I tell [the boy], 'you have a sister too, right? You don't say that to her!' I don't want they talk bad about [my daughter]. If you don't like her, don't talk about her. I hate when the kids they talk behind the back.

American kids grow up very fast. Most people not listen
to parent at all. I worry sometime to let [Touch or Srey] go or
not to go. Sometimes Touch, Saturday, Sunday, or Friday
went to [a] club. I worry about what kind of people he meet or
what he doing or what kind of kid he go out with, drinking
kid, smoking kid. I worry about that, and loud music car. I
am very strict like that, that is why. I work very hard to take
care of him.

Rath names her children, her mother, and her father as the people
she most admires. She especially admires her father because he has
always loved and protected her. She states that he was always very
generous to her when she was growing up. Her personal role model is
someone who doesn't smoke, drink, and is respectful to family
members and elders.

I admire my children, my mother, and father. My father, he
support me, he give me everything I need. He love me very
much. He don't care how much he spend.
I respect people who are nice. I don't like them to swear
too much or drink too much, or steal. I don't look down if
they do, but I just feel like they do wrong or are very hard to
help or to understand.

But Rath has always perceived the high education person or the
Buddhist monk to be the most successful person in her culture. "I
really admire high education person who is really respectful to the
family, obey the parents, and is respectful to elders. The person who
don't take education for granted."

To Rath success would be inconceivable without knowing the
Buddhist Way. Without the comfort of the monks Rath would not have
the strength to keep her children on a good path. As a result, Rath's
religious devotion is considered high praise in the Forest City
community, especially since her children are respectful of elders and
are good scholars.

Buddhism is very important to me because I don't have
anything to help me but the Buddha or monk. I just pray and I

> believe they are going to help me. I cry inside my heart, very
> painful. Nobody know. I just pray and the monk understand.
> I worry too much and I learn from the monk. They make me
> feel like I am clear. I understand everything. They help me a
> lot.

Rath, like her mother, is instinctively generous; when she cannot give money to people she sees in the streets, she prays that they not be hurt or unhappy.

> Sometime I see a family; they are unhappy and I feel bad for
> them. I pray, give them to be good, and don't get hurt. I don't
> care how they do bad or good, but anyone get hurt I feel bad
> for them.

Finally, Rath believes the successful person is one who is willing to change. She thinks of herself in the middle between the traditional ways of her mother and the modern ways of her daughter. She sees merit in both perspectives and works to sustain the one and cautiously encourage the other.

> Some family who are old like my mom are very hard to
> change the old religious ways. But the young, my daughter's
> age, they change, they not stay the same. I think some choices
> in life are open and it is very good for the person. They know
> how life can be provided. Sometimes it is good to be change.
> Cambodians want to have a good future, but we cannot stand
> on old ways. We have to change.

She is passionately devoted to helping her children become successful American citizens, and so she is willing to listen to her children's choices and their opinions. While she is often afraid that her children are not strong enough to resist the temptations of the too fast and too liberal American culture, she fundamentally trusts them to follow the right path. Above all else, Rath loves and enjoys her family. And the secret of her success, I believe, is the way she is able to remain strong as well as gentle, supportive as well as strict, and fun-loving as well as hard-working.

American woman really free and I say it is very good. In my
country when we meet a boy one or two times, the Cambodian
community call you very bad, look down on you and you feel
funny. When a woman have one husband and they get
divorced, the community look down on you.
  I don't know, we change a lot. I feel like we want
everything. We support children and make so happy family.
We don't care about whether we poor, so we happy family.
We support children, go to school, grow up good life.

Rath's family, like Pirun's family shows the cultural epistemology
operating through three generations. Long's frame of reference is
grounded in a 1920s-era Cambodian reality and models of success for
Cambodian women that included arranged marriages, foregoing school
in favor of her brother, and working hard to support her family. It is
unlikely that she conceived of her retire [sic] years being spent in the
United States, and so it is not surprising that she considers her life in
America to be "living in heaven." She is a person of high praise in the
Forest City community because she is a generous and devout Buddhist,
but also because she is, at age 72, a new American citizen.
Nonetheless, her perceptions of success for her grandchildren are still
quite traditional.

Rath's frame of reference draws from the 1950s-era Cambodian
reality of her childhood, which was very poor and in which education
and free choice in one's marriage partners were also not part of her
experience as a Cambodian woman. The war and her displacement to
Forest City have presented her with a different reality. Rath can
choose divorce and not be stigmatized by her community. Even though
she is illiterate in her Khmer and virtually illiterate in English, her
children will graduate from college in America. Rath, who would like
to move back to Cambodia where she can spend her retire years serving
the monks in a temple, also wants to become an American citizen, and
she champions women's freedom to choose their husbands and their
careers. She struggles to raise her children balanced between these two
cultural belief systems, and her story is a reflection of the tension she
experiences in holding the middle way.

Kusal states that his mother taught him to be polite, respectful,
generous, and disciplined. His perception of what it means to be a

successful Cambodian is to better your life by accomplishing your
goals.

> Success people could be you or me as long as they accomplish
> [their] goals in life. It takes from bottom to be on top, it
> doesn't take from top to [be on] bottom. I would say if I
> would be successful [it] is just being better off in life.

Kusal's goals are strongly connected to the Buddhist ideals instilled by
his mother. Specifically, he wants to help others. He is nice to
everyone; he is over-generous to friends and acquaintances to the
despair of his family. He even describes himself as an "easy touch"
because of his lack of selfishness or greed. The fact that people
frequently take advantage of him and that he often loses everything he
has, does not seem to alter his behavior.

> I just want to help. If I see an old lady crossing the street, I
> will go over and help her, carry her across the street. It is just
> the way I am. I can't help it, I can't ignore it, I can't pretend
> not to see it. My mom notice that when I was little, she knows
> that, "See what happens when you so nice, they take
> advantage of you. You are so nice, you give [to] everybody.
> If they ask [for] something, you give it to them." It's OK,
> you know how moms are, but I can't deny who I am. I can't
> lie to myself, I can't be greedy, I *can't*. I can't be selfish or
> jealous of other people.
>   The [disadvantages of being so generous] you lose
> everything. People take advantage of you, [but] it feels good.
> People need help, everyone need help. No one know
> everything, everyone need a helping hand. In my past, no one
> really [help me] everyone just mean to me cause I am so nice
> to them. [I] don't get mad if you joke around with me, I am
> just calm. No one nice to me [but] I am nice to them, you
> know, no matter what.

In spite of his life-long dedication to helping others less fortunate
than himself, Kusal wishes that in the past he had had successful role

models like a father or an older brother or sister to look up to, someone who could have taught him right from wrong.

> I could [have] accomplished a lot of things, but I haven't no one to look up to, nobody, no dad, no nothing.... My family don't encourage [me] 'cause I come from a broken home. The family not together and plus I am the oldest, it is a lot harder for me. If I have an older brother, sister, this is much better cause I can look up to 'em. I have no dad to look up to, my dad don't live with me.

Today, Kusal's mother and grandmother (and his siblings) come the closest to being role models for him. They "lecture" him on the right way to live and to be responsible to the family.

> I would like to have all those qualities [my mom has]. My mom is a hard-working person, a very hard-working person. I really admire and respect her. She is an integrity person. She is very caring, supportive and I would say a strong person. She is very generous. My mom has taught me always to be polite, respect people, and discipline.
>
> My grandma taught me [to] always help each other and always do good to people and be nice, be faithful and treat everyone like you are going to be treated, equal. [She say] don't be hitting or killing, or swearing or stealing from people or doing bad things to people because when you do bad things, what comes around goes around. What you don't have now, [if] you leave, you will have it. [If you are good in this life, the next time] you will be a lot better off.
>
> The most important things my [mom] has taught me is to come home. I never really like to come home, I always want to be by myself. [But] my mom really miss me or she didn't want me to be on my own, I might end up dead. Moms worry too much about their kids, they want to see their kids *there*, like next to you with or without nothing, they don't care.

In an ideal sense, Kusal names Mother Theresa and the Pope as the role models who inspire him to help others. He states that he would like to travel around the world helping others like they do.

> If I wanted a role model [to be] someone I look up to, it would
> be Mother Theresa. She is my role model. She travel around
> the world and she helps people. I want to be just like her, I
> like to help.

He also names Pirun as a person who inspires him because of the way Pirun helps out in the community.

> [For a Cambodian person] I respect Pirun. He is a hard-
> working man. He helps a lot. He deals with a lot of people
> [and] he helps a lot of communities. He is a nice person, an
> integrity person. He has helped my family to get jobs, to get
> educated.

In his narrative Kusal returns often to the theme of role models and his regret that he, like many of his peers, did not have a strong role model to guide him down the "good path." Had Kusal grown up in Cambodia, this role model might have been one of the monks in the absence of a supportive father. The absence of a large and vibrant Buddhist temple, for the Khmer, affects the life paths of all three generations in America.

> If you come from a good home and you hang with the good
> home people, with a lot of love, support and encouragement,
> they do really well. If you hang with a crowd like no father,
> no discipline, probably child abuse when they were little, that
> crowd just don't care what they do in life. Life [is] just kill
> time, just see time fly.

Kusal's friends appear in his narrative as *unsuccessful* role models. Kusal does not have a best friend because there is no one in his life he trusts.

I don't choose a best friend because I would say your best
friend one day would be your worse enemy. They would
know everything about you and I can't trust people. I put out
100 percent and they only put like 50 percent. I see who is
good and who is not; who has been mistreating or rumors,
gossip people. It is why I choose not to have a best friend. I
would never tell my secret my deeply personal life to another
person. I just keep it to myself. I think one day [my friends]
would use my words against me. [That happened to me] one
time a long time ago. All it takes is just one time, you know.

In fact, he refers to his friends as the "wrong crowd." When Kusal
dropped out of high school, he sought independence from his family
but immediately attached himself to a group of other high school dropouts. Kusal's experiences with this group have led to his "mistakes,"
his lack of trust and occasions when people have taken advantage of
him.

All it takes is the wrong crowd for anybody. If you are in
school, work, anywhere, [if] you hang with the wrong crowd,
you got to be accepted. I did the wrong crowd. I have been
there. Me and my friends just go party, drink, sometimes do
bad things to ourselves. I wasn't that person, but I was
influenced by that person, so I have to do what they have to
do.
    I thought it was cool to hang out with that crowd instead
of the geeky crowd, like the nerd crowd, the smart ones. The
smart ones, the nerd ones really get somewhere in life and I
am hanging out with the bad crowd in a corner over there.
Now I regret it. I just wish I had got the right crowd, but I
didn't know what is right and what is wrong, no one tells me.

In 1983 when Kusal became a student, the Forest City public
schools were just beginning to create English as a Speaker of Other
Language (ESOL) classrooms, and the majority of the teachers who
began working with the Cambodian and Vietnamese refugees were not
certified in either ESOL or bilingual education. Kusal's description of
attending these early ESOL classes is tragic and speaks to the effect of

cultural bias and lack of critical training on these young people. Without sensitive and competent teachers, these children have little choice but to turn to their ethnic cohort for safety and acceptance.

> When I first came to the U.S. I wasn't really interested in school because I was older. I was a few years older, a lot older [than my classmates.] They know so much [and] I feel like I am left out of everything. You just shake your head 'no, yes, no, yes' [and] you don't have a clue what they [are] talking about. Every time you raise your hand to ask questions, sometimes they talk back and it isn't quite what [you are asking]. They say like ten sentences and you only pick up one sentence.
>
> I don't think the teacher really take the time to teach, they just do it for the money. Most of the time, they just don't really care. I remember I used to get a test, open book test, and the teacher would come over and [point], 'the answer is right there, B, B, B.' I would get good grades and we passed. They don't take time to explain it.
>
> If the teacher take the time and help one student, really help them instead of pass them [by]. I mean teachers have favorite students, so they go to favorite student. We are not dumb. I am just saying that we learn slowly and they don't want to bother. They leave that person alone.
>
> I want to learn more English or more reading [but] they don't really teach us how to write the pronoun and all the adjective and all the words. And when we write we don't know how to spell [or use] the past tense. [And] they don't really correct it, they just look at it [and say], 'oh, well that's good.' They don't really take time.

Kusal's story about his schooling experience speaks to the complex problem of perpetuating a culture of resistance and low self-esteem by withholding opportunities to participate in mainstream classes while at the same time supporting a cultural identity.

> You don't learn as much doing the ESL, well you do, but mainstream is a lot better cause you learn much more, you fit

into all the other people. You hang out with different groups
and your English get better. In ESL we don't really speak
English, to our friends we speak Cambodian to each other. It
doesn't help us [learn] anything about English. It would help
us more if we train English with the Americans.

The crowd I used to hang out with is just not the right
crowd cause we are always goofing off in class cause we
really didn't know what was going on. We were like, 'Oh,
this is too much stress,' so we forget about going to learn. The
English, it is too hard for us and we start to speak Cambodian.

Without anyone to interpret or mediate the racism he experienced from
his white peers, and faced with unskilled and possibly indifferent
teachers, Kusal eventually gave up and dropped out. Unfortunately, his
is not an uncommon story.

Regrettably the Forest City school system has not kept records on
retention and promotion of this one and a half generation. It is my
impression that most of the young people who were part of the first
wave of Cambodian refugees and whose parents were educated, were
more successful in school than students like Kusal. Refugee parents,
without any schooling prior to resettling in America, were unprepared
to assist their children with the transition into school.

My parents, all they know of their life, they just work [as]
farmers and no school. They can't really help me much to set
my goal, they just like "You need money or something? Here
just take it." They just hand money to help us financial [and
give us] a place to live. I don't think they encourage you, they
just give you lecture and they yell at you.

My family is so busy, they don't really help us. The
Asian culture, we don't really, you know, help. I mean, they
help you with money, but they don't help you with English or
sit down and explain [to] you [about America] cause they are
not American themselves. We have to go out there and study
the world and compare and then we can help ourself.

Now that Touch is in college and Srey is preparing to attend
college in the fall, Kusal has seen that educational success is possible

within his own family. Although he believes he is not as smart as his siblings, he wishes he could complete his GED and continue on to college too. But Kusal is still very naive about school, and without committing himself to a full-time English tutor which would interfere with the requirements of his current job, he is unlikely to connect further schooling to his future.

> If I had [my GED] that would be a lot better than what I am doing now. My life be a lot simpler. I be more happy. I be like I accomplish something, I could move on, go to college and not work as hard.
>
> I always want to go to college, but you know here I am, working. I could go to school and go to work [at] the same time, but if I do that I think I can't keep up with school. I want to do education, it's just the job, it is in the way. I go to work and come [home] late and sometime you can't get to sleep until like one or two cause you still wide awake. Sometimes if I go [to school] in the morning, I will be too tired and won't focus right.

When I first met Kusal he told me he wanted to own his own business, a small music club or restaurant. He was a bit vague on how he would ever have enough money to finance such a business, or where he would gain the expertise to manage the business over time, but it sounded like fun to him and not too much work. Today, Kusal knows how long it takes to work your way into a full-time job with good benefits. He also knows how long it takes to save money and what kind of credit banks require before they loan money on new businesses.

In our second interview, Kusal began to talk about another kind of career that sounded much more consistent with his character and his experience; he stated that he wanted to become an ESL teacher. I speculate that in light of the experiences mentioned above, Kusal recognizes how important it is to be given a good foundation in reading and writing English if one wants to get ahead in American society. He is inspired by the prospect of helping other refugee children be successful in school by making sure they do not get stuck in ESL classes where they are in danger of falling behind or of falling into the wrong crowd.

If I have a choice [I would study] to be a teacher or maybe like an ESL teacher. People who spoke another language, [I would] just help them out with their English. If I go to college I would probably go for that, I will be studying education.

If I were an ESL teacher, I would take a student, test to see how they work in math and science. If they do average work, OK I will send them out there. Not to a mainstream, but to like a high level, send them to a basic mainstream first. If they do good in there, I will send them to the general and if they do better, I will kick them out and just leave them there. I will leave them there for the college courses. [If they don't do well in English], I would help them, practice them, keep them until they correct mistakes. Make sure they are learning, get it right. If that doesn't work, I will tutor them extra time, just volunteer to help them accomplish the way they want to go.

Although Kusal believes he is much more successful now that he is married, working full time, and saving for the future, he still thinks of work as an inconvenience. He believes he is still a little young to have such weighty responsibilities, and continues to visualize work as an opportunity to work with people he likes, to see different kinds of jobs, or volunteer with an organization like the Peace Corps or the Red Cross.

The hardest part [of my life] right now is finding the right job 'cause a lot of jobs you need a college degree or school. At work I bounce around, I like to see different jobs. I stay for a while and then move on. I have to be working where I like the people. Sometimes I don't like working with the public because people just get on your nerves. There is good customers and there is mean customers. There is a lot of mean ones, rude ones.

In middle school, sixth grade, I was interested in Peace Corps. I wanted to join, but no one really helped me or showed me [how to do it]. I don't know where to go cause my English is really poor in middle school. All the kids wanted to do other stuff, but I always wanted the Peace Corps. The teacher said, 'Oh forget it, you don't want that.'

Volunteering or calling to help people, I will do it even [if there is] no money, less money, I will still do it cause I like doing it, it would be fun and [it] would be like helping, be a teacher or doctor or something like Peace Corps. I want to join a team like Blue Cross, Red Cross or go out and help. I think it is fun for me, I like that. That is where I want to be, I like to help.

Helping and having fun continue to be strong themes in the way Kusal connects his perceptions of success to a conventional story of getting ahead. In Pirun's model of the three stages of life, Kusal is clearly at the productive stage of life without having successfully completed his formal education or first stage even though he has learned the Buddhist principles from his mother and the monks. Kusal continually negotiates between two cultural models in his mind. One requires that he work hard, plan, save money, and provide for a secure future for his family. This model is balanced by the conviction that making a lot of money and being very stressed are less successful than being happy, having fun, and having the time to help people.

When asked about making money as a criteria for success, Kusal—like MP, Avy, Alyana, Srey, and Touch—indicated he would like to have a lot of money, but he also believes that having a lot of money just brings problems.

[I don't like] charity people because they feel bad for me or take pity on me. Like if I am poor, I be poor and if I am rich, I be rich. I don't want to [have someone say] here take a dollar, you have no money, you have no clothes. I don't like to feel like [they] judge you or something, just let me be who I am. I am happy the way I am.

[Wealthy or powerful] people they got problems. They not really success. Yeah, they success, but they not happy. I would rather be happy, you know, poor happy. [I would rather have] a full happiness and having something that our family have. Like we don't need a million dollars to be successful. Successful is in our own mind, in our mind.

[Success is] not like, "Hey, I got $1,000! Look at me!"

No that money is going to be not good. [It] could help to buy
items and take you places, but it is only mind [that is]
successful. As long as you are happy, successful is
everywhere in yourself.

Kusal states that he will teach his children about Khmer
culture—the language, the food, the customs and the religion, although
he will not force them to accept the culture if they resist. Kusal
believes that the most important Cambodian tradition is Buddhism, and
as a future role model for his children, he will pass along his belief in
the Buddhist teachings which have always sustained his family.

My culture is very important 'cause I don't [want] to forget
where I come from, my background, because where I come
from is who I am. The culture things we do, the language, the
tradition, the food, every little detail that is just me. I was
brought up as a Cambodian, my religion is Buddhism. I will
stay that way until I probably die.
    My kid can do whatever they want, they can believe
whatever they want, and they don't have to accept the culture.
I will teach 'em the language, I will teach them the food and
tradition and some of the stuff that should be really important
to know. Stuff [that's] not important, they don't have to worry
about it 'cause if you put too much stuff into a kid, the kid
going to find it boring and they going to [say,] "Ah, forget this
culture. It's too much."
    Buddhism is very important to my family. My family
always practices that culture, that religion. Every ceremony in
a year or every month they attend that temple [in Forest City]
or sometimes in L. They always get me to go with them.
[When] we get there, we just pray to our God and worship and
ask him to look after each other and for forgiveness. It is
really important because Buddhist tradition has been for
generations of my parents [and] my parents' grandparents.
They have been telling us to go with the Buddhist way.

In a stunning transition from the concrete analysis of success
according to the amount or type of schooling he has, or the kind of

career that would be best, Kusal moves into a discussion of success as the inevitable unfolding of his destiny. His narrative is one of the most powerful examples of a deeply held Buddhist model which claims that each person is born with a destiny which unfolds over time. In spite of Kusal's struggle to make something of his life to this point, he passionately believes that he is being saved for something important.

> My grandparents told me you can change [your destiny] for the worse or better, [it just] depends on where you are going. I think it is something you did in your past life. If you do good in this life, you will do better in your next life, way better. You will be more happier, more secure.
>
> I think I am being saved for something. I haven't accomplished my destiny yet. I have a destiny to be on this earth, [and] once I accomplish my destiny, I will be able to rest. If I try to die on purpose, I will die, but if I don't die on purpose, in an accident, something will save me. My time hasn't come yet. I am here on purpose to do something.
>
> Only I will know; no one else will know. There is no one else who knows your destiny. I don't know your destiny, you don't know mine, so [when] you reach that destiny that you really have to be, [you can say,] "Okay, I am done," and you feel like *wow*, I did it.
>
> So if I die [it is] because [I have] already done my work, I already have kids, I already have fun, I already accomplished some success, own a business. [In the meantime, you just] keep doing whatever you are doing. Yeah.

Kusal is particularly sensitive of his need to balance the two parts of his identity. Kusal considers the years when he was pulled off center by the gang who influenced him to experiment with alcohol, drugs, and lawlessness to be major life mistakes, and in this regard he sees himself as an example for his siblings—a model that was *not successful*. It is perhaps why in our interviews, Kusal reflects on the difficulty of having a Cambodian and an American mind without knowing fully what his heart wants to be.

I like both [Cambodian and American way] because I know
two things. If I know [only] one thing, I will do that mistake.
If I do my culture way, I might be wrong. So I have two
cultures in my mind when I do something. I always think
twice before I say something, before I do something.
    You don't just think American way, "Yeah, let's go party,
drink, and hang out." "What about school?" "Wait a minute,
I go to school." You have to weigh both sides. [One side
say,] "Let's go, no time to waste, we have a schedule, come on
we have a schedule booked up. [The other side] say, "Take
your time, take a deep breath, a calm second."
    Most Cambodian people I see are more Americanized
than Cambodian. They know very little about Cambodian
culture. Most teenagers I know are more Americanized and
mostly get into trouble. Even though they come from a good
home, they turn themselves in a bad way. Only a few
Cambodians that I know [are] really dedicated and loyal to
their parents and very faithful, but if they hang with certain
groups, like the thugs or drugs, they will do a lot of problems.

Finally, Kusal voices a central and enduring concept in Cambodian
Buddhism—that the most successful life is one in which the person
remains flexible and balanced—able to follow the bends in the river
and adjust to the underlying currents. Like the familiar Khmer
proverb, Kusal sees his future success as something crafted on the
lessons of his past.

I am just going with the flow, where life take me I just go.
Wherever it leads me, it just leads me. By doing that I learn a
lot from my mistakes. We are going to go out there making
mistakes [and] we will learn from mistake. We can help us
out and improve ourself better. By doing mistake I learn from
mistake, so I go to my younger brother and sister and I will
tell em, that's the wrong thing. Don't do that, don't do this
cause I did already and I don't want to happen to them like
what happened to me.

In the section above Pirun states that the most important knowledge for the successful Cambodian is to train the mind "to operate within the frame of the culture. If the mind operate within the frame of the culture then the whole understanding, the whole thought is going in the right direction. But if the mind has been pulled to the left or right by an unfaithful friend, a gang or an enemy, then the mind can lead the body to do something not within the norm of the culture." Kusal has clearly struggled to keep his mind centered in the right way of living as taught by his grandmother, mother and the Buddhist monks. On the one hand he believes he has not had a strong, older male role model who has taught him the difference between right and wrong, but on the other hand, he intuitively acts on principles of generosity, helpfulness, kindness and forgiveness modeled by his family and his religion.

Touch states that "success is just something I enjoy doing like having fun." Having fun to Touch means volunteering endless hours tutoring children, playing soccer, taking challenging courses and helping his Cambodian friends get into college.

> Success is just something I enjoy doing like having fun. I do a
> lot of community service and I tutor a lot of ESL kids. I want
> to help other people because I feel like it is fun cause there are
> just so many things you take for granted. It goes along the
> lines,'you don't know what you have until it's gone.' I mean
> you don't value it unless you lose it.

Touch credits his mother with teaching him what is right and wrong; what it means to be a good Cambodian. He looks to his mother for qualities he wants for himself—understanding, loving, openness, and the ability to handle stress. Touch states that he is respectful of everyone because his mother and grandparents have persistently taught him to respect his elders and to avoid conflict.

> [The qualities in my mom I most want to have] are
> understanding and loving, open and sometimes naive when it
> comes to certain things, like how to handle stress and pressure
> because my mom handle[s] that pretty well. [In] talking to my

mom, she said all the things she had to do like coming here, trying to live in this Western society where the values are different. I guess it is her ability to handle [stress] and not break down [that I admire]. I don't see her break down that much. [She has had to] overcome genocide and still have optimism for the world. I am a pretty respectful person around when it counts. I am respectful of everyone because it is the way I was brought up.

Touch and his mother don't honor the Buddhist religion in the same way, still, he admits that he bases his moral decisions on what feels right to him. In fact "doing the right thing" dominates Touch's narrative from fulfilling his responsibilities at his summer job to giving a friend a ride home. For Touch, doing the right thing is not an abstract moral law, but a code that guides his daily thoughts and actions.

I am not a saint [because] I do all these right things, but for the most part I try to do the right thing. I base my moral decisions on what feels right. It just felt right to help out [a friend]. She said she was really grateful and I told her that I am just another squirrel in the world trying to do my part.

Taking leadership is another form of success for Touch, primarily because he enjoys working with groups of people. From Touch's perspective, leadership is not about exerting power or authority, but in teaching the people he supervises to work as a team.

For the most part I am [comfortable with positions of leadership]. There are some drawbacks like when I was making people's schedules [at the M. Industries job]. I had to make moral decisions about this person who needed to so many hours to pay their rent. It worked out pretty well.
   [I am a good leader at the Country Club] because I communicate with them and they trust me. That is what makes a good leader, if you trust them; like, I will follow you blindly like a prophet. Whatever I say, they do and they respect whatever I say. We get things done faster as a team when they listen to me cause I know the ropes. I try to put

myself in their situation, I try to understand. One of the first
things I teach when I train people at work [is] you tell them
that we are a team. If you are falling behind, I will help you
out and vice versa, cause I am not going to get out unless you
get out.

The kind of people Touch looks up to as leaders and role models
are people who have a strong, internal sense of right and wrong and are
motivated to better themselves. "For me a role model would be
someone who is just successful. I look up to them because I sort of
want to be like them; I want to have that success. A good role model is
someone you want to follow because they are doing the right thing."
Touch's heroes are simple people, who are educated, who enjoy their
work, are involved with their families, and are compassionate to others.
By the same token, Touch recognizes that he has become a role model
for other Cambodian young people. A few, whom he once envied for
their advantages in life, have not done much with their lives. While
they have turned to gangs and drugs, Touch has pursued his dream of
college and a good future.

> I look up to my boss at the Country Club. He is a chef and he
> runs the place. He has worked hard and he has paid his dues.
> I look for what features can I try to learn from him. He says
> be a fast and efficient worker, and I try to do that. That is
> why I sort of look up to him someone who has proven himself.
> I want to adapt, sort of take a little bit from them and expand
> it.
>   I try to be like Tom because he is always helping out,
> always looking the other way. I want to be like that; that is
> what I strive to be. Tom is basically what I thought is an All-
> American person. I like his personality, his kindness in his
> heart. He is just this nice guy, everyone likes him. He is not
> that charismatic, but you know you can trust him. You can tell
> him anything. He is not stuck up; he is open minded, and he
> will help you out in a jam. He is not that rich; he is middle
> class. At school he won the nicest person award. It is the way
> he was brought up and his sister is like that too. If there were
> more people like him in the world, it would be a better place

because he is always doing community service and helping out when he can. I think that would be successful to be like that.

[The most respected adult I know] would probably be my uncle. [He] is the one with the semiconductor job, new car. He is high praise because he has a degree, he went to job corps, he has his own house, his own land, and he is raising a family. To our community he is high praise because he is able to educate himself.

Someone like MP is high praise because he is clean cut, he works, his family is successful, they own a store. Some people think I am one of them too because when I call they are so glad I called their house. When I call or [when] MP calls, parents love us, they treat us really well. They try to feed us because they feel like it might trickle down to their kids, you know.

Touch reflected that as he slowly lost interest in trying to "fit in" with the popular American students at Danforth Academy he went looking for people who were more normal.

Sometimes I try too hard cause it sort of comes into play with my psychological, like wanting to fit in, wanting to be liked, so I try harder to be liked. [But] I am not out to go and hang out with kids that are really snobby or cliquey as much as I was. I was trying to be cool, now I am more into finding people that are just like *normal*.

Even though Touch was easily accepted as part of the sports group or the elite group, he eventually found himself drawn to the "nerdy" kids. He came to admire their intelligence and the things they could teach him about computers. Perhaps from his perspective as a minority, Touch was able to move beyond peer pressure and stereotypes and find friends who had the same passion for learning as he.

Some of my friends at high school were kind of nerdy. A lot of people wouldn't invite them to parties [but] I found out that they are really cool people. They are like incredibly smart. They are going to Williams, one went to MIT. They can

program [computers], they made their own video games. I
have learned some cool computer things from them. [It]
would be cool if I could do half the things they do. I admire
these guys a lot, [even though] they don't play a thing of sport.
I got laughed at a lot because I was always hanging out with
them, [but] I learned a lot with them with the Mac and the
IBM so, ten years from now, hopefully it will pay off.

For Touch, the concept of "getting ahead" is complicated. If
Kusal's perceptions of success have been formed by his experiences
with people at the "bottom of the hourglass," Touch has formed his
perceptions of success through his experiences with the people at the
very top of the hourglass. On the one hand he has some appreciation
for what it means to be truly wealthy. He has seen the advantages as
well as the tremendous responsibilities that accompany young people
who inherit sizable portfolios upon turning twenty-one.

At [Danforth school] we get a lot of kids who have the luxury
to do whatever they want. It is kind of sad because there are
inner city kids that don't have the luxury of that. There is not
a [safety] net for them. There are some kids [who] are taking
a year off and they are going to Europe, they are going to
Asia. Most of the [Cambodian] kids I know don't even know
how to get into college yet.
My [wealthy] friends are just oblivious to the fear [of
failure]. They just see me working and [think] 'Oh, that's
cool.' They don't see this fear of failure because most of them
pretty much have a safety net. Their problem might be 'Oh,
what am I going to do now?' 'cause they *have* all these funds.

On the other hand, Touch has a profound appreciation for the
"immigrant work ethic" which fuels the ambition of many people in his
community to better their lives. Touch uses the phrase "fear of failure"
to explain the immigrant's constant drive to work two jobs, buy a
house, or accumulate status symbols such as cars, televisions and
clothes.

For the Asian community the fear [of failure] is like not being
able to make it; to be able to do something that has meaning
to your life or something that gives credibility. Fear of failure
would be like me ending up working at McDonalds for the rest
of my life. So I am afraid of failing and like working the third
shift of something.

The difference between the [minorities] and the lower
people that are white is that these minorities are willing to
work the third shift like 12 to 6:00 and the other people would
rather be unemployed. And then they get labeled the
immigrant worker ethic which is sort of true because they
come from a country [where] there is not much to have and
here if they work at it, they will get it.

Given their place in the American economy, most immigrants do not
have a financial safety net to fall back on in times of stress. Touch is
confident that the opportunity exists for him to earn the career he
wants, but without a financial "safety net" he must survive or fail on
his own. It is why his discussion of getting ahead is saturated with the
concept of having to prove himself and being afraid of failing to do so.
Similar to MP, failure appears to represent being stuck in a
meaningless job, working the third shift for the rest of his life.

[My Cambodian friends] are in the same boat as I am. They
don't want to end up working at Konica from 11:00 at night to
8:00 in the morning everyday for the rest of their lives getting
$5.75 an hour. Most of my friends just want to do something
that is worthwhile; something that is not the normal.

What makes it more complicated is that Touch frequently weighs
career success on the scale of his Danforth friends against the success
of someone like his uncle who has a good job in a semiconductor
factory and is considered highly successful within the Cambodian
community. Touch is intelligent enough to recognize that each
generation of his family uses a different point of reference to gauge the
progress of success. For his family a middle class job in an American
technology industry is more successful than life as a poor rice farmer.

However, Touch aspires to something more personally meaningful and fun.

> To [my Cambodian friends] going away to college is sort of a
> dream. Most of them just expect to graduate and probably not
> go [to college]. Best case, they might go to the university, live
> at home, and work. Not all of them have the opportunity or
> the luxury to actually go away to college like in another state.
> Most of them just have to get a job somewhere and work,
> probably get a wife from mail-order bride from Cambodia.
> They will be married and it starts over again.
>   I have something to prove [to society] because I want to
> establish myself and do something well. That is one of my
> motivations. I want to be one of those guys, [lawyer, doctor].
> I want to try and establish myself, I don't want to just do
> something minute.

While Touch would like to be well established and comfortable in life, he also wants to be in the position to help minorities get ahead. He has noticed that it takes connections as well as hard work to get ahead in American society, but, in his experience, minorities have few connections. Instead they are the people who make the world work, who do all the little things that no one else wants to do. Touch's narrative reveals a certain sense of pride in these humble, but honest endeavors, along with a yearning for the opportunity to improve his status in American society.

> I just want to see if I can help [minorities in my job]. I know
> everybody has to overcome hardships but minorities have that
> extra step or two with the language and just trying to get their
> foot in the doorstep. Most minorities can't get those high jobs
> because they don't have connections. The only connection is
> probably their uncle working at a food place or a brother
> saying, 'come on man, there is an opening,' and that is where
> they end up for the rest of their lives because they don't have a
> person to open the door for them.
>   We are basically a bunch of merchants and peasants. We
> basically do the little things that [makes] the world go around.

Like we are the ones working in sweat shops, we are the ones working at the sea urchin places, we are the ones working on the farms doing all those little things. We Cambodians are the guys you find at the farms picking strawberries and green beans at 2:00 in the morning. We are the people you find mowing lawns or [picking] sea urchins. You don't see many of us in a corporate place at all, and if you do we are either cleaning the toilets or being a teller.

Touch has gained a perspective on the kinds of work he likes to do and the kind of work he is good at doing. He comments that he prefers teaching and working with minorities the most because it is fun and it gives him the opportunity to help people who are less fortunate than he.

I enjoy teaching. It is training for long hours and you don't get paid that much. When I go back and visit my middle school teachers, they seem like they have aged so much more. I mean they [say] they don't do it for the money, they do it for the love of teaching. When I talk to some of my teachers about how they feel, they are getting paid so much less than all their friends, but all their friends talk about their job as a job, and he is talking about his job as like [his life].

I just want to do something that is able to give back. That could be whatever job is available that is appealing and can offer me a chance of some freedom to do things for the community. I don't want to confine it to just a lawyer or a teacher or some sort of communications job. It could be like working for Coke or being a manager and being able to open clinics, sponsoring clinics for kids and at the same time endorsing Coke.

Unlike Kusal or Srey, Touch expresses many conflicts over religion. He went to the temple with his grandparents, mother and siblings until he was old enough to stay home by himself. Touch remembers a time when he believed in the power of the monk to do almost anything. However, when he entered high school, Touch turned his back on Buddhism and declared he was a "child of the enlightenment," a rational scientist.

> I am pretty scientific. I guess I know like the ten
> commandments like thou shalt not kill. I guess all that stuff I
> sort of believe, [but] I am more like one of the people of the
> Enlightenment, like Voltaire, you know. You have ten
> principles of enlightenment and that is how people are. One
> of them is like you can be an atheist and the moral part of that
> is everyone is basically equal. That is how I view people.

There is a continuing tension between Touch and his mother over showing proper respect to the monks and proper adherence to the Buddhist precepts. For most Cambodian elders the monk represents the wisdom and selflessness of the Buddha. They say, "Attend to the words and not the actions when choosing a path for your life." Pirun who is perceived as high praise for his generosity toward the community, understands that most young Khmer especially in the United States will reject the formal demands of the religion while they are young—but if the patterns of the culture have been instilled in infancy, young people will internalize a way of behaving and a set of values that are consistent with the "mind of the culture." In spite of his skepticism, Touch acts out of a value structure that is highly correlated with the guidelines set down by his mother and grandmother.

> Cambodian society, we are really religions. We are always
> going to temples and praying. I have sort of moved away
> from that. My mom is always wanting me to go to New
> Year's festival and L. where they have these big [festivals]
> where they sit for five hours and they pray and chant. I just
> don't want to do that, I would rather stay home and watch
> football. I think it is all a waste of money and time.
>   I don't think [religion] is a significant role [in my life.] I
> am pretty positive that all the kids my age don't really take
> religion that seriously. We feel like it doesn't apply to us; it
> is for the old people. I remember going [to Temple] as a
> child. I just felt like I saw through it. I felt like it was more of

a scam cause I realize how has it helped my family. It hasn't
done anything.

It is obvious to me that Touch has internalized most of the Buddhist
way and follows a highly moral path, nonetheless, Touch states that,
for him, religion is a waste of time, that it has done nothing to help his
family or him. He bases his conviction on his study of comparative
world religions in high school, which he contends proves his point that
religion has manipulated people for centuries. He further illustrates his
opinions by pointing out the many hypocrisies prevalent in Cambodian
culture from arranged marriages to considering dating as a sin. The
tension is revealed in Touch's observations that much like MP, his
indifference to Buddhism drives a wedge between himself and his
culture.

> I don't know what my destiny is. I don't believe in
> reincarnation. I have taken all these classes in religion and I
> just see that most of the time religion manipulated people and
> made them unhumanistic and how time and time again
> religion was proved wrong. Well, the Christian religion
> anyway.
>   Basically I am not religious. It is kind of sad because I
> kind of lose out on my culture because my culture is heavily
> religious. But it just doesn't appeal to me. I just refuse it. If I
> don't believe in something, why bother?

Touch stated that in the past year he has become conscious of what
it might mean to lose his culture. He still speaks Khmer with his
friends and family, but notices that his cousins from a mixed marriage
do not.

> I think it is important to [speak my language] because like my
> other uncle, he is married to a white woman and his kids are
> mixed, they are brought up [as] American. He doesn't talk
> Khmer to them at all. It is kind of weird cause they don't
> really understand the certain rituals. They have their Barney
> and their power rangers, [but not having their language] is just
> going to come back to haunt them. I am glad I had the ability

to speak both. For me it would be kind of demoralizing, like
you know, I can't speak my own language, I got some issues.

He is aware that many Cambodian young people feel ashamed to be
Cambodian and quickly adopt American dress, behavior, and speech.
Faced with the extreme contrast between cultures in high school,
Touch has become more intent on maintaining his own cultural
traditions, at least those that do not require him to attend the Buddhist
temple!

I find most kids [are] sort of embarrassed to be Cambodian,
like in public schools. They more associate themselves with
being Black and they don't really speak Cambodian well.
They just push it aside, like it is all American. I think the
reality [is that] they want to fit in. No matter where you are
you [are] always going to be viewed differently because you
are, you know, different.

On the other hand, he recognizes that the need to "fit in" is fairly
compelling for most young people. Touch refers to this dilemma as the
"clash of two cultures," but does not seem to have a strong sense of
how to resolve the incommensurable differences.

I am sort of at that crossroads. Most of my life I was always
trying to fit in. I was always trying to be American. My
friends had baseball cards, so I started buying them and I had
no idea what they were even for, I just bought them. I tried to
play sports and all my friends would be playing T-ball and
little league and farm league. They would all be playing [in]
these football leagues and I would always be a kid watching.
It is just weird growing up like that always wanting to sort of
be like that. Now I am at this age where it is like in reverse,
where I sort of have to bring back my culture because I realize
it is diminishing.
    A lot of people say that is the price you pay for the
melting pot. We have to compromise certain cultures so it
will be like a medium and a lot of people disagree. They say it
shouldn't be that way, [we] should emphasize each culture and

point out the beauty of each culture and not omit certain things because it is not appealing.

Keeping a foot in both cultures has required him to negotiate issues of race, beliefs and especially social class. Even though Touch has always had Cambodian and American friends, he has made the decision to keep these two worlds separate. He does not feel up to the task of trying to make his American friends understand what it is like to be a Cambodian, nor does he believe his Cambodian friends will ever understand the life of a wealthy American.

> I kind of keep those two worlds sort of [separate]. There is the life of the minority side and the life of the, I don't know, bourgeoisie, the middle class side. [And the rich], there are some pretty well off people [at Danforth school.] It is pretty tricky. I know I am lucky to be there and I just try to enjoy it. I mean if you don't enjoy it, you will drive yourself crazy.
>
> If [my friends] are wealthy, like they have three condos and I live in an apartment, I don't talk about that. I sort of filter out what I say. We talk about sports, school. We don't talk about [the fact that] they go away every vacation to the Bahamas and stuff. It is not like that cause there is just a comfort level.
>
> Even though they are my closest friends I don't tell them half the things. They wouldn't understand. It's like, 'do you want the truth or what you want to hear?' and you tell them what they want to hear. Cause the truth; they wouldn't understand the truth. They have to go and experience it themselves. They want to hear just the fascinating stuff, but they don't want to hear. That is how most people should be and that is probably how most minority [people] are like to the Caucasian people. It's like we try to explain everything and you still [don't] understand.
>
> I am pretty cool with my Cambodian friends, MP and B who lives down the street because we are all minorities so we can talk about serious stuff. But I wouldn't talk with them about my other friends. So it is kind of like a double life cause

they are always making fun of me saying I sold out by going
to a private school.

Although Touch experiences the clash of two cultures more
directly with his school friends, his family represents the third place of
conflict for him. Touch is highly sensitive to the way the Cambodian
community attaches praise or censure to a family based on the
children's reputations, so Touch interprets his mother's perceptions of
success in light of what he believes is his family's obsession with
appearing successful in the community. Rath's sensitivity about people
looking down on her family is justified according to her children who
are acutely aware of how many Khmer families gossip about one
another.

The [most important things my parents taught me] were to
succeed. Like my mom wants [her] son and daughter to be [a]
success. She wants everyone to be successful because she
doesn't want our life [to be like her life]. I guess the biggest
thing she has taught me has been like fear, fear of failure. It is
just key cause she doesn't want people to look down on her
family, so she wants us to do well.

My mom says how we should always marry UP and try to
move up the caste system and how I shouldn't hang out with
people who aren't as smart as me or who aren't as well off as
me because they are going to bring me down.

To my mom [Tom and my boss at the Country Club]
would not be successful at all. My mom would probably be
like that would be a nice person, but she wouldn't want that
for any of us if she had a say in it. To her it is how people
look upon the family. It is how our status is. She wants us to
be well respected. To be a nice guy is great in the American
community, but in the Khmer community, you are just viewed
as a blue collar worker that hasn't done much. You are just
like a guy that works at a restaurant which is a great
opportunity, but you are not the guy who works at
semiconductor where you have a parking space and you wear
a white coat.

Touch is an exemplary student, a popular and a generous individual, yet in spite of his lack of interest in gangs and drugs, Touch believes that his mother does not trust him. No matter how much he proves to her that he is not following the same path as Kusal, Touch cannot convince his mother that his accommodation with American culture does not clash with his Cambodian ethics. Consequently, Touch also keeps himself separate from his family, locking himself in his room and refusing to discuss what he is thinking or doing with them.

> The [clash of two societies] is mostly values and traditions. I am always going out with my friends and my friends are good people, they are not druggies. [When] I come home at 10:00, 11:00 or midnight, [my mom] thinks I was at a party. She has never given me the benefit of the doubt cause my brother, he is always doing stuff like that. It is so frustrating sometimes. I sometimes ask myself why do I even bother like doing the right thing when I don't get credit for it. The reason is, it doesn't appeal to me.
>
> I guess I got that [privacy] from my mom because she likes to keep everything inside. I am sure she has a lot of stuff I don't even know that she doesn't tell me cause she doesn't think I can handle it. That is how I am towards people too. There is just a lot of stuff that I keep inside. There [are] a lot of things I don't feel comfortable telling to people, so I guess the lock [on my bedroom door] is symbolic for that.

In the year since he has been at college, Touch has become more open and interactive with his family, and the tension between him and his mother has lessened. Her lectures on not getting into trouble have more or less ceased. Rath calls and goes to visit Touch frequently; she takes his favorite food and what little money she can spare, and she comments that Touch is always very glad to see her. For Touch, the clash between him and his family no longer appears to be as potent.

> I realize that most American families aren't really that close; Khmer families are so much closer. Like they all want to live in the same house or in the same city. It has been like that in

> my family and I realize that *wow*, when I get older and get a
> job and it causes me to move away to another state, then what?
> You lose touch. It is really weird. I don't know if I could find
> a job actually in Forest City where my mom is and keep this
> tradition going because eventually you are going to have to do
> away sometime. I think by growing up in America you kind
> of have to change because it would be hard not to.

Srey's perceptions of success are much like those of Avy, Alyana
and April. She wants to complete four years of college and a possible
two additional years in pre-med. Srey enjoys her high school biology
and anatomy courses and has applied to colleges that offer either a
nursing or a pre-med major. However her mother cautions her not to
reach too high suggesting that Srey might find nursing to be a less
stressful, but just as fulfilling alternative.

> I want to go as far as I can in education, like four years. I want
> to reach for a career in pre-med. I think about that all the
> time, thinking in my mind what advantages will I have being a
> nurse and attending a four year college and being a pre-
> medical for a couple of years to become a doctor, what
> advantages will I have? Will I be happy and satisfied that I
> have accomplished my goal so far, or do I want to extend my
> goal, or do I want to stay where I am if I am happy. I want to
> be proud of myself for what goal I have reached, and also I
> want people to know, like 'Look at this one girl staying up all
> the way and accomplishing a strong career.'

Srey also wants to have a good reputation in the Cambodian
community as a respectful daughter and a good Buddhist. Three years
ago Srey challenged her mother and grandmother over the rules
imposed on girls by Cambodian culture, but as she has matured, she
has come to value her identity as a modern, Cambodian woman. She is
very thoughtful and generous toward the elders in the Forest City
community and she attends all religious ceremonies with her mother
and grandmother. As a result, she is highly regarded in the Forest City
Cambodian community for the way she is following Cambodian
customs and for her achievements in school. For those young women

who aspire to similar goals as she, Srey wants to be a role model for Cambodian girls who will follow in her footsteps.

> I want to prove a Cambodian person can succeed and accomplish their goals and be in a major career that they want. They may judge themself that Cambodians cannot do this cause they are Cambodians; think only the Americans can do that. But I want to *prove* it to them that it is not just Americans, a Cambodian *woman* can do that too. And young girls could look up at me and see me as their role model so they can follow along my footsteps.

> Tong praised my praised my high reputation in the Cambodian community and warned me to be careful of other Cambodian girls who do not have such a high reputation, that they will try to tear me down. He said to be sure I tear down the wall before they do. The wall is my [status] as a Cambodian refugee and my good reputation as a Cambodian woman. I will tear down the wall as a refugee as I succeed in school and a career, but jealous people might tear down the wall of my reputation through envy and gossip.

Srey rarely mentions success in terms of wealth. Although she works ten to fifteen hours a week during the school year and full-time in the summer, the money she has accumulated is set aside for her tuition, books and expenses at Elizabeth Seton. Whatever is left over is reserved for college. When asked about money, Srey states that she wants to have enough wealth to afford a big house and a car, but being happy is more important than being wealthy. "With my career I want to be happy and have wealth. I don't really think much about the wealth, but I want a huge house and a car. The wealth doesn't really matter, I just want a house and a car, and I will be happy."

Over the past three years that I have known Srey, she has increasingly used metaphors to describe women who are full of combat and power. Many factors influence Srey's perceptions that women need to be strong and resilient in order to survive abusive relationships, compete equally in school and the workplace, and to build their self-esteem. While she states that she would rather be a member of a group, her narrative is full of language that marks her as a leader. Unlike April, Srey is compelled to voice herself in public because she has opinions and ideas that she wants to share. In the role of leader, Srey describes the successful person as "strong," "courageous," "standing tall," "powerful," a fighter for beliefs and against prejudice.

> Being a leader you have to be a strong-compassion person. A strong-compassion person has a strong strength, no one can go against you or walk through you. You have to stand tall and whatever they say, you can't be affected by their comments. You have to fight as hard as you can to be a leader if you really want to accomplish things. If some people are weak they are just going to put their head down and walk off, but if some people are strong, they are going to fight back, nobody step on top of me.
>
> Anybody come across this person she will try everything that gets in her way to accomplish something. She will try to make the obstacle and reach for what she want to accomplish and then she will be happy when she succeed. I want to reach. If I don't get that goal, I don't give up. I will keep on going, and going, like the battery energizer, just goes, and goes, and goes.

She is inspired by the story of Zorah Neale Hurston who overcame the barriers of color and gender to become a powerful role model to African-American women.

> Zorah Neale Hurston was just a powerful woman which I truly admire. She is a role model [and] I want to follow in her footsteps to let people know in their mind that she is a strong, powerful woman and there will be other strong powerful women that can follow along like her.

Srey's descriptions of her mother as being strong and powerful provide clues to Srey's concepts of success. Srey is a testament to her mother's fierce battle to protect her from bad peer influences, and to push her to go as far as she can with her education.

[My mom] had a sacrificing life, like going back on her feet having her husband be so awful. Like falling back on the ground, laying flat. She got back on her two feet and knew she could go on and knew she had things to succeed and three children to take care of. She needed to move on and start a new life cause she sacrificed. She sacrificed so many things in Cambodia living her childhood, she was poor, coming to America, new country, knowing no English, no person to depend on. She knew she was the only person. She had to depend on herself, hold strong and try to stand for herself.

[My mom] will let no one push her around, not even her friends or other elders. She will just stand on her ground, she will fight back. When she hear rumors or something is going on about our family, she will just compare their family to ours and say at least my kids are not like yours. She compares her children and she compares herself and she is just like that strong voice.

She won't let us, like Touch and I, be against her like how we sometimes just say no to her if she tells us to do something or just be stubborn or we just be really mean to her. She won't take that, she will fight back. She will just voice herself back. No many women have the strength to fight back on what they truly believe. Not many Cambodian women.

As she grows older, Srey is more willing to listen to her mother, trusting that on major issues like arranged marriages they can agree to take a more modern approach to choosing a husband. I find it interesting that Srey seeks a career in nursing which is the career Rath would have chosen had she been able to attend school in Cambodia.

In learning how to combine the strengths of both Cambodian and American cultures, Srey thinks a great deal about what makes a good role model. She studies the people around her for qualities that she believes are important and she chooses friends who have qualities she especially admires.

When I was little I made up a role model in my head. I don't really think this person exists, but it is kind of a mixture of one person that I see my perspect what I like. I take that little piece from her and put it together and form one person in my mind. It is like stealing an idea from them of how I want to be like them. I just put it in my mind and each time I would just think about it, but it is not formed of one person. When I accomplish high school next year it will form. On that day I graduate there will be one role model for me.

A good role model would be a woman, definitely a woman because I am a woman. When I see a role model I just admire what a strong powerful person she is. I tell myself how to be strong as that person and how I can have the warm heart as this person and how this person is not like closed, shell, this person is open herself up and make everybody's life happy and light their faces up with light.

Consistent with the other young women in this study, Srey's mother and her grandmother are her strongest role models.

I admire my grandmother. She is just a wonderful cook and I want someday to be a wonderful cook like her. I admire how she is so intelligent in arts and crafts. She goes to temple and prays. She has a cassette of monks praying and she went to learn how to pray with him. She will try to do that at night while she is sewing. She listens to the tape and prays to have the bad spirit inside go away and have the good blessing be upon her.

[I admire] how she take care of the grandson and granddaughter, which I cannot do. And just how she cooks for us, how she takes the time to come over and prepare something for us instead of just staying at her house and doing whatsoever. She has the love inside her and the caring to walk over to our house, make something good for us and staying at our house having company so my mom won't be alone. If [my mom] feels unhappy my grandmother will be there to be like bring light to her and if anybody is not home [my grandmother] will stay home and make sure everything is going right in the house.

My grandmother is successful because she can read and write English, not fluent but quite well and write in Khmer.

She is so talented in doing all these things and how she is so
generous. She is like this generosity heart. She would send
money to Cambodia to help the temple do a celebration. Then
she sends money to her family, like second cousins because
they are single parents with five or six children. She sends
them every month $50 or $20 . What I admire most is how
old she is, sometimes she goes to work with my mother. She
tries really hard and my mom says 'oh, stay home you are too
old,' [My grandmother] says, 'no, need the money to send to
Cambodia.' She sends the money to Cambodia or gives it to
the temple in Lowell whatever would help out the community,
so it is both places. She does not keep it to herself.

Srey is especially insightful about what makes a successful
learning environment and what it takes to be successful in school. As
noted above, Srey skipped her eighth grade year and started the ninth
grade in Berwick High School. Berwick is a very progressive public
high school and is organized as one of the Coalition of Essential
Schools. The teachers are strong advocates of the team approach and
work with one another to design theme-based units that incorporate all
content areas and last from six weeks to an entire term.

At Berwick High School each person in the team was
responsible for certain things so the team would do well. We
were evaluated as a team so it was important for everyone on
the team to work together and help the team look good.

All classes are on a full block schedule which allows the teachers and
the students to study material in depth. The student body is
predominantly white, but includes a small percentage of Cambodians
and African-Americans.

At Elizabeth Seton classes are 50-minutes long and the students
have eight periods a day; the first period of the day is an all-school
morning prayer held in the auditorium. The teachers are a combination
of nuns and secular men and women, some with state teaching
certificates and others without. The classes are small, the curriculum is
rigorous consisting of a few regular classes with the rest either honors

or AP classes. The student body is completely white; Srey is the only Asian.

The contrast between Berwick High School and Catherine Seaton causes Srey to speculate at great length on which environment is more successful for a student like herself. It is obvious that being a successful student is clearly a high priority for Srey, and she maintained a nearly 4.0 average when she was at Berwick High School. By these standards, she is not as successful at Elizabeth Seton and this has forced her to evaluate her success at this school in different terms.

The concept of "expectations" especially gets her attention. She states that many of her classes at Berwick High School had minimum expectations, but that she was motivated to put in more effort in order to create something that pleased her, that was beautiful.

> At BHS we work together as a class with the teacher, it isn't
> just the teacher throwing out material. We work together to
> accomplish that thing. The teacher wasn't pressuring you and
> the students weren't pressured by the parents or their friends.
> They wouldn't feel bad if they got a C and their friend got a B.

At Elizabeth Seton the teachers have high expectations and try to model the demands of a college curriculum. While Srey pushes constantly pushes herself to meet these expectations, the effort she expends is less rewarding because it is demanded. She has also discovered that this pressure to get "good grades," pushes a number of students to cheat on tests and assignments.

> At Elizabeth Seton, some students are just so closed up, they
> don't want to let anything out. They have their own friends,
> they are always hanging out with best friends and they don't
> open up. And they *cheat*, and that is terrible! We do not do
> that, no matter what, we *do not cheat*. I was just so terrible
> knowing how far they would go just to achieve a good *grade*
> cause that good grade will not lead them to success in life, the
> *education* will, not the grade. At Elizabeth Seton, we have
> this quiz and this girl wrote all the questions and gave it to this
> girl. At Berwick we would not do that, I know that for a fact.

Srey's discussion of expectations highlights one of the paradoxes in her narrative as she tries to rationalize her strong preference for the more relaxed and less challenging climate of Berwick High School with her belief that she is getting a better education in the intense and competitive climate of Elizabeth Seton.

> At Berwick, the kids work together. They don't have cliques or groups. In classwork we work together and outside we always work together. We rely on one another if there is a question in our schoolwork. We work together even though we despise that person, well not that many people hate one another, just little things, they don't let that come across them. They just talk to one another, laugh at one another.
>
> But at Elizabeth Seton, it is challenging and I am motivated. I like working by myself, I am like an independent person. I like to be independent, but at Berwick I don't like to be independent because we work in groups and if you are independent, [they will] probably think you are weird. It is more independent at Elizabeth Seton, you are just an independent person.

Srey has learned that sometimes a student who is successful in one setting can become inhibited and shy in another setting. At Berwick High School it was customary for the teachers to encourage an open, non-threatening group discussion before each class. Srey and her peers enjoyed the wide-ranging discussions where they learned things about one another that contributed to a shared bond among them. In a more traditional setting, like Elizabeth Seton, the teacher controls the discussion by singling out individual students to call on. Srey, personally does not mind this approach since, as her history teacher stated with great pride, she is not afraid to be wrong when he calls on her and is willing to test out her opinions in the public forum. Nevertheless, Srey regrets the loss of community that she experienced with the more open, collaborative classroom.

> Some students are just tight, they will not open up. If you do things independently, like a traditional learning way, you call on one person and you want *that* answer, or the students has to

raise their hand. Its like the teacher saying a question and you have to raise your hand, it's like the center of attention and everybody turns and look at you. You are going, 'no, I have this opinion and I have this idea in my mind, [but] I am not going to say it, I am going to keep it to myself.' That point will not get across because that opinion may be helpful for other students to learn.

If the class is open, wide-spread, then everybody is talking, everybody is listening and knowing about one another's opinion. One of the students, at least 50 percent of the students will get something out of another person's opinion and learn from that opinion, or go along with that opinion from the teacher's topic.

Srey offers another perspective on the concept of expectations when she talks about classrooms that are more diverse such as those at Forest City High School. In this instance, Srey believes that the immigrant students should not be held to the same expectations as American students if they are not fluent in English. She suggests that the pressure to constantly achieve causes them to "lose their intelligentness." On the other hand, Srey is convinced that with encouragement and time, the immigrant students will surprise their teachers by moving ahead of their American peers.

Cambodian students suffer more than Americans because they have to go through many different steps to feel that they are welcome in this country, even though they were raised here. [Because] they are from a different ethnic group than Americans they have to go through discrimination. They have more challenges voicing themselves. I am a different ethnic group, from a different country, but I was raised here and am an English student. I have another language that I speak and another culture that I relate to. Some students judge you because you are a different color, for your face, your language, the way you act, the way you are.

Some teachers think you have the same strength as other students. Some can [have the same strength], some cannot. [But the teachers] want you to be the same way, they want you

to be in the middle range with the other students and expecting
more from you than what you can accomplish. I know at
Forest City High School it is a diverse school. The [teachers]
won't expect you [to be] as high as other students. The
teachers know that they are having trouble with their English
and the [student] know they have the teacher to rely on and
that teacher will give them that consideration and know that in
Forest City High School [there] is a diverse culture from all
over the world not just American students. Maybe they will
be so surprised to know that some of these diverse students
can achieve higher than *their* American students and they will
be really pleased.

I believe that Srey's preference for the education she is getting at
Elizabeth Seton is linked to the fact that the high school has a good
reputation among college admissions officers particularly in this
region, and the high achieving students from Elizabeth Seton all appear
to get into top competitive colleges. However as Srey gets closer to
submitting college applications, she has begun to look for a good
program with a nursing concentration, but that isn't intensely
competitive. She has stated often that after the intense pressure of the
past two years at Elizabeth Seton, she would like to enjoy a more
relaxed college life.

I should point out that Srey has chosen a career in medicine
because she wants to help people in Cambodia who cannot afford to go
to hospitals. I have never heard Srey talk about choosing a medical
career because of the high social status it confers. She consistently
refers to her career as her good deed in this life to make up for bad
actions in a previous life which she believes contribute to all the
illnesses she has had since she was small.

My mom and grandma lecture me, 'You know in your last life
you probably were a terrible person and that is why you have
to live this life having a lot of illness.' I think they said I
wasn't really a generous-heart person, like I wasn't generous
enough in my last life. Going to Cambodia and doing
[medicine] with no charge is my generosity for my soul. I
want to do this with my heart and soul, doing it with no charge

and cure the sickness so in my next life I won't be sick as this
any more. That is how I thought of it.

Srey has a large extended family; her four uncles and their families
live within a 100-mile radius, and they get together often. Even though
Srey doesn't have cousins her own age, she prefers to spend all of her
free time with her family. Srey's family is an important component in
her perceptions of success because over the long term, they care about
and support one another. I have witnessed numerous day-to-day
interactions where the confinement of six people in a five room
apartment caused an eruption of bad tempers and copious tears. But I
have come to expect a depth of caring and compassion among this
family that transcends the pressure of poverty and prejudice with which
they live every day.

> Our family are kind of close together. We watch out for one
> another, like I watch over Touch and he watch over me. [If
> there is a problem] we as a family, we discuss it. If we do
> something wrong, as a family we [have] compassion with that
> person to let him know what he did wrong, [and] not to follow
> that stuff again and try to avoid that. We will be sitting
> around the room and we will start up something, sometime
> about Touch, sometime about me, and Kusal. We have issues,
> we just work it out as a family.

One outcome of my interactions with Srey over the past three years
has caused her to think more deeply about the nuances inherent in
being a Cambodian and American *woman*.

> Not many Cambodian women have the strength to fight back
> on what they truly believe. They put it in their mind they are
> weak women who must depend on their husband, living on
> their husband and they get less confidence and low self-
> esteem.
>   There is always a voice in Cambodian woman's head
> saying you are low, you lean on your husband, you are not
> intelligent enough, you don't have a lot of wealth cause he
> does, you are just a woman. He could divorce you and you

would be alone. The woman has to be really careful with her
husband or he will take advantage of her in every way.

My questions along with my profound respect for her culture and her
family have caused her to weigh the advantages of both cultures. She
despises the racism she experiences in American culture and equally,
she rejects the sexism in her own culture. Clearly, these are large
issues which she may not resolve until she begins to raise her own
daughter and decides how she will pass along what she has learned
from both cultures.

> The questions you ask help me know what I want to do in life
> and give me a clear view in my mind. It gives me an
> open[ing] to family discussion about a person's education or
> just graduating looking for a job. The questions you ask
> makes my goal or my dream seem like more success, so I
> could reach for it; like it's reality.

Srey wants to tear down the wall of prejudice that she feels as a
refugee in American society, but she wants to protect the wall of her
reputation as a compassionate and respectful Cambodian woman. Srey
states that she wants to "fit in" to the society in which she lives, and
she wants to "bring the two cultures together." One of the poems she
wrote as a junior in high school is a powerful expression of how she
experiences these realities.

America
Being raised as a baby
to a teenager
Living the life in America
Having two conflicts to live.
Being an American
and Cambodian person
Being laughed at for not
pronouncing words correctly.
There would always be
sad feeling inside myself
not letting anybody know
that I am

truly hurt
by insult of your words.

I go to school trying to fit in
as an
American,
then I come home
to be
A Cambodian daughter.

When sitting in class
I would look around
seeing the different
faces
of my classmates.
I was a very lonely person
and different from the others.
I always remember the whisper
behind my back,
"why is that girl in our class who has
slanted eyes
and an accent?"
I would just close my eyes and ignore
the voices.
I wished it would not affect me.
I tried very hard
but still
the voices behind my back,
the whispers,
and the laughs
hurt me.
I scream a question –
Why do the kids have to treat me this way?
Will this prejudice ever end
when I get
older?

CHAPTER 8

Discussion of Findings

*I live my life knowing that I am an individual, free-type person, but I also have
my traditions to follow. I don't want [the elders] to see that this girl is
breaking the traditions just because she is away from home. I will have to do a
lot of thinking on what decisions I will make because if I change one tradition I
have to change all of them.*

—Srey

INTRODUCTION

My purpose in undertaking this ethnographic study was to learn more
about the dynamics of culture, spirituality, and success in the lives of
three generations of three Cambodian families. As the previous
chapter reveals, their perceptions of success are at times consistent with
one another and at other times conflicted—even within themselves.
Nonetheless, the epistemology of success as these eleven individuals
describe it represents a powerful quality of knowing that is grounded in
Buddhist philosophy and practice. It is not a knowing of facts, it is a
deep knowing of how to survive, how to reclaim pieces of their culture,
and where they are going. The adolescents capture this knowing in the
way they describe what it means to become a successful Cambodian

and a successful American. But, for a couple of them, that knowing does *not* connect a Cambodian identity to their perceptions of success.

The discussion of my findings requires the reader to first review my three central research questions:

1. What does being successful mean to Cambodian refugee parents and adolescents in this group?

2. In what ways do these adults connect their perceptions of success to cultural models represented by Theravada Buddhist beliefs, Cambodian institutions, and/or American institutions?

3. In what ways do these adolescents connect their perceptions of success to cultural models represented by their parents, Theravada Buddhist beliefs, and/or American institutions?

I identified five general categories that represented qualities of success to my informants: Goals, Expectations and Norms, Role Models, Family, and a category that I call Bicultural. This chapter is first, a discussion of how each family perceived success; second, a comparison of the adults' perceptions of success, and third, a discussion of the adolescents' perceptions of success within these five categories. The cultural models that emerged from their narratives can be matched with the concepts that I found among the adults in my pilot study.

PIRUN'S FAMILY

Goals

Pirun and his wife Rany have achieved a number of goals since arriving in Forest City in 1981. They own a duplex in a middle class neighborhood, and they own two cars. They share their house with their four children, Grandmother Yeang, and—recently arrived from France—Rany's sister, her husband, and their four children. Pirun is an American citizen. He holds a certified nursing degree from this country, and he currently works for the Forest City public schools serving his community as a parent liaison. Rany is not a fluent English speaker, nor is she a citizen. Rany owned an Asian grocery story for five years before selling it recently to her two brothers. Pirun's family still lives in Cambodia, but Rany's family live in Forest City and a bordering state. All of her brothers and sisters are married with four children; none have ever been divorced.

According to Pirun, the successful Cambodian person has a choice: He can become a Buddhist monk, in which case the goal is enlightenment resulting from a life of compassion and generosity. Alternately, a Cambodian can become a "full human being" by passing through the three stages of life. The goal of the full human being is to bring oneself to the "top of the mind" and to operate within the "frame of the culture." In the first stage of life, the adolescent must go as high as he or she can in school using Buddha as the greatest teacher and role model for learning. Whereas in Cambodia this might have been a high school diploma, in America a degree from a university is the coveted goal.

The goal of the second stage of life is to find a good, secure job, work hard, marry, and provide shelter, food and material things for one's family. A further goal is to teach one's children the norms of the culture and guard their good reputation within the community. The goal of the third stage of life is to have a wonderful time giving back to the community and the temple. It is a time to enjoy one's grandchildren and the fruits of good deeds.

MP is Pirun and Rany's oldest son. He graduated from Forest City High School in June 1998 and is currently enrolled at Tufts University. Gaining admission to a "good" college has been his goal throughout twelve years of school. Once he completes college, MP's goal is to find a good job and then consider the next stage of his life—finding a wife and starting a family. Making money is a goal for MP because it provides him with security. But while money "will take you places," it is not what fulfills him. Because of this, MP strives to find ways to give back to his community—to improve himself and to better society. One goal which eludes MP is to follow his father's example and spend time serving as a novice monk in a Buddhist temple. He feels his faith tradition slipping away as he focuses on completing his education, yet he emphatically believes that religion is the most important part of being Cambodian.

Avy is a year behind MP and is preparing to achieve her first goal, to be accepted to a four-year college. Avy wants to stay close to her family, so she has applied to colleges within a three-hour drive from Forest City. She has considered working in a family-owned business, but has more recently changed her goal to a career involving some kind of travel. Along with her career, she wants four children whom she intends to raise in the Buddhist faith. Accumulating wealth is not one of Avy's goals; accumulating knowledge is.

Alyana is on the threshold of high school. Her goals are absolutely firm—she intends to complete school through her master's degree, then complete the training to be a medical doctor. Alyana, who was born in the U.S., also wants to remain close to her family throughout her schooling, yet she thinks of herself as very independent. She sets her own goals, has the discipline to achieve them, and accepts the risks or rewards that come with her accomplishment. Two years ago, she decided she wanted to study and perform classical Cambodian dance, and today she is well on her way to realizing this goal.

Expectations and Norms
Pirun's expectations for the successful person closely follow Buddhist and Cambodian norms. They are characterized by the concept of balance—parents should be "not too strict and not too loose" with their children. He and Rany encourage their children to share their opinions, even if those opinions challenge traditional customs for girls such as dating and going out with friends. Pirun and Rany trust their children to strive in school and to choose their friends wisely. They emphasize the Buddhist concept that competition is only with oneself.

MP's expectations for the successful person are rooted in the concept of *karma*. He accepts responsibility for his actions and is careful to do good and not harm to other people. On the one hand, MP is self-motivated as he strives to meet his goals; contentment or "getting stuck" in the same place represent failure to him. On the other hand, MP seeks the middle way with regard to his future. He prefers being a member of a group rather than the leader, avoiding the pressure and back-stabbing that can accompany positions of leadership. He sees himself as another person in the work force, not the "limelight person." MP plans his life in stages, one step at a time, so that he does not lose sight of what is going on now. Bettering himself, and doing good for others, is his way of ensuring himself a good next life.

Avy and Alyana find the expectations for women restrictive in Cambodian culture, but understand the rationale, and have voluntarily chosen to limit their freedom in order to sustain their family's good standing in the community. While they advocate for more lenient rules about dating and going out with friends, both young women admit that the successful daughter (and granddaughter) guards her reputation and saves face for her family.

Role Models

Pirun's role models, not surprisingly, include Buddha who is Khmer culture's best role model for the strong, compassionate, and wise person. Other role models are the "high education person," the parent who balances strict with lenient, and the individual who gives of his time and resources to help others. Pirun's children consider him their role model in all these respects, yet they frequently complain that he is often more devoted to helping someone in the community, than he is to helping his family.

MP's role model is the "rags-to-riches person" who had nothing and made something of himself; the person from the working class who understands the value of hard work and the power of money. This is a person who sets a standard and doesn't stray (too much) from the middle path. In MP's perspective rich people, as a rule, do not make it to the status of role models, especially if they have a lot of money but neglect to do good with it. The rare person who shares his wealth abundantly with those around him, MP considers successful.

Avy and Alyana both describe their father and their grandmother as their role models. Their father because he gives time and resources to help others, and their grandmother because she sets the rules for the family to follow. They respect and revere their grandmother because she is highly respected in the Cambodian community for her generosity and her faith. What Avy and Alyana know about Buddhism and about their dreams they have learned from their grandmother.

The Family

For Pirun, Rany, and their four children, the most potent concept of success is rooted in their family. Avy and Alyana aspire to make their family (primary and extended) proud when they are accepted into college and complete their degrees. MP values the closeness of his family and finds that they have become more important to him as he has gotten older. Pirun admires the family as the highest representation of the Cambodian universe and points out the damage to young people when the family becomes broken by divorce or abuse. Being successful, then, has to do with maintaining a dynamic and close relationship with the family—learning what it means to be Cambodian, what it means to be Buddhist, and being supported in striving for the future.

RATH'S FAMILY

Long and Seoun, Rath's mother and father, live in a small, four-room apartment in downtown Forest City just a few blocks from Rath's family. They live on SSI benefits and contributions from their five children; they have a telephone but do not own a car. Occasionally Long works preparing sea urchins for export or helps her daughter at a local farm. The money she earns goes to the temple in Forest City or to rebuild temples and schools in Cambodia. As a person in the third stage of life, Long is considered "high praise" in the Cambodian community because of her spiritual devotion and her warm-hearted generosity. She has also become an American citizen, learning how to speak and write some English in the process.

Rath is a single mother who neither reads nor writes Khmer or English. She speaks English well, but sometimes loses the nuances of discussions among her children. Her English is not good enough to assure her a full-time job, so she works long hours at seasonal jobs. She receives welfare benefits and housing subsidies which help support her five children. She owns a car (cosigned for by her brother). Their apartment is five rooms and usually houses seven people; still it is clean and comfortable. Rath is also considered "high praise" in Cambodian society because of her spiritual devotion, her consistent generosity to other families who have hard times, her commitment to help her parents, and for the good reputations of Touch and Srey.

Goals

Rath's goals are entirely centered on giving her five children a good life. Once her responsibilities to them are completed, Rath wants to go to school to learn how to read and write—both Khmer and English. Like her mother and her children, Rath wants to become an American citizen, but she still longs to spend her "retire years" in Cambodia serving the monks in a temple and meditating.

Kusal's goals have changed in the past three years. From age sixteen to twenty-one, Kusal went with the flow, wherever life led him, he followed. He regrets that this attitude led him to go with the wrong crowd where he learned about the consequences that go along with making mistakes. Today Kusal is married and living with his mother. He and his wife Sarem (who is a traditional Cambodian woman), want to have at least three children. Kusal has a full-time job with benefits and has begun to save for a future business and a place of his own.

Kusal believes he would be more successful if he could complete his goal of finishing the GED and going on to college. When he was in the sixth grade, his goal was to join the Peace Corps where he could help people; more recently he weighs the idea of becoming an ESL teacher and devoting his life to helping children overcome the stigma and frustration of learning how to speak English. Sarem's goals are to complete her ESL courses and find a better job. Kusal states that he would like to have money, but believes that while money can take you places, it can't make you happy. Being part of a loving family that supports him is of greater value than being wealthy.

Touch has achieved the first of his goals and is currently enrolled at Clark University. He has not chosen a major field, but dreams of completing his master's and Ph.D. as long as his resources "and his pockets" hold out. Touch thinks of himself as a leader as well as a hard worker, and when he envisions the kind of work he would like to do, it is in some field where he has the influence to open doors for minorities. He especially enjoys working as a team toward a shared goal, and as long as the work is fun, he doesn't mind putting in long hours or sacrificing his spare time. This explains, perhaps, why he is drawn to teaching—not because of the money, but because it is a way of life that is fulfilling. From his affluent peers in high school, Touch discovered that wealth is a responsibility and often a burden. While he would like to have enough money to be secure and provide a safety net, money is not his goal.

Srey, who is one year behind Touch, is about to achieve her goal of being accepted into a challenging college. She intends to enroll in a pre-med program with the goal of becoming either a nurse or a doctor (if the pressure and stress of school are not too overwhelming). Srey is not drawn by the money or status which is commensurate with the medical profession, but by the opportunity to return to Cambodia and work in a free clinic. She states that this is her "generosity-goal" for her soul.

Srey has an equally demanding goal which is to be a good Cambodian daughter and a good Buddhist. She has a high reputation in the Cambodian community because she attends all the Buddhist ceremonies, has performed classical Cambodian dance, and is a respectful and obedient daughter. From her status within the society, Srey has set a goal of changing her culture by challenging the most restrictive and repressive customs for women. Srey intends to raise her children in the Buddhist faith, and she also intends to teach her daughters to voice their opinions and stand up for what they believe.

Expectations and Norms
Long sets high expectations for herself in following the Buddhist norms of helping others, praying for her sins, and giving as much as she can afford. She follows the rule of "No and Yes" which she interprets as knowing when to be strict and knowing when to be lenient with her children and grandchildren. For instance, Long does not tolerate disrespect to her or any elder person, and she is firm with Srey about issues of dating and achieving in school. But she is always ready to treat her grandchildren to ice cream or a rental movie.

Rath's first years in the U.S. were difficult with three children and an abusive husband. Not understanding American culture, Rath allowed Kusal too much freedom which she now regrets. She has learned how to implement the rule of not too strict and not too lenient as she charts a course between the traditions of Cambodian culture and the ways of American culture. As long as her children are successful in school and obedient at home, Rath is willing to listen to their opinions and trust them with their friends. She maintains her spiritual balance by trying to be as generous with the people in her family, her neighborhood, and her community as her time and resources allow, and she heals her soul by meditating and seeking guidance from the monks.

At least four times in his life, Kusal expected to die from accidents or abuse. The fact that he is still alive indicates to him that he is being saved for something important. Kusal believes that his destiny is to help others, which, he admits. often causes people to expect his help and generosity whenever they ask for it. Kusal has come to accept his role as the oldest child in the family, and he is helping his mother with finances and child care. He reminds his younger siblings that the route he took as a teenager was the wrong path and did not lead to success.

Touch likes to challenge his family and peers' expectations of him. He enjoys teaching language to minority children, working with the Special Olympics, helping minorities find good jobs, and training the people at his workplace to be fast and efficient workers. He sets high expectations in school, realizing that his academic excellence may take him farther than his pockets will. He seeks out friends who are motivated to get ahead as he is; he is not drawn to people who are ambivalent about their future.

As the oldest daughter, Srey is expected to carry a great deal of responsibility in the home and in school. She is an outspoken and highly motivated student at school, and at home she helps her mother with the cooking, cleaning, and supervision of her younger siblings. By meeting these high expectations, Srey is able to gain concessions from her mother and grandmother in adopting certain American norms.

Role Models

Long and Rath admire their children as role models—the daughter who is dependable and can be relied on to help, the son who is in college and respected as a hardworking employee, the granddaughter who makes the honor roll and volunteers to tutor refugee children. The high education person or the Buddhist monk is the person Long and Rath name as a role model

Kusal's role models are his mother because she is strong, hardworking, caring, and has great integrity; his grandmother because she has taught him about Buddhism and the value of helping others; and Pirun for the same reasons. When he thinks beyond his family and his community, Kusal considers Mother Teresa to be the person he most admires because she lived in poverty and devoted her life to helping people.

In discussing the people he most wants to be like, Touch names his mother who is understanding, loving, open, and hardworking. He especially admires the way she handles stress by keeping her worries and fears to herself and never breaking down. He admires his uncle who has gotten his degree, bought his own home, is raising a family, and has a secure if monotonous job, working in a semiconductor plant. He admires two friends for the same reasons—one Cambodian and one white. They are hardworking, they come from very close and loving families, they go out of their way to help people, and they are people he can trust and in whom he can confide. Finally, Touch admires the "nerds" because they are down-to-earth and very intelligent; they are going somewhere in life by using their minds and by teaching others.

Srey's role models are all women. She admires her mother because she is a "strong-compassion person," someone who has fought back against abuse, poverty, and lack of education to be a powerful role model. Her grandmother is a role model because she is a great cook, a creative artist, a loving companion to her mother. Srey admires women who have spoken out against racism and sexism. She especially admires women who have taken the time to listen to others, to learn about Cambodian culture, and to help in the community.

The Family
For Long and Rath, being a successful Cambodian means having a successful and happy family. It is why they are so strict about the kind of people their children spend time with, why they attend Buddhist ceremonies with the family both in Forest City and a neighboring state, and why they are so vigilant about the kind of education their children are getting.

For Kusal, the family has been both a prison and a sanctuary. He, more than his siblings, suffered when his parents divorced and broke up the family. As a teenager Kusal abandoned his family to experience the world and to discover himself. As a young adult, he has returned to the family ready to help his mother and his siblings achieve their dreams, and to begin his own family. He is mindful of the kind of family he wants to provide for his children and the cultural traditions he wants them to understand.

For Touch, his family is both supportive and problematic. He respects the closeness of Cambodian families compared to the families of some of his American friends, yet he keeps his family separate from his friends, and himself separate from his family. Touch, more than the others, has witnessed the tremendous socioeconomic disparity between his family and the average American family. As he grows older, he recognizes that it will be up to him and his siblings to continue the family tradition of remaining close and supportive of one another.

Srey grounds her identity and her ambitions in the context of her family. She spends her free time with members of her family; she is proud that she brings honor to her family by her good deeds, and she aspires to raise her children in a family much like the one in which she was raised. Her frame of reference for success is influenced to some extent by academic measures, but fundamentally she knows she is successful because she has met her family's standards.

CHINDA'S FAMILY

At age 45, Chinda is wholly engaged in completing her college degree. She subsists on public assistance and the income from part-time and work-study jobs in order to free her time to study. She has a mixed relationship with the Cambodian community. On the one hand she is a valued interpreter and a sensitive social service case worker with elderly Cambodians. On the other hand, because of her independence and the freedom she gives her two children, she does not have a high reputation among some Cambodian elders.

In spite of the fact that April is an honor student at school, the Cambodian community is critical of her reputation because she is free to go to clubs and movies with her American friends. Mam is a significant problem for Chinda; he has dropped out of high school, can't keep a steady job, and has a thirteen-year-old girlfriend.

Chinda subscribes to similar goals as Pirun in seeking to live within the Buddhist way. She studies with Buddhist masters and understands the meaning of the Eight-Fold Path. Her goals are a mixture of being independent and of serving others. Her education allows her to be independent and choose a career that suits her; her faith inspires her to choose a career that helps people who experience discrimination and prejudice from a more powerful and indifferent society.

Goals
April's pragmatic goals are simple. She wants to complete her senior year in high school in Florida in order to establish residence in the state. She intends to apply to South Central Florida State for the Fall of

2000 and major in business. April's more expressive goals are to find a "family structure" which is open, respectful, trusting, and bounded by sensible rules.

Expectations and Norms

Chinda confronts the cultural expectations for women by resisting some and ignoring others. Although Buddhist practice is somewhat misogynist, Chinda seeks the guidance of Buddhist monks to keep her on the right path. She takes responsibility for her actions, trying not to do or say something that would harm another person. She tries to take a middle way with her children, listening to their opinions but demanding their respect. Chinda ignores the cultural norm which states that she is too old to go to school, and she lectures her children to stay in school and to stay away from bad influences. Chinda does not push her children in a particular direction, realizing that the more she tries to control them, the more they resist her. She grieves that neither of her children speaks Khmer, attends the temple, nor knows much about being Cambodian, and she prays that someday they will reclaim their culture.

April has internalized her mother's expectations that she be independent, self-reliant, and a good scholar, and she has adopted the lifestyle of a conventional American teenager. The fact that this separates her from her culture does not seem to affect April, who states that she does not seek to maintain her Cambodian identity. She does not believe in Buddhism, yet she seems to maintain an internal sense of right and wrong and avoids peers who are going down the wrong path.

Role Models

Chinda's role models are, above all, strong and liberated women. She refers to ancient Cambodian folklore where the women were the most powerful until they were suppressed by the Hindu religion. She also admires Cambodian couples who have strong marriages and successful families. The strength of the marriage, she states, comes from the fact that both partners are well educated and treat one another equally in the family. For role models April names neither her mother nor her father, but rather friends and teachers who support her and give her good advice.

The Family

In spite of the fact that Chinda considers the "beautiful family" a role model for her, she has not experienced success within the family context. She felt misunderstood and confined in her family of origin, and so she has apparently gone to the other extreme in her own family. Chinda's passion for freedom and independence appears to take precedence over the traditional close-knit family structure—none of her extended family live in the U.S., she does not communicate with her oldest son, and her daughter is leaving to live with another family. Yet, both she and April talk about the ideal family as one where the parents put more time into their children than into their work and the pursuit of money. April, paradoxically, admires parents who set rules and spend time with their children. It may be significant that the family she is joining consists of adults more like surrogate *grandparents* for her—a cultural model that is consistent with the other two families.

ANALYSIS OF SUCCESS FROM THE ADULT PERSPECTIVE—CONTROL, BALANCE, FLEXIBILITY

I consider that the above adults—grandparents and parents—perceive success as a fine balance between traditional Buddhist norms and select American norms. There are two members of the third generation in this study, Long and Yeang. While I did not interview Yeang, her grandchildren provided me with extensive descriptions of her life and her lectures to them on Cambodian ways of being. Long and Yeang are approximately the same age. They were both successful businesswomen in Cambodia in spite of each receiving only a sixth grade education. Both are monolingual Khmer speakers, and Long knows how to read and write that language.

Long and Yeang are faithful members of the Buddhist temple in Forest City and travel frequently to a larger Buddhist center in a neighboring state. They observe Buddhist holidays and attend the numerous wedding and funeral ceremonies hosted by families in the community. Yeang and Long are acknowledged as the heads of their extended families because of their position as elders, but even more because of their reputation as devout Buddhists.

Yeang and Long anchor their families in traditional ways of being Cambodian. They instruct their granddaughters about guarding their reputations within the Cambodian community and about proper duties to the monks and the temple. They counsel their grandsons in the roles they must play as husbands and as the guardians of their parents' *bun* which can ensure their parents good future lives.

In spite of the fact that both grandmothers' frame of reference is rooted in an early twentieth-century Cambodian reality, each woman is referred to as the person her children most admire. Because they are in the third stage of life, they are able to spend all of their time helping their families or helping in the community. As a result, their perspective of what it means to be a successful individual carries a lot of influence with their grandchildren.

Pirun and Rany, Chinda, and Rath are successful individuals and parents on a variety of levels. Pirun and Chinda are both college educated. They are fluent in English and Khmer, and they both work or have worked in white collar jobs. However, Pirun owns his own home and Chinda lives in subsidized housing. Pirun is highly respected in the Cambodian community for his intelligence, his good deeds, and his knowledge of Buddhism. Chinda has an uneasy relationship with the Cambodian community, and while she is respected for her learning she is criticized for her independence.

Rany and Rath are not literate in Khmer, and their English skills are modest. Nevertheless they are perceived as strong women with great integrity and honesty. Their poor English skills account for the fact that each works in manufacturing and seasonal employment. Yet, both are devout Buddhists and are considered high praise in the community for the way they practice their faith and for the way they have raised their children.

Chinda is far more Americanized than Pirun, Rany, or Rath. Her perception of success is to be free and independent. She has instilled this model in her daughter and to some degree in her son. The greatest conflict Chinda seems to face is an internal one between her Cambodian and American selves, the former far more than the latter perceiving the close, respectful, and generous family as highly successful. She condemns Cambodian families who spend all of their time working or gossiping and ignoring their children. Yet because of her desire to complete her education and her inability to find a professional, part-time job, Chinda has spent the past two years working part-time in another state, leaving her children to fend for themselves. In her story, the Cambodian ideal of self-reliance appears to have taken precedence over the ideal of the beautiful family.

Although they have taken slightly different paths, these four parents have moved toward becoming bicultural individuals. They maintain their traditional beliefs in the most basic tenet of Buddhist philosophy—control, flexibility, and balance. Pirun states that successful parents raise their children in the frame of the culture—specifically the concept of "not too strict and not too loose." From the narratives of MP, Avy, Alyana, Kusal, Touch, and Srey I feel confident in claiming that Pirun, Rany, and Rath are successful parents from the point of view of Cambodian culture. Chinda has also tried to instill Buddhist principles in her children. While April claims to know little about Buddhism and Cambodian culture, she nonetheless ascribes to many of their principles.

To their Cambodian worldviews Pirun, Rany, Rath, and Chinda have also added American concepts of success. These include such ideas as equal opportunities for men and women, higher education, and secure, middle class jobs. They have opened lines of communication with their children in a willingness to listen to their opinions, recognizing that their children have much to teach them about American culture. The women in particular have embraced varying degrees of autonomy for women, and are moving away from certain cultural traditions such as arranged marriages. Nonetheless, all continue to subscribe to the cultural model that connects the success of the children to the status of the family.

ANALYSIS OF SUCCESS FROM THE ADOLESCENT PERSPECTIVE—BECOMING BICULTURAL

While there are many similarities among these eight adolescents when it comes to defining success, the differences among them can be attributed to their family structure, their school experiences, and their immigrant history.

MP, Avy, and Alyana live in a two-parent family and are surrounded, literally, by an extensive, extended family. MP was almost three years old and Avy was one when they arrived in the U.S. Alyana was born in America. All three adolescents are fluent in Khmer and English although none of them can read or write Khmer. All three have attended public schools throughout their school careers. Their elementary and secondary schools were predominantly white, and they have spent very little time in ESL classrooms. All three have or will attend Forest City High School which is the most racially diverse high school in the city. MP and Avy also work ten to fifteen hours per week at local retail stores.

Kusal, Touch, and Srey live in a single-parent family with grandparents, aunts, and uncles close by. Kusal is a member of the 1.5 generation; Touch and Srey were ages one and two when they arrived in the United States. All three adolescents speak fluent Khmer and English although none of them read or write Khmer. Kusal dropped out of school in the tenth grade. After attending public elementary and middle schools, both Srey and Touch completed their high school educations at exclusive, private schools. Kusal works full-time at a meat-packing plant; Srey and Touch work ten to fifteen hours a week at the exclusive Forest City Country Club.

Mam and April are the most different from the other adolescents in this study. Mam was age two when he came to the U.S., and April was born in the United States. They have grown up in a housing development surrounded by other Cambodian families. Neither Mam nor April speak Khmer, and they understand very little of what elderly Cambodians say to them. Mam, like Kusal, dropped out of school in his junior year; he works at a car wash. April has gone through public school without attending ESL classes. She transferred from Forest City High School in her freshman year in order to attend the majority white Stevens High School. She works part-time at a credit-card telemarketing company.

Numerous conversations with these adolescents revealed that all of these young people know each other. They grew up playing at one another's houses and participating in activities within the Cambodian community. According to their parents, they were good students and obedient children until the end of middle school. High school appears to be a serious watershed in the ways these adolescents are constructing their bicultural identities. While their parents and grandparents are fairly consistent with regard to modeling and instilling a Cambodian identity, it is the school experiences which provide the greatest contrast with regard to their "American" identities.

MP, Avy, and Alyana attend racially diverse, public schools. They interact with other students of color who adopt a variety of strategies in order to cope with the structural racism that is part of the school climate, the curriculum, and the wider community. According to them, Cambodians in Forest City High school are frequently stereotyped as gang members in spite of the fact that many Cambodian students, MP and Avy among them, are taking honors courses and succeeding academically. Possibly, because of the greater ethnic polarization, these three adolescents tend to have more Cambodian than white American friends both inside and outside of school. Their role models also tend to be members of their family rather than teachers or American peers.

At no time did MP, Avy, or Alyana indicate that achieving high academic honors stigmatized them in the eyes of their Cambodian friends—doing well in school does not equate with "acting white". They are "American" in dress, language, recreation, and aspiration, giving full definition to the hyphenated concept of Cambodian-American. In fact, the language that dominates their narratives is one of "rags-to-riches," "self-reliance," "proving oneself," and "striving." These phrases seem to fit with American middle class notions of goal-orientation, independence, and self-made success.

Nonetheless, their standard for success seems to be grounded primarily in the family. MP strives to get in to a good college so that he can have a good career; Avy and Alyana strive to do the same. This standard is set by their father and by their uncles, and it is connected to their belief that they must make it on their own. The motivation to do well is inspired by wanting to prove to their *families* that they are capable of achieving their goals which, in turn, proves to the Cambodian community that their family is "high praise."

Kusal's experience as a member of the 1.5 generation places him painfully between two cultures. Kusal has strong memories of his life in Cambodia, but the twin traumas of exile and divorce left him without a strong male role model to ground his Cambodian identity. He met with ignorance, indifference, and racism in Forest City's white, public schools. This prejudice coupled with lack of sufficient academic scaffolding and access to mainstream classes caused Kusal to gravitate toward underachievers, both Cambodian and white. As a result, Kusal does not have a particularly positive bicultural identity.

Touch and Srey have both achieved the same academic success as MP and Avy; they will attend good universities with full scholarships. However, the experience of private school has given them different perspectives, specifically when it comes to defining their "American" identities. Both Touch and Srey describe middle school as their favorite time when they had teachers who "really understood them" and friends from many ethnic groups. High school has been very different. Srey and Touch are minorities of one and five respectively in their high schools. The curriculum is rigorous and not particularly multi-culturally inclusive. While Touch has maintained friendships with MP and a handful of other Cambodians, most of his friends are white Americans. Srey has no Cambodian girlfriends; her friends at Elizabeth Seton are white, although she has become close to one student who is an immigrant.

Success for Srey and Touch is measured both by their family's standards and also by the upper middle class standards of their high school peers. They are more self-conscious of the family's socioeconomic status and, at least for Touch, more willing to keep personal life separate from public life. Although I believe Rath's family to be very close and respectful, I have witnessed much tension between siblings and between Rath's expectations and those of her children. This tension is the most evident in the language that Srey and Touch use such as "the clash of two societies," "fitting in," and "fighting back." My sense is that for Kusal, Touch, and Srey, being bicultural means in one context they are Cambodian and in another context they are American, resulting in identities that are artificially joined by the hyphen.

April and Mam are at the other end of the continuum. It is, of course, impossible for me to gauge Mam's relationship to his Cambodian and American identities, although he seems to have followed a path similar to Kusal's. April appears to consider herself completely American. She is one of very few Cambodians at her high school. Her friends are white Americans, some of whom are honor students while others are into drugs and parties. April's standards of success are grounded outside of the Cambodian community and outside of the Buddhist belief system. She maintains her high academic standing which she knows will allow her to attend a good university. She idealizes the close family structure in which parents spend time with their children listening to their opinions and trusting their judgment, so she has opted to live with a former white teacher and his wife. April is convinced she does not need to maintain her Cambodian identity since being Cambodian is connected to old-fashioned traditions that are out-of-place in modern American society. Although April does not concern herself with becoming a bicultural individual, she nonetheless is struggling to find a place to belong.

RELATIONSHIP TO PILOT STUDY, 1997

The seven Cambodian adults whom I interviewed for my Pilot Study are also part of the Forest City community. Three of them are a part of this case study. The four who are not are married and work for the Forest City public schools; one works for himself. Their children attend public schools, and their lives in many ways mirror the stories narrated above. My questions to them also focused on being successful, and their answers implied that they believed in two paths to success for Cambodians. One path to success included owning a home and having material possessions, cars, and enough money to do as one pleased. The most direct route to this standard of success was through school. The more successful the individual was in acquiring a college degree, the more successful he or she would be in acquiring the status symbols that represented "success."

Beyond the pragmatics of achieving material success, each adult spoke at length about what it meant to be a successful Cambodian. The successful Cambodian is a devout Buddhist who follows the principles of the Eight-Fold Path and who is mindful of the law of *karma*. All but one of my respondents accepted the concept that the successful life is lived in three stages—school stage, productive/family stage, and retire stage. They spoke of the middle stage as the most difficult during which families had to work hard in order to survive and provide sufficient security for their later years. Because of this, they stated that spending a lot of time helping out in the community or attending the many cultural ceremonies and Buddhist holidays was a burden, both financially and in terms of time.

They believed that their most important task was to raise their children to speak the language, know something about the culture, attend Buddhist holidays, and feel high self-esteem as Cambodians.

They trusted to their children's innate gifts and qualities to make sense of the public school system and succeed according to their talents. Occasionally, one of the mothers would comment that the more Americanized their children became, the harder it was to bring them back into the culture. Observing the law of not too strict and not too loose, these parents resolved to not pressure or restrict their children, but remain flexible and patient that the middle way would, in the end, be the most successful tactic.

SUMMARY

This discussion covers an analysis of my research questions by revealing the themes which emerged from the narratives. The themes that represent success to each respondent include first of all their *goals*—successfully maneuvering the three stages of life, going as far as they can with their education, finding a good career, making enough money to be secure, and becoming free and independent individuals. The second theme has to do with the *expectations* these people have for themselves and those they have internalized from the family, from the culture, and from Buddhist beliefs. Being successful in meeting Buddhist expectations is inspired by a desire to be helpful to others which in turn brings good merit and ensures a good next life. At the same time, meeting the expectations of teachers to achieve in school or the expectations of the family to be respectful and obedient confers a high status to the individual and, by reflection, to the family. The families who are considered "high praise" in the Cambodian community receive their status more from a perception that they are in balance with one another—they are neither too strict nor too loose with their children, and they are generous and compassionate to others.

The third theme reveals their perceptions of success through the naming of *role models* and the people they most admire. With only two exceptions, the people most admired, trusted, and respected are members of their own families or people in the community who are considered to be exceptionally kind and open-hearted. This perception holds true even though the parents of two of the families are divorced and the adolescents do not have close relationships with their fathers. The perception also holds true in spite of the fact that the day-to-day reality in each of these families is a struggle for income, for space, and for security.

Finally, the narratives revealed a powerful theme I call *bicultural success*. Although most of the parents and grandparents do not struggle with issues of cultural identity, they are deeply aware of this struggle in their children. The Cambodian nature is to be flexible and adaptable, seeking the middle way between extremes. However, without a strong understanding of the norms of the culture, the language, and Buddhist beliefs, one's Cambodian identity is fragile and is easily bruised in the racial hostility that characterizes much of Forest City society. Yet, the young people seem instinctively to know that becoming too Americanized is dangerous; denying one's culture does not automatically allow one to fit seamlessly into American society. They are pulled between two cultures with part of their mind in the frame of Cambodian beliefs, history, and expectations, and the other part competing for resources in the fight to get ahead. While they have each come to terms with the clash of the two cultures in slightly different ways, I believe that those who will be the most successful will be those who sustain their identity in both cultures.

CHAPTER 9
Conclusion and Implications

There is an external life which is educated at school, taught to read, write, cipher and trade; taught to grasp all the boy can get, urging him to put himself forward, to make himself useful and agreeable in the world, to ride, run, argue, and contend, unfold his talents, shine conquer and possess. The inner life sits at home...it loves truth because it is itself real; it loves right, it knows nothing else; but it makes no progress; was as wise in our first memory of it as now; is just the same in maturity as it was in youth.... It lives in the great present; it makes the present great.

—Emerson[1]

INTRODUCTION

The patterns of success which are revealed in these three families can be connected to Cambodian history and the philosophical tradition of Buddhism in both pragmatic and expressive ways. While it is the parents who primarily draw on their country of origin as their frame of reference for what it means to be successful, deep patterns of culture such as the caste system remain even in the Cambodian community in Forest City. Khmer language reinforces these differences because of its stratified construction. The level of education and English facility for some Cambodians may have lifted them to a higher status in the

U.S., but high character remains, for all Cambodians, the successful ideal.

Trueba et al. and Caplan et al. have suggested that there are certain middle class values which transcend cultural specificity and guarantee success in a modern society. Clearly, the adolescents in the study have confronted these expectations and have found themselves on familiar ground with some and alienated by others. Rumbaut and Ima's analysis of socio-cultural qualities that characterize the Khmer has undergone some revision in light of these findings. And Kiang's analysis is supported and elaborated by the perceptions of success held by the three generations in the study.

The ethnographic work undertaken by a few Cambodian scholars is validated in my findings, particularly with regard to the influence of the family structure, the resilience of Buddhist norms to guide and sustain the culture, and the speculation that the movement toward a bicultural identity is—for the second and third generation—likely to produce the most successful outcomes both psychologically and socially. There is, however, disconfirming evidence that for many Khmer youngsters, there are more advantages to becoming Americanized as long as certain Cambodian cultural models continue to stigmatize and restrict young women from aspiring to independent goals. While the institution of the family remains a central one, the need to hold on to Buddhist practices and beliefs may, for some, be diminished. As young adolescents increasingly internalize the United States as their frame of reference, it may become more and more difficult to sustain their spiritual identities in competition with the secular American culture.

Finally, the implications of this case study can be connected to pedagogy, curriculum design, and classroom practice in emphasizing the importance of cultural belief systems. This in turn has the potential to influence dropout rates, post-graduate aspirations and accomplishments, and strategies for parental involvement.

RELATING CONCEPTS OF SUCCESS TO CAMBODIAN CONTEXT

The criteria for success as represented by Cambodia's social classes and the status of men and women are reflected in the narratives of Pirun, Rath, and Chinda. Pirun, as a male, took advantage of the temple system to be educated through high school and a three-year nursing program. He also received seven years of training as a Buddhist monk. His status is further enhanced because he is a classical Cambodian musician. Even though Pirun is lower-middle class in the United States, he is very high status in the Cambodian community.

Chinda, who was born into an affluent family, was not allowed to complete high school because she is female, although she did learn to read and write Khmer. Born into poverty, Rath received none of these advantages from education. But while Chinda receives status in the United States because she is a college student, Rath receives status from the Cambodian community because she and her family are considered to have high character.

According to some accounts, Cambodian society valued scholars and artists more highly than industrialists and financiers. The children of privilege were frequently educated in Europe or studied with prominent national artists, and they ultimately took their parents' places at the cosmopolitan center of the society. The middle classes sought civil service jobs, jobs which one could attain with a high school degree and hold for life. The richest person in the village was a person with the most rice fields. In all these contexts, the more children one had, the more successful the family. Families depended on their children to help with farming and fishing; civil servants received an increase in salary for each child they had. It is not surprising then that the adults in this study continue to connect success and achievement to the family, education, and high character. This belief holds true for many Cambodians in Forest City while their perceptions of *Americans* in this society are that education, competition, and making money are connected to success.

Another important point that connects Cambodian history and philosophy to the narratives in this case study is the evidence that Cambodians have always been bicultural people. Their society has managed to exist with two seemingly incompatible cosmologies—the Hindu-based, militant elitism of the Cambodian royalty with the Buddhist-based, humble passivity of the Cambodian middle and lower classes. This biculturalism is played out over and over throughout their history, even in the figures of the ultra-nationalist Pol Pot and Prince Sihanouk juxtaposed with Maha Ghosananda, Cambodia's most venerated man of peace.

RELATING CONCEPTS OF SUCCESS TO SOCIO-CULTURAL THEORY

Trueba et al. argued that Asian families who internalized a certain constellation of middle class values and behaviors ensured that their children would have successful outcomes, primarily in school. The values they identified were parental factors, study habits, community service, and popularity. Parents are perceived as advocates for their children securing special tutoring, auxiliary experiences including travel, and the latest in technology. They predicted that parents who became personally involved in the life of the school or in political participation on behalf of the school would have a positive influence on their adolescents' commitment to school. The authors also theorized that extracurricular activities such as sports, music, or clubs along with popularity with a wide variety of social groups were indicators that pointed to a well-rounded child with high self-esteem and inter-personal skills. Finally, the child who maintained disciplined study habits and worked independently to solve problems or think through complex ideas would be successful in moving up the educational ladder through college and post-graduate programs.

Pirun and Rath, plus the other adults in their extended families, see their responsibilities as good parents to make sure their children are raised to experience and understand cultural norms, specifically the different religious expectations. They expect the school to prepare their children for American society.

All the parents in this study work long hours and are rarely available to assist their children with homework, although they do lecture their children on its importance. MP states, "I never got that much [from my parents] anyway. I got a little bit from my teachers. 'Good job on that test. Good job on this year.' My parents never said, 'You did a great job in school this year.'" MP and his siblings accept that their parents must work to support the family and that the children must do well in school to make the parents proud and make the sacrifices worthwhile. It is this commitment that motivates these adolescents to be self-reliant and independent students.

The parents in these families are strong advocates for their children in school. Rath has put two of her children through private high schools, and she is now pushing to get her youngest son into mainstream classes when he enters the third grade. She made sure that Touch was given a tutor at Danforth Academy. Yet, with the exception of Pirun, the only school functions that these parents attend are semi-annual teacher conferences.

In the case of Kusal and Mam, schools did not meet their responsibilities to these young men and the two are now outside the system. Because Kusal lacks the English proficiency to complete his GED, his skills confine him to a manufacturing job where, with long hours and hard work, he may achieve his goal of self-sufficiency. However, if he and Sarem have a child, the likelihood that either of them will complete their education grows more remote.

Along with maintaining his Cambodian identity, Kusal is also learning a different set of cultural codes—those, suggests, which are part of the underclass. His siblings, along with MP, Avy, Alyana, and April, are learning the cultural codes of the American middle class which give them better access to higher education.

Community service as a criteria for middle class success is clearly commensurate with Cambodian values. These adolescents have discovered that community service hours "look good on their college transcripts." However, while community service is a prerequisite at Danforth Academy and Elizabeth Seton, it is voluntary at Forest City and Stevens High Schools. With the pressure to maintain honors grades and the necessity of holding part-time jobs after school, MP, Avy, Alyana, and April are not involved in structured community service programs. Avy and Alyana, however, are very involved in community and temple activities, especially around Cambodian New Year when Alyana performs classical Cambodian dance.

All of these young people are popular, but they struggle with having to "fit in" to American culture—a struggle they find stressful. MP and Touch point out that they have both American and Cambodian friends but that they feel more relaxed, more assured with their Cambodian friends. Touch comments that he keeps his groups of friends separate from one another, believing that they just would not understand the other's culture. MP says,

> It is good that I have friends outside my race, but it is just as
> important to have friends within your race. You kind of need
> that balance. I used to be friends with white kids from about
> seventh grade till now. [We're] still friends but not as close.
> We were really close, but people change.

Only one of these adolescents believed she would trust friends over family. As a result, most of them seem to prefer being with their families when they want to relax or have fun.

Caplan et al. come closer to a prediction of success for Asians that is consistent with my findings. The adolescents respect the person who works hard and gets ahead with persistence and drive. They are incredibly optimistic about their goals to complete college and go for advanced degrees or find fulfilling jobs. Even Kusal, who has been shut out of the educational conduit to success, believes he is being saved for something important. In addition, the young women, especially, want to make their families proud that they can be both respected Cambodian women and successful Americans.

The point that needs to be emphasized is that prior levels of education or socioeconomic status have not influenced the persistence, optimism, or self-reliance of these nine young men and women. The family has been a powerful influence in all three cases, primarily from the young people's belief that they have been given unexpected opportunities which should not be taken for granted, but rather seized and enjoyed. While delayed gratification is a common middle class value in achieving success, I believe the Cambodians take a more pragmatic view. Balance is the most important virtue—it is not good to play all the time, nor it is good to work all the time. This is one cultural model they have sustained.

Rumbaut and Ima interviewed Khmer, Vietnamese, Hmong, Lao, and Vietnamese-Chinese families in order to describe cultural beliefs and behavior toward family, work, and education. They paint a portrait of the Khmer family and individual that seems to explain the Khmer lack of educational and economic success as compared with the other four groups. While the Rumbaut and Ima analysis corresponds to much of my own data, I believe there are some significant differences in approach and in outcome.

Rumbaut and Ima describe the Khmer family as primarily nuclear, female-centered, and neolocal. The children as well as extended family members see themselves as individuals, and there is a perception that they have a choice about whether to help a family member or not. In some respects this is consistent with Pirun's belief that the good parent does not expect his children to take care of him when he is old; that it places too great a burden on sons and daughters to raise their own families as well as "raise" their parents. Kusal states that he has *voluntarily* agreed to come back and help his mother with the family expenses and childcare. However, he and his wife are also saving rent and food money by continuing to live with her. Rath spends half of her time caring for her aging parents, often without the help of her four brothers who live nearby and are far more affluent. Nonetheless, over the past three years I have witnessed the family proceed with an elaborate wedding, a pre-funeral ceremony, New Year celebrations, and costly citizenship applications, all of which would have been impossible without the generous support of Rath's brothers.

Rumbaut and Ima found that Khmer families report working in low status jobs specifically in the service sector, or jobs that do not require higher education and sophisticated English skills such as those in manufacturing, industry, or seasonal work. The jobs are usually found through family or friends.

After fifteen years of residence in the United States, Rath continues to work in seasonal jobs as does her 72-year-old mother. However, one brother has completed his degree and has a white-collar job in a semiconductor plant, another owns his own business, and a third is completing a degree in electronics in a neighboring state. This disparity in career outcomes is most likely explained by the education Rath's brothers received prior to fleeing Cambodia—an education which prepared them to do well in American schools. Rath's children aspire respectively to be a nurse, a lawyer serving minorities, and an ESL teacher. They have chosen these careers because they are helpful to others while being fulfilling for themselves. Still, attaining these careers requires discipline, planning, and long-term commitment to education and further training.

Pirun is a certified nurse as well as the parent coordinator for the Forest City Public Schools multilingual program. He assists with grant writing and presentations of the center's innovative curricula for ESOL learners. His wife, who has owned her own store, now works in the food processing industry. Her brothers and sisters own family businesses in Forest City and a neighboring state. Pirun and Rany's children also aspire to careers in medicine, travel, and possibly mathematics. Their selections of careers are guided as much by suggestions from their parents as by their desire to find something that is personally meaningful and fulfilling—something that can be helpful to others.

For nearly ten years Chinda has pursued her associates degree while working part time in social services. There is no question that Chinda will eventually make her career in social work focusing, I would guess, on the needs of refugee women. April is highly motivated to complete her education and enter either marine biology or business management. It remains to be seen what her brother Mam will do about his future given his lack of discipline in completing his education and in finding work that leads to a secure financial future.

Rumbaut and Ima point to education as a path through the bottleneck for these Southeast Asian families. However, they observe that the Khmer are content with high school diplomas or two-year associates degrees, frequently in technical colleges. They point out that the low educational levels of the primarily female heads of households is often a factor in low educational attainment and persistence of the children.

This study has fully documented the importance of education to all of the people who participated in the interviews and observations. Although Rath is functionally illiterate in her own language, she understands implicitly the need to place her children in mainstream English classrooms rather than leaving them too long in ESL classes. While she would like to provide the supplementary help in reading and writing for her younger children, only Srey can provide K and J with that kind of help, and she is already under tremendous pressure to maintain her academic standing at Elizabeth Seton. Based on Kusal's experiences in ESL classes, Rath is also concerned that K and J will attach themselves to the "wrong crowd" and lose interest in school and getting ahead. She holds the school accountable for their progress and indicates that she is willing to move them to another school if they do not succeed. Rath's commitment to seeing her children succeed in American schools in no way conflicts with her commitment to raising her children to speak Khmer and to know proper Buddhist rituals and behavior.

Pirun and Rany have also been proactive in their children's education, although they chose the more diverse Forest City High School instead of Stevens High School which has a very small percentage of Asian students. From my observations, the quality of education in these two schools is virtually the same, although the teaching staff at Forest City High School appears to be more sensitive to culture and differences in learning style.

April has always attended schools which are predominantly white, and she has excelled academically. Maintaining a high grade point average in exchange for more personal freedom is the one rule Chinda enforces with April. When I observed April in school, it was obvious that she received a great deal of reinforcement from her instructors. They all indicated that she was consistently one of the hardest working and best prepared of the students in the class.

Kusal and Mam are representative of a number of Khmer in Forest City. I have already pointed out that Kusal entered first grade at age eight without any previous schooling experience. He encountered a school system and an instructional staff that was not prepared for a large multilingual student population. Though her efforts seem to have failed, it must be noted that Kusal's mother was his advocate, moving him to two different schools trying to secure for her son the help he needed to move ahead academically. I can only speculate on the effects of racial prejudice, alienation, and the negative impact of his parents' divorce on Kusal's lack of success in school. Perhaps because he was the oldest, Kusal felt the divorce trauma more; the family was certainly more unstable as he embarked on his educational career. On the other hand, the fact that his brothers and sisters have found ways to withstand these same stresses and succeed in school may mean that the problems were developmental ones for Kusal as an individual. It is important to reiterate that neither the socioeconomic status nor the fact that two families are headed by single women has adversely affected the educational attainment or persistence of these adolescents in school.

Rumbaut and Ima describe characteristics of Khmer parents and Khmer individuals that refer more to expressive qualities. For instance, they state that Khmer parents typically exercise less discipline over their children; that they try not to push their children in one particular direction, encouraging them to go "step-by-step" toward their goals instead of making long-term commitments. The authors imply that one of the outcomes of the close relationships between children and parents sets up a long-term dependency on the mother (and grandmother) which delays their separation from the family and accounts for an apparent lack of ambition and independence.

Rumbaut and Ima describe the Khmer individual as primarily passive, fatalistic, and reactive. One outcome is that the children appear to be less oriented to hard work and personal effort; they lack competitiveness and prefer to remain in the background or withdraw from situations that become too stressful or marked by conflict. The authors seem to equate a belief in *karma* with a fatalistic perspective that they suggest leads to a tendency toward self-gratification and a relaxed, unhurried coping style. If one's life course is essentially set and cannot be changed with hard work or personal effort, Rumbaut and Ima imply, then the goal in life becomes seeking personal happiness and fulfillment above other more stressful goals. The authors find the Khmer more preoccupied with expressive matters such as festivals, weddings, celebrations, and reunions than with pragmatic goal-oriented strategies for getting ahead.

In observing these three families, I heard them speak often about the rule of "no and yes," or "not too strict and not too loose." They are familiar with other families in Forest City who operate at either of these extremes. As a result, they have seen children either rebel against oppressive restrictions or become disorganized, confused, and lost as a result of the lack of structure in American society. So Pirun, Chinda, and Rath try to balance Cambodian norms that *they* know with American norms that their *children* know. They work hard on developing a base of trust with their children, exchanging knowledge and experiences interactively and equally. Because the family represents the one place where children can be understood and trusted, it becomes the place where young people work out their problems, either with one another, with their peers, or with the institutions that control their lives outside of the family. They consistently emphasize the Buddhist belief that *if the path is too stressful it is the wrong path.*

The tendency of these individuals to plan their lives in a "step-by-step" approach is directly related to a Buddhist model of living in the present moment. This model has been validated in the case of Cambodian refugees who learned not to plan too far in advance while living under the Khmer Rouge when the next day could bring betrayal, death, or relocation. I think it would be difficult for most refugees, even after fifteen years in a host country, to change such a deeply internalized cultural model. The young people have their own perspective on the step-by-step approach as they begin to leave high school and enter college. Many of them want to go to "good" colleges where the tuition is far beyond their family's resources. A few want to go on to graduate school. Taking their educational goals step-by-step (seeing how "far one's pockets" will take them) is a realistic and pragmatic approach for young people who know they do not have financial safety nets to ensure the achievement of more ambitious goals.

Another Buddhist model evident in these narratives is the concept of competition. Pirun's perception of success is a vivid illustration of an individual competing only with himself in order to bring himself to the top of the mind. This pattern recurs in the narratives of MP, Avy, Alyana, Srey, Touch, Kusal, and April. As a rule, each adolescent prefers working collaboratively with a group or a team to accomplish goals; most do not seek to be leaders except as facilitators of teamwork. I find MP, Avy, Alyana, Srey, and Touch highly competitive, pushing themselves to improve grades and learning. While not perfectionists, they expend effort to be creative, and are disciplined about meeting deadlines and expectations. The motivation may come from an internal sense of wanting to do their best, and prove to their families they can achieve; it may also come from the realization that without high achievement, they will not be able to accomplish their goals of college.

Kusal has successfully completed and passed each of his GED requirements except for English. He wants to complete this final step, but without tutoring, it will be difficult for him to do so. He now works full time, clocking eight to ten hours a day, six and sometimes seven days a week. Each of the adolescents works ten to fifteen hours a week outside of school and helps with family chores. In the summer Touch and MP both worked two and three jobs at a time. Clearly, hard work, effort, and persistence are not the issue for these young people.

In each narrative, regardless of whether it is an adult or an adolescent, the individual speaks about a desire to have a life and a career that is personally fulfilling. They refer to Americans as going out to conquer the world, while for them it is more important to look within. These individuals have many goals in life—some are ambitious, some are modest—but the most consistent goals are to maintain those "expressive matters" that bind the family together and bind them to their Buddhist heritage. It is not a matter of which is more pragmatic; it is simply the way to live a good life.

Reflecting back on Rumbaut and Ima's characterization of Cambodian norms as influencing their "lack of success," I think it is critical to expose the cultural norms which judge these strategies to be flawed. American culture is obsessed with a single-minded, relentless drive to get ahead. Demanding a balance between family, religious obligations, and career is not highly valued in mainstream American life. While comparisons between the two styles of status mobility may be valuable, one must not assume that the Cambodian tendency to withdraw from stressful and highly competitive situations means Cambodians are destined to fail in this society.

SUCCESS RELATED TO CAMBODIAN SCHOLARS' THEORIES

This case study validates the findings on Cambodian families in the research of Sin, Welaratna, and Ebihara. Sin's categories of Cambodian families as either *high achievers, financially concerned,* or *under achievers* is consistent with the narratives in these three families as well as my observations of other Cambodian families in the Forest City community. I would place Pirun, Rath, and Chinda's families in the category of high achievers. The parents maintain open communication with their children. They have added select behaviors from American culture while maintaining core beliefs based on Buddhist traditions. There is a degree of mutual trust among grandparents, parents, and children, in spite of the push and pull of daily life.

This study also confirms Sin's analysis that socioeconomic status is not a significant factor in determining which families will be high achievers or underachievers. And at least in the case of Touch, MP, Srey, Avy, and Alyana, maintaining a strong self-concept as Cambodian has allowed them to compete successfully in a system which frequently does not have high expectations for people who are non-Caucasian.

Welaratna's analysis of Rumbaut and Ima's theories about Cambodian coping styles matches my own. Our findings are consistent in the way the individuals spoke about the significance of money to their perceptions of success. Welaratna points out that generally individual Cambodians who became successful in the United States rarely kept to themselves accumulating more and more wealth. Instead they shared their resources with their immediate and extended families, providing opportunities for family members to acquire more education or move into better careers. As for material wealth, Welaratna documents that good character was more highly valued than being rich, and that happiness and fulfillment were the rationale for selecting one career over another. "Cambodians have felt little compulsion to succeed in a material sense. Acquisitiveness is not a dominant characteristic; adequacy is the objective in life."[2]

I was intrigued to find that when I asked if my respondents equated wealth and power with success, they invariably said no. MP was the most outspoken as he analyzed his feelings about money, being rich, and wealth:

I really don't think that the trickle-down effect works at all. That is pretty much the basis of capitalism, you help the rich get richer and if they get rich [enough] then maybe they will help out the middle class and then the middle class helps out the lower class. I think it stops with the rich. They give out little handouts to people, so there is even a bigger separation.

I don't have as much respect for [a person who was born rich, or stays rich, or gets richer] as I would a person who had bettered himself. If you are born rich you are given almost everything so you don't really have to work, you don't feel that hunger that need to do this or I am stuck here.

Income level is not really that important. I would like to have a lot of money, but money is not going to solve the problems. Money will help with the problems. Money is never the answer, but you are not going to solve all your problems with money.

There is only so much to wealth. There is only a certain amount of money that you can have before it is nothing anymore. There is only so much money you need. You don't need the MBA contract type of money; there is no point in having that much money. You know you can't spend all that money.

You can have all the money in the world but that's not

really achievement and fulfillment of what you want. If
money is what you are after and you get that then there is
nothing for you to want. There is no point for you to go on
'cause you already have what you need. But if you have that
hunger inside of you then money might be your goal to a
certain aspect, but when you reach that you are going to want
to get more because you know that is not all there is in life.

Touch, Srey, Avy, Alyana, and April echo MP's sentiments about
money stating that education is more important than wealth because
knowledge allows one to find a good job. All of these youth observe
that the rich seem to be more unhappy than the middle class. Touch, in
particular, has witnessed the pressure that extreme wealth places on
individuals and how difficult it is for them to lead simple lives, unsure
if people like them for themselves or for their wealth and influence.
This does not mean to imply that these young people are averse to
making money, buying cars, audio and video equipment, and clothes,
or dreaming of large houses and their own successful businesses. It
does, I believe, reveal that emotional fulfillment, high character, and
generosity are not simply abstract concepts passed along by their
parents, but have found their way into the narratives of the next
generation.

The thrust of this study is to describe the extent to which each
generation continues to draw on Buddhist epistemology as the frame
for being successful even though a few of the adolescents do not
ascribe their beliefs to Buddhism. In his book *Culture in Mind*, Bradd
Shore develops a theory of cultural models as biologically constructed
cognitive concepts that match with external, conventional behavior and
artifacts. His point is that a model may be active at a deep cognitive
level and still adapt to changes in context and meaning.

Cultural models are born, transformed through use and
eventually die out. Their continued existence is contingent,
negotiated through endless social exchanges. Such shared
models are a community's conventional resources for
meaning-making. To gain motivational force in a community,
these models must be reinscribed each generation in the minds

of its members. In this way conventional models become a personal cognitive resource for individuals.[3]

Venerable Maha Ghosananda is the Supreme Patriarch of Cambodian Buddhism and travels the world offering insight into the true nature of Cambodian values such as control, balance, generosity, and compassion. His parables bring these concepts to life as he encourages Cambodians to build bridges of unity, understanding, and peace, to "eat time" by living in the moment, and to take the middle path. Each person in this study speaks about her or his relationship to Buddhism and its meaning in his or her life. The adolescents speak about the importance of being good, doing the right thing, helping others, giving all one has, and not judging others. While a few do not connect these values to being Buddhist, they nonetheless behave as their devoutly Buddhist parents have instructed them.

On some level each person understands that every action in life produces a consequence for the actor and that the consequences, whether good or bad, are not resolved in one lifetime and must follow the individual into the next life. The law of *karma*, even imperfectly understood, is a potent part of their belief system; it recurs again and again in their narratives. The adults give of their time and resources with a full and warm-hearted generosity. They believe this will bring them merit in the next life. The adolescents are cognizant of the actions which bring merit to themselves and to their families, and they strive to meet those expectations. They have little sympathy for those who become the victims of their own foolishness or ignorance, but they have great compassion for those who have entered this life with bad health or misfortune. Far from being fatalistic, I believe that their interpretation of Buddhist philosophy motivates them to "catch the best future life" by achieving their goals while being generous to their families and compassionate to others.

Their religion and their families inspire them to lead lives of caring and generosity. They strive for the future, but they live in the moment. More often than not, they encounter a society which demands that they not waste time, that they compete for limited resources, that they know facts and not themselves, and that they must help themselves at the expense of helping others. While the spiritual philosophy of Buddhism is similar to other spiritual traditions, the point to consider is the depth to which Buddhism inspires these young Cambodians to aspire, to become successful. They may chafe against cultural traditions that seem old-fashioned and arbitrary in American society, but they intuitively accept the rationale behind them. Good actions are connected to a good reputation. Their good reputation is connected to the status of the family which earns respect, admiration (and envy), much like what happens to people who become very successful. Their faith tradition inspires them to care for and about others. It is the motivation for personal merit, it is the substance of role models, it is the most important element in career choice, and it is the foundation of the good family. It is also very, very difficult to maintain over time—especially in a society that is so preoccupied with the self-centered individual.

There is evidence in these narratives which also contradicts some of what I just said. Touch sees hypocrisy in monks who are revered by elders but who to him are simply human and fallible. They can't produce miracles and they appear to manipulate people through their faith. Touch, Avy, Chinda, April, and Srey see hypocrisy in elders who profess generosity and kindness but gossip about others based on external assumptions and rumors. Rath comments on parents who know the importance of family but sit around playing cards and ignoring their children. Touch points out the tendency of Cambodians to respect people who have good jobs and material possessions but act like "assholes" to the people around them. He challenges the notion that someone who works hard doing a job that he loves, even if the job does not have high status in this culture, deserves as much respect as someone who works for an electronics firm. The young women argue against the cultural norms which seem to repress women when Buddhist norms suggest that all people are equal and are encouraged to take themselves to the highest level of the mind. And while they are close to their families, day-to-day interactions can erupt in anger and jealousy.

Other paradoxes occur when Khmer look at American society. From images prevalent in popular culture, Americans appear to be preoccupied with material things, power, high status jobs, leisure. Their families seem to be artifacts, part of the well-rounded portfolio. Education is oriented toward the technical, toward whatever makes money. And religion is alternately virtually hidden or sensationalized when verging on the cultish. The Khmer look at all of this out of eyes that are centered in family and religion. Their world is constructed between these two boundaries, so self-reliance is encouraged because the person who takes responsibilities for her actions understands the norms of Khmer culture as well as American culture and thus brings merit on herself and her family.

The adolescents in this study observe, first hand, that their parents and many others lead lives of sacrifice. That because of language and the lack of education, they are poor, but that the parents are rich in the capacity for caring. Parents anchor them in the home and in their ethnic identity. The family is low stress (at times), it is fun, it is supportive, it is the role model. The adolescents reciprocate as the culture brokers and provide for their families as they get older. Control, balance, flexibility, and compassion are core Cambodian cultural models. The way in life should be balanced between too much stress and complete disorganization—the middle path. Too much success brings worry about how to manage it all. Too much wealth is a burden just as too much poverty is a burden. The goal is personal and emotional fulfillment which is not achieved through material things. The movement toward a good future is taken step-by-step.

IMPLICATIONS FOR EDUCATION

Kiang's charge to future researchers of Southeast Asian students was to understand more about the effects ethnicity, socioeconomic status, and culture have on shaping the self-image, aspirations, and development of a "minority" group identity. He also called for more research into the meaning of success as defined through the daily lives of individuals and their families. This case study provides such a window into a Cambodian point of view. The respondents have described what it means to be a Cambodian adolescent or adult in the Forest City community. The respondents provide graphic detail on their goals and expectations for education and future jobs, combined with their desire to remain close to their families and their religion. Are these *families* successful from the point of view of the Cambodian community? Are these *adolescents* successful from the point of view of their parents and from the point of view of the community? Are these *adolescents* successful from their own point of view? I believe they are. This case study documents how profoundly their spiritual beliefs infuse concepts like the family, self-reliance, competition, aspirations, hard work, or withdrawing from conflict and stress.

For educators looking to find ways to support a cultural epistemology of success that is founded in spiritual values, one approach is to become more familiar with instructional practices that are effective with language minority students.[4] Huerta has found that there is a strong relationship between a supportive classroom environment where students use their language and cultural experiences along with appropriate mainstream knowledge on the one hand, and the tendency of many of those students to persist in school and achieve at high levels on the other. The thrust of Huerta's analysis is the need for educators to take an active role in encouraging bicultural identity.

Marcelo and Carola Suárez-Orozco are looking at similar indicators for bicultural identity development through a longitudinal study involving five immigrant groups from China, Central America, the Dominican Republic, Haiti, and Mexico. They are finding that strengthening those institutions which ground the ethnic identity (specifically family and faith communities) is essential to the development of an equally strong American identity.

> Some of the youth will achieve bicultural and bilingual
> competencies which are an integral part of their identity.
> These youth respond to negative social mirroring by
> identifying it, naming it and resisting it.... They are able to
> network with equal ease among members of their own ethnic
> group as well as with others from different backgrounds.
> There is considerable evidence that those who develop bi-
> cultural efficacy (that is to say social competence in both
> cultures) are at a significant advantage over those who are
> alienated with a part of their identity.[5]

Another resource is Nel Nodding's book *The Challenge to Care in Schools* (1992) for instructors who see advantages in constructing a curriculum that builds on cultural models such as compassion, generosity, and collaboration. Noddings lays out a detailed curriculum organized around "centers of care: care for self, for intimate others, for associates and acquaintences, for distant others, for non-human animals, for plants and the physical environment, for the human-made world of objects and instruments, and for ideas."[6]   Given the rich narratives of these Cambodian students around their desire to give back, to help others, and to better society, such a curriculum, I believe, might inspire these young people to achieve to the full extent of their potential.

In addition to crafting a curriculum of care, educators might take advantage of other resources found in Khmer communities. Given the high regard for education and for cultural retention among most Cambodian families, educators might consider utilizing parents or grandparents to teach students the native language and culture in such a way that it is integrated into the school day. When students are ready to be moved out of ESL classrooms into mainstream classes, providing tutors to help with English grammar and construction should be considered. Older Khmer children would, as a rule, make good peer tutors and role models for younger students. The family is an ally. Instructors should take time to visit students in their homes instead of expecting parents to come to the school. It is important to support the parents in their desire to pass along cultural values and behaviors by encouraging those choices the Khmer perceive are successful.

Maha Ghosananda, Cambodia's most venerated spiritual leader, opens all of his presentations with the following verse which captures, eloquently, the qualities that represent success and fulfillment to the Cambodian:

> *The suffering of Cambodia has been deep.*
> *From this suffering comes Great Compassion.*
> *Great Compassion makes a Peaceful Heart.*
> *A Peaceful Heart makes a Peaceful Person.*
> *A Peaceful Person makes a Peaceful Family.*
> *A Peaceful Family makes a Peaceful Community.*
> *A Peaceful Community makes a Peaceful nation.*
> *And a Peaceful Nation makes a Peaceful World.*
> *May all beings live in Happiness and Peace.*

NOTES TO CHAPTER 9

1. Emerson, op. cit., p. 292-293.

2. Chhim in Welaratna op. cit., p. 275.

3. Bradd Shore, Culture in Mind: *Cognition, Culture and the Problem of Meaning*, (New York and Oxford: Oxford University Press, 1996), p. 47.

4. Teresa Huerta, *A Humanizing Pedagogy: Effective Instructional Practices for Latino Students*, Qualifying Paper, Harvard Graduate School of Education, 1998.

5. Carola Suárez-Orozco, "Identities Under Seige: Immigration Stress and Social Mirroring Among the Children of Immigrants", in Anthony Robben and Marcelo Suarez-Orozco, eds., *Cultures Under Seige: Violence and Trauma in Interdisciplinary Perspective*, (Cambridge: Cambridge University Press, in press) p. 20.

6. Nel Noddings, *The Challenge to Care in Schools: An Alternative Approach to Education*, (New York and London: Teachers College Press, 1992), p. xiii.

Mythic Journeys, Multiple Paths

INTRODUCTION

For the past eight years in April, the international students at Forest City High School have staged an Annual Cultural Heritage and Fashion Show. The graduates who started this resplendent tradition now sit in the audience (some with children of their own) and cheer their younger siblings and friends. On one particular Friday evening in April 2001, couples, parents with children, grandparents, mothers with babies, and students of all ages file into the high school auditorium. They fill every seat, then the aisles, and finally line the walls of the hall eager for the show to begin. The excitement is electric as performers and audience members flow up and down the stairs, brandishing video cameras and greeting one another with hugs.

The International Club at Forest City High School was formed by a growing population of refugee students who wanted a safe and open space to share their experiences in a new and often hostile environment. Within the club, some talk about the effect of meeting racism and stereotyping for the first time; others exchange stories of what it feels like to discover that their white peers and some of their teachers know nothing about their cultures or the values they share with their families and communities. They have come to believe that this ignorance is intentional, the legacy of a mainstream attitude that regards non-white cultures, traditions, and values as inferior—an attitude that assumes assimilation is the goal of all immigrants.

I do not know precisely how the Annual Cultural Heritage and Fashion Show first began, but it has had a profound effect on the immigrant community in Forest City and indirectly on the white majority of Forest City residents. The evening's performance combines elegantly choreographed displays of native dress from such countries as Cambodia, Vietnam, China, Korea, Yugoslavia, Somalia, Sudan, Ethiopia, Russia, and India, with traditional dances from most of these countries. This year for the first time, students from five or six ethnic groups present their version of hip-hop fashion and dance. Rooted in traditional African rhythms, the hip-hop dancers fuse contemporary music with ancient dance structures in a wildly provocative and exuberant performance. The audience goes wild with appreciation.

What stays with me long after we have left the auditorium is the fierce pride which infuses the faces of the performers and is heard in the voices of the audience as they cheer and cheer and cheer for every performance. In some small way, one can see living traditions being passed down to a new generation even as one appreciates the subtle nuances of gesture which distinguish the Vietnamese from the Cambodian dancers and the eloquence of village rituals which distinguish the Somali dancers from the Ethiopian. It is full of the ongoing immigrant story at the heart of American culture, and it reveals the strength that comes from sustaining one's cultural roots while making a way in American society.

Just as the young people on stage on this particular Friday evening show us the varied ways in which an individual can be both Sudanese and American, so too are the young people in this study constructing who they are as they take their places in the Cambodian community and the larger American society. As indicated in the introduction, I have continued my friendship with the parents and the adolescents in the families of Pirun, Rath, and Chinda, and during this time I have informally kept track of their aspirations, achievements, and detours. As more narrator than scientist, most of my observations are products of the casual give and take of interactions in living rooms, restaurants, school dorms, and workplaces. Nonetheless, my extensive portrait of three generations and their transformation from Cambodian villagers to American citizens would be incomplete without a final reflection on the pathways they now follow, step-by-step.

PIRUN'S FAMILY

Pirun continues his responsibilities with the multilingual center as liaison to the Cambodian community. He personally shepherded a number of Cambodian elders through the rigorous citizenship process, helping them memorize facts about American government and history such as the make-up of the U.S. Houses of Congress, the names and number of the original American colonies, and the leaders of the Civil Rights movement. As is common for new citizens, the Cambodian community in Forest City became intensely interested in the Bush/Gore Presidential election. Starting in September 2000, Pirun began broadcasting information about candidates and referendum questions over the weekly Khmer radio program. His goal: "To motivate people becoming an active citizen." His listeners' goal: "To be an informed citizen, analyze and making decision on voting." One morning in late October, Pirun asked me to present the positions of the two presidential candidates on such issues as welfare, education, immigration, and health care to the radio audience. Fortunately, there were no call-in questions!

Recently, as more and more young Khmer men and women approach their senior year in high school and think ahead to college, Pirun has applied some of the lessons he has learned in helping Avy and MP with their college finances to providing assistance to parents in the community. He asked a local man to donate a couple of days in January to help families complete federal financial aid forms and college scholarship applications. Slowly, Pirun is teaching his community that America provides resources to low-income, immigrant families to help send their children to college. Whereas ten years ago, Cambodian adults were proud of their high school diplomas, today their children recognize that a college or technical degree is important to their future, and is also within their grasp.

College has been good for MP in providing different pathways for him to achieve to his abilities. He is completing his Junior year at Tufts, with a double major in computer science and engineering. He spent the summer of 2000 in San Diego working as an intern for a software development company, and for the first time in his life did not return home for the school vacation. He has excelled in his major field, and he has participated for three years as part of a tutoring program for kids. When I first interviewed him, MP set his goal on completing college; today his goal is to go for a post-graduate degree when he completes his bachelor's degree in 2002.

Avy is completing her sophomore year as a pharmacy major at Northeastern University, and she will graduate in three more years. She has managed to enjoy the freedom of college while maintaining close ties to her extended family with whom she spends her weekends. If anything, she has become closer to her cousins, one of whom attends the same school.

Alyana is finishing her freshman year in high school. Unlike her siblings, she attended Stevens High School, but like them she is a high achiever. College is still within her sights, but "not much conversation for now," according to her father.

CHINDA'S FAMILY

In some ways the changes in Chinda's family have been the most dramatic of the three and are a startling validation of my theory that the Cambodian family is a powerful component in their epistemology of success. Early in 1999, Chinda became very ill, and her ex-husband Soeun came to take care of her during her slow recovery. Nearly eighteen years before, Soeun and Chinda divorced because she had wanted the freedom to pursue her education more than she wanted to maintain a traditional family. With independence no longer an issue between them, Chinda and Soeun admitted that they no longer wanted to live alone. More important, both parents knew that their children wanted to be part of a whole family. Soeun brings a traditional perspective to this Americanized family in that he speaks primarily Khmer and demands proper respect from his son and daughter. While Chinda continues taking college courses and working part-time, Soeun goes to work and takes care of household responsibilities. He is more often waiting for April or Mam when they come home from school or work.

In December 1999, April began a regular e-mail correspondence with me, which represented a significant change in our relationship. After almost three years of knowing April, I have finally come to a place where she is willing to trust me and begin constructing a one-on-one relationship. Chinda confirmed my impression and stated that April was generally slow to trust adults and the fact that I have maintained a connection with her mother and indirectly with her, establishes a foundation on which she is willing to build.

It was also during this time that April sent me a poignant poem she had written about a Cambodian woman she had known since infancy and who had died the year before. April referred to her as "grandmother" and accepted her as part of the family, "I was very close to her. We had this bond." April never mentioned this woman to me during our two formal interviews, and her enduring memories of a woman whom she considered "my best friend" caused me to reconstruct my earlier analysis around April's concept of family.

In January 2000, April consulted me on college applications, financial aid forms, and how to request transcripts. Just before her graduation, she announced that she had decided not to go to college in Florida but rather to attend the university in Forest City. A week later she announced that she would delay college so that she could spend a month with her older brother in Australia whom she had never met. April graduated from high school in June, having made high honors four times in her senior year; she was nominated by one of her teachers into the National Honor Society. Unable to attend April's graduation, I made it to her graduation party which was held at a local Thai restaurant owned and operated by a long-time Cambodian friend. The other guests included Chinda and Soeun, a brief appearance by April's brother Mam, April's school friends, Chinda's friends, including Rath and Srey, and a scattering of community elders. My conversation with April was brief, as she talked about her upcoming trip to Australia, but there was no mistaking her joy and pride at having friends and family celebrate this passage from school girl to young adult.

A year later April is planning another major trip. The journey this time is to Cambodia to meet her mother's family for the first time. After receiving a letter from her grandmother stating, "she doesn't have long to live," April has begun to save money for this visit, reflecting that "Cambodia will definitely be another big adventure." I questioned

Chinda about the implications of this visit for April given that she does not speak Khmer, nor is she familiar with many of the traditional customs of Cambodian culture, particularly for women. Chinda admitted that it will be a shock for April, but a number of her cousins speak English and are prepared to help her acculturate during her month and a half in the country. Chinda does not plan to accompany April, but I sense that Chinda is hoping the visit will inspire April to reconnect to her culture, to perhaps reclaim some of her language, and to give her some grounding in an identity she has up until now superficially rejected.

April's decision to delay college became more understandable when in a series of e-mails she revealed that her application to the local university was rejected. She interpreted the rejection as due to her low scores on the SAT tests stating that,

> [The university] rejected me last year and that's why I took a
> year off. I have this problem, I can't take tests under pressure,
> and I can't sit in class. I get very fidgety. I want to take
> classes independently. I know that [the university] offers that
> program but they rejected me last year so they aren't going to
> accept me for the fall term. I need to get back into school and
> get motivated and work on my degree.... I just refuse to go to
> class.... Internet home classes anything...to do at home I will
> do...like correspondence classes...I will do...I just need to
> know how to get it.

I was surprised by April's aversion to the classroom and conventional course work given her academic success in high school. All through high school April talked about attending college in preparation for a professional career, and there was no question that college represented a way out of Forest City, and into the mainstream society.

My sense is that April is more motivated by the thought of travel in which she is indirectly reconnecting to her extended family. April's search for family, for community—a place where she belongs—is still an underlying theme in her narrative. Perhaps, she will be able to construct her own identity only after she has integrated some of these missing pieces, and only then will she decide which path points the way to her future success.

Mam's story is also greatly changed from the picture I painted in 1998. He completed his GED in one year, passing the tests with ease. He applied to and was accepted in the Forest City Police Academy where he received straight A's in both semesters. Simultaneously, he joined a part-time program with the Marines and spent the summer of 2000 training with his unit. He has returned to the Police Academy for his second year, and has recently gotten his own apartment. He remains in frequent contact with his family, and especially his father with whom he has a close relationship

RATH'S FAMILY

There are profound changes in Rath's family narrative which have had an influence on the choice of paths each is now following. Rath continues to work in seasonal employment which allows her time to take care of her ailing father and keep track of her two youngest children after school. Rath continues to be proactive about K and J's schooling, pushing the school to begin moving K from the ESL classroom into the mainstream classes. K is not as academically motivated as Srey or Touch, and Rath wants him to have a strong foundation in English before he reaches middle school. Without the confidence to succeed in mainstream classes, she knows he may go the way of Kusal and drop out of school before graduating.

Rath also takes responsibility for communicating with her extended family through organizing and participating in regular celebrations, some of which are woven around traditional Buddhist holidays. In late December 2001 Rath was contacted by her brother Sareth who had disappeared during the Cambodian holocaust. He was married, living in Phnom Penh, and had recently received a visa to travel to the United States. Sareth spent some time with his uncle in California before making his way to Forest City where he now lives with his mother and is applying for permanent residency. This small miracle was profoundly moving as I observed Rath's extended family integrate Sareth into their lives. They are actively working to keep him in the United States while simultaneously applying to have his wife join him. They asked if I would consider being a second sponsor, and I agreed without hesitation.

Kusal and Sarem have both found jobs in the electronics industry and have moved into their own apartment. They are also the parents of a son who was born in Spring 2000. Kusal talks wistfully about his former life where he had the freedom to go where he pleased, but he accepts his responsibilities now as parent, husband, and as the surrogate head of his mother's family. This latter responsibility is more evident after the death of Kusal, Touch, and Srey's father, also in the spring of 2000. Although long estranged from his father and his second family, Kusal shaved his head and donned the robes of a monk in respect to his father and in accordance with Buddhist custom. This act of respect reflects on Kusal's good deeds in this life, thereby "cleansing his *karma*," and brings great merit to his mother and their family.

Touch completed two years at Clark University where he continued his study of history, particularly focusing on classes which explored issues around genocide and mass murder. These classes gave him opportunities to talk with fellow students and his professors about the Khmer Rouge holocaust. Touch spent time gathering narratives from his family members and other community elders about their wartime experiences. He was somewhat surprised to discover that many elders, including his mother and grandmother, "really don't want to talk about [the war]. To this day they do not want to emphasize Pol Pot policies at all."

Like MP, Touch has formed his strongest relationships with international students. He stated that he chose Clark,

> because there are so many people there who are not
> Americans. At Clark, even though it is very diverse, everyone
> is proud of their heritage. But it sucks because there is not a
> big Cambodian population; there are two. One of the reasons
> I went to Clark and get away from [home] was to be around
> more Cambodian people.

However, in spite of these new relationships, Touch chose to come home at every opportunity. When Touch's father died, he seemed to lose his focus and eventually took a leave of absence for the fall semester of what would have been his junior year. Touch took a job working ten to twelve hours a day, precluding a lot of interaction with his family. Tensions became strained with his mother and siblings, as Touch withdrew from virtually all family activities in favor of spending his leisure time with friends.

I interpreted Touch's response to losing his father, even though the two of them had not been close, as a catalyst which on some level forced Touch to reexamine his goals and who he was. Touch did not attend his father's funeral, nor did he participate in any of the Buddhist ceremonies around his father's death. Pirun, on the other hand, is convinced that Touch has a

> strong tool inside him which allows him to go a different way. He is not interested in Buddhism, does not believe in it. But Touch is very strong inside, very confident. He provides a good role model for his peers and siblings. Touch will always fight back; he stands outside the circle because he has his own way to do things. He does not seem to feel regret because of this strength.

Touch returned to Clark for the Spring 2001 semester, and he has taken up his studies again. Rath urged me to talk with Touch about his commitment to finish college, but even though we had a few conversations before he left, Touch kept his future plans to himself.

Srey is completing her sophomore year in a private college an hour from her home. College has provided her many opportunities to explore her American identity beginning with her freshman year in which she lived on campus and enjoyed the heady independence of dorm life, parties, and dating. Discovering an internet site for Cambodians based in the East, Srey began to meet young Khmer men who thought nothing of driving 100 miles to meet college-age Cambodian women nearby. Over time she began to date one young man (who calls himself Ziggy) on a steady basis and who attends a university in the southern part of the state. Pulled by her increasingly difficult academic courses, a busy social life, and her weekend job, Srey gradually withdrew from many cultural and family events, which strained Srey's relationship with her mother.

Srey made a decision to live at home in her sophomore year and commute to college. Her decision was primarily motivated by the need to focus on her academic courses and by the knowledge that I would be able to continue as her tutor. The tension with her mother decreased as Srey resumed her roles as caretaker for her younger siblings and interpreter for her mother and grandmother.

The clash between Cambodian and American culture came to a head in the late Spring 2001 when Srey failed to score high enough on a series of difficult multiple choice tests in her nursing foundation course, and the professor failed her in the course. This action forced Srey to withdraw from the four-year nursing program and request acceptance into the five-year program. The director of the program agreed to accept her only if she attended an ESL class in the summer. Srey is mystified by the requirement since she has a B average in her theology and philosophy courses, which calls into question the implication that she is unable to write and interpret English.

Srey has struggled to make sense of this "failure," observing that there is no longer a single Cambodian student, or any student of color in the nursing program. After contacting a number of her peers who had transferred out of the college, she discovered that they, too, were unable to pass the tests in this course and were dropped from the program. The fact that Srey had received As in all of her clinical work did not make up for her failure to pass the examinations.

Srey is at a crossroads. She is committed to becoming a nurse, but she will find it difficult to fund an additional year in order to receive her RN. She does not want to drop out of college and go the technical route as a college degree has always been her goal. Moreover, the evidence from all her other academic work is that she is more than capable of graduating in two years. Much as she tries to avoid the connotation, Srey increasingly suspects she is encountering discrimination because she is a minority. Becoming Americanized holds less and less appeal for her because of this.

In contrast to this experience, she and Ziggy recently brought their two families together to celebrate their formal engagement ceremony in front of the whole Cambodian community. Traditional Cambodian society does not approve of casual dating, thus it is customary for a young couple who want to spend time with one another in public to become formally engaged. The two sets of parents finally agreed on a date for this event and approached two prominent elders to represent each family. Over 100 people turned out to witness Srey and Ziggy's vows in a traditional ceremony. Having been privy to many conversations between Srey and her mother over the year, I know how difficult it was for the two of them to balance these two paths. In one scenario, the parent is obligated to arrange an engagement for a son or daughter which respects and enhances the reputation of the entire family. In another scenario, the adolescent wants to make an independent choice about a future partner. The resolution of this situation is a testimony to Rath"s perspective on change and her willingness to adapt old traditions by paving the way for her children to be successful in American and in Cambodian society. Later, Srey reflected on what the engagement ceremony meant to her:

> The people of the community praised my mother. They were all saying how lucky she is to have a wonderful daughter like me. Everyone admired on how I am so well educated and on how I still hold on to my Khmer traditions. Everyone complimented on how Ziggy and I are a good match because we are both good and well educated people with high expectations.

MYTHIC JOURNEYS, MULTIPLE PATHS

Ethnographers tell life stories and in this telling and retelling, the stories often reveal larger than life themes. Dr. Robert Atkinson (1995) discusses aspects of the life story in his book *The Gift of Stories: Practical and Spiritual Applications of Autobiography, Life Stories, and Personal Mythmaking.* Narrative forms of story telling have a number of variations from autobiography to personal myth, and it is the sacred quality of the personal myth that has particular relevance to the lives of the Khmer in my story. The archetypal human journey from separation through transformation and return is at its deepest level the journey toward identity and wholeness, and for the Khmer this is a story as old as their culture. According to Atkinson,

> A personal myth is what is most deeply true about our own experience of life. It is our expression of those personally sacred and timeless elements of our lives. It focuses on the experiences, beliefs, motifs and themes of a lifetime that have

ordered, shaped and directed our lives. It is our personal
expression of how the pattern of separation-initiation-return
has played itself out in our life. This is what links the
individual story we have lived to the collective story we all
share. The personal myth teaches us about the universality of
life.[1]

The metaphor of the mythic journey is embedded in Cambodian
epistemology through its connection to the legend of Siddhartha
Gotama. In the legend, Lord Siddhartha separated from his life as a
royal prince to wander among the people of India until he was
transformed as an enlightened human being. Thus the mythic journey
to enlightenment orders the Khmer universe and defines the pattern by
which the Khmer identity is formed. A variation of this pattern is seen
in the building of Angkor Thom, the exodus, and its rediscovery
thousands of years later. Today, the identity of Cambodians is
profoundly influenced by the knowledge that their ancestors are the
architects of this magnificent city.

Cambodian Buddhists in the United States reenact the mythic
journey as they experience the separation, transformation, and return
common to all refugees. In order to become whole, a culture in exile
must reinvent the mythic universe of their homeland. Traditional
customs, life cycle ceremonies, language, and gesture take on even
greater significance in the diaspora, and identify one as a member of
the community. The Cambodian family sets the pattern by selecting
those cultural values which are the most important to their identity as
Khmer, gradually incorporating other values from the new society
because they are seen as essential to success, and allowing a few values
die out.

As this study shows, Buddhism, the community, and the family
control the boundaries of the Cambodian universe. But flexibility and
balance are powerful metaphors in this culture and provide precedent
which allows one generation to accommodate the movement of the
next. Pirun, Rath, and Chinda function as bridges between their
parents' generation and their children's, and they have interpreted the
need for flexibility in different ways. Their children have begun their
own journeys of separation and transformation, some through the
experience of college, some through the death of a parent, and others

through the actual process of travel. The children are faced with divided identities—American, Asian-American, Cambodian-American—each of which brings different expectations and levels of belonging.

When they begin the journey back, to what will they return? What part of their archetypal story will endure, and how will the story change to reflect who they are? What will be the nature of their success? American tradition teaches that success is always the upward movement on a ladder from one level to another, but Khmer tradition accepts that success is often a step-by-step experience—the path is rarely straight, and detours are understood as part of the journey.

As indicated in the introduction, the immigrant family plays a crucial role in the assimilation process when children are unsure whether to become fully Americanized or not (Zhou, 1997). Increasingly studies of refugees and immigrants provide evidence that families who understand and support bicultural identity development increase the opportunities for their children to lead balanced and productive lives. While my study confirms this theory, in the case of these three Cambodian families, the pathways taken by the adolescents have not been predictable. For MP and Avy, separation and transition have been empowering. For now, they are not eager to return to Forest City. April, too, is eager for separation from her family in Forest City, but is drawn to connect with her extended family in Cambodia. Kusal has returned to take up his role as surrogate parent to his mother and actual father to his new son. The traditional pathway is familiar for both Kusal and Sarem, and they have begun the process of blending both cultures in the way they teach their son about who he is. Touch appears to have the most difficulty with separation and return, and may feel more deeply the larger loss of culture and identity that is the legacy of the Cambodian exile. Without the role model of a father, or a strong Buddhist *sangha*, Touch will have to work out his place between two cultures on his own. And finally there is Srey who is carefully negotiating her way between her goals of a college degree and a nursing career with her commitment to her family and the Cambodian community. She is unusually insightful about this journey in which she has so much at stake:

I never knew I was bicultural until you pointed it out. It never occurred to me; I never asked myself that. I just followed the Khmer traditions at home and tried to fit in at school. I think it is better now that I have different limits and I understand myself better. Now I think ahead and ask if what I want to do is the Cambodian way or American way; is it the right way or wrong way for me. I don't try to fit in as much; I just go with the flow.

Theravada Buddhism teaches that selflessness, wisdom, and compassion are what identify the ideal person in Cambodian culture. The overwhelming evidence gathered over ten years with this small community is that these values are not only expressed but they are enacted in the three generations who are part of my story. Their journeys may inspire them to become members of a much more cosmopolitan community, but I believe that they will always retain an identity which embodies the Cambodian characteristics of balance, flexibility, and control. They will balance the desire to live a fulfilling life with the practical tasks of education, family, and career; they will live in the present moment, not planning extensively for an unpredictable future, and they will follow their own paths, step-by-step, remembering the words of the Buddha: "If the path is too difficult, it is the wrong path."

NOTES TO THE EPILOGUE

1. Robert Atkinson, *The Gift of Stories: Practical and Spiritual Applications of Autobiography, Life Stories, and Personal Mythmaking,* (Westport, CT: Bergin & Garvey, 1995) p. xv.

Pilot Study I: 1992-1994

This case study was initiated and funded by the Pluralism Project, founded by Dr. Diana Eck, Chairperson of Harvard's Committee on the Study of Religion. The research included both a descriptive survey of the religious landscape of "Forest City" and a more detailed study of the Cambodian Buddhist community.

The research was completed in two cycles: initial entry into the community Fall 1992; preliminary study Spring 1993; research grant for Summer 1993 to focus specifically on two cases—one involving the Khmer and their attempts to establish a Buddhist temple; the other an examination of the confrontation between traditional Khmer beliefs and practices and Western medicine; analysis and write-up of the project Fall 1993 through Spring, 1994.

The research questions for the first study were:

1. What world religions are represented in the metropolitan area of "Forest City"?

2. How are the religions self-identified, maintained and practiced in this setting?

3. What adaptations, if any have they made in this setting?

4. What adaptations, if any, have the social institutions (particularly the school) made in response to the religious beliefs and practices?

I conducted over twenty-five personal interviews, five of which were recorded and transcribed; the rest were recorded as field notes during the interview. Subjects included bilingual and monolingual Cambodians (educators, monks, Kru Khmer) using an interpreter when the respondent was monolingual. I analyzed documents on Cambodian resettlement from the Refugee Resettlement Center, videotapes prepared by school or health providers, and audiotapes from a conference on refugee health care. I participated in and observed traditional celebrations and temple fundraising activities.

The religious landscape study revealed the presence of a large Muslim community of people from Afghanistan, Africa, the Near East, Turkey, and Malaysia. The men had established a small prayer group led by a Saudi Imam which met weekly on Fridays. The prayer group was open only to men, and I learned of no movement to establish a mosque. The equally large population of Cambodians had established a Buddhist center in a tiny house located in an outer suburb. The practice of the Buddhist religion, for the Khmer, was limited to major celebrations (New Year, Ancestor Festival, marriages, and funerals) when a monk had to be imported from a nearby state. Forest City also has Interfaith Council which includes most Protestant denominations (including a Korean Presbyterian church), Catholics (Polish, Irish, Italian, and Vietnamese), and Jews.

The impact Buddhism and Islam had on the schools was varied. One of the high schools was required to set up a prayer room so that students could complete their daily prayers while attending school. The religious holidays of Christians and Jews as well as Chinese and Cambodian New Year were recognized and "celebrated" at the elementary and inner city middle schools. Other than this, many mainstream and ESL teachers did not see the role that these faith traditions played in the lives of the refugee students as relevant to their success in school.

Pilot Study II: 1996-1997

A primary purpose of the pilot study was to describe and analyze cultural meanings of success and schooling for Cambodian refugee families in "Forest City". One of my goals was to use the framework of cultural ecology theory to identify Cambodian folk theories of success and status mobility and the extent to which cultural models that represented success in Cambodian culture were being reinterpreted and transmitted within the family.

My research questions were:

1. What does being successful mean for Cambodians in America?

2. How do Cambodians negotiate different meanings of success?

3. How does their view of success vary depending on the context of the school or community?

My sample included seventeen individuals who comprised seven Cambodian families and two resident Cambodian Buddhist monks. Data collection ran from December 1995 through December 1996. I collected personal history, educational, and occupational information with a questionnaire. Primary data were formal and informal interviews conducted in person using audiotape and transcribed. Participant-observation activities included Even Start (ESL) classes for refugee mothers and their pre-school children, citizenship classes for Cambodians, weekly guest reader at a fourth/fifth grade multilingual class, and attendance at major religious festivals.

Data analysis involved multiple readings of transcripts and field notes. The readings were organized to 1. understand the context or landscape of the narrator, 2. understand the narrator's personal experiences (actions and consequences) with regard to success, 3. understand the narrator's interpretation of these experiences, and 4. discover key linkages in the data that pointed to a single phenomenon. (Erickson, 1986)

Once the themes had emerged, transcripts and field notes were color coded and organized into categories. Each audiotape transcript was checked with the narrator, and language, explanations, interpretations and biographical data was corrected and clarified. Contact summary sheets were used to summarize themes for each transcript and field note and to mark follow-up questions. Interpretive commentary was checked with Cambodian informants and doctoral colleagues for feedback and critique.

Finally, biographical and narrative vignettes were member checked with respective individuals. Each individual was asked to give me a name that I could use in the final document. In three cases the informants wanted to use their own names, and I had them sign permission forms. I disguised the city, the demographics and the school statistics in the final report.

Findings showed that Cambodians believed in "American way" concepts of success : having a lot of money, a good business, power and influence, a large house, and material possessions. In addition, the Cambodians in my sample articulated four central themes which each interpreted as essential to understanding the Cambodian approach to a successful life:

1.   Buddhism as Cambodian culture

2.   The responsibility of the Community

3.   The three stages of life

4.   You are your own action

(1) Everything in Cambodian culture is referenced to Buddhism which is syncretized with the folk religion. The folk tales which teach clear values between right and wrong, also teach problem solving, critical thinking, being observant and using practical reason rather than aggression; Buddhism teaches the concept of right way of life which is based on taking responsibility for oneself and one's community.

(2) The entire community is responsible for teaching the child: the parents, the teachers, the monk, and the community leaders all have interlocking roles and duties in helping the child to find the right path in life which is the central and overriding goal for all Khmer.

(3) The most successful Khmer progress fully through three stages of life: children and adolescents must attend school and learn the ways of the culture; adults who become parents must raise a healthy and respectful family. They must provide material sustenance through good, non-stressful jobs which meet the needs of their families; and finally the elderly who retire from work may go to live in the temple or contribute time and funds to support the monks and activities of the temple.

(4) The most important concept is that each individual is born with a particular destiny which is the result of actions accumulated in past lifetimes. It is up to the individual to take responsibility for his or her own action in this lifetime, and that is why Cambodians place great emphasis on being self-reliant, independent, and responsible.

I also found individual interpretations of the meaning of success. The single-parent families (all mothers) stated that the true meaning of success for them was being independent and free to take advantage of opportunities in America that had not been possible for women in Cambodia. For them, education was the single most important guarantee of personal success.

The dual-parent families each seek upwardly mobile professional jobs, education beyond high school, their own homes, and material possessions. At the same time, they display a commitment to maintain and grow the Buddhist temple and teach their children to speak Khmer and to respect the cultural traditions. The most successful families (by middle class standards) appeared to confirm Gibson and Sin's theory of multilinear acculturation in which they showed positive engagement with values of both American and Cambodia, culture, and transmitted those values to their children.

Bibliography

Altheide, David and John Johnson. "Criteria for Assessing Interpretive Validity in Qualitative Research." in N.C. Denzin and Yvonna Lincoln eds. *Handbook of Qualitative Research.* Thousand Oaks: Sage Publications, 1994.

Atkinson, Robert. *The Gift of Stories: Practical and Spiritual Applications of Autobiography, Life Stories, and Personal Mythmaking.* Westport CT: Bergin & Garvey. 1995.

Baizerman, Michael, Glen Hendricks, Ruth Hamond, Norah Neale, Phuc Nguyen. Study of Southeast Asian Refugee Youth in Minneapolis. Report prepared for office of refugee resettlement family support administrations, U.S. Department of health and human services by the Southeast Asian refugee studies Project Center for Urban Regional Affairs, University of Minnesota. Washington, DC: Government Printing Office. 1987.

Balzano, Silvia, Ronald Gallimore, Claude Goldenberg, Leslie Reese. "The Concept of *Education* . . .". *The Annual Meeting of the American Anthropological Association.* Los Angeles: University of California, 1991.

Becker, Elizabeth. *When the War Was Over: The Voices of Cambodia's Revolution and Its People.* New York: Simon and Schuster, Inc., 1986.

Becker, Howard S.. "Generalizing from Case Studies". *Qualitative Inquiry in Education: The Continuing Debate.* New York: Teachers College Press, 1990.

Bempechat, Janine Mordkowitz. "Achievement Motivation in Cambodian Refugee Children: A Comparative Study". paper given at the Society for Research in Child Development. 1989.

Berger, Peter L.. *The Sacred Canopy: Elements of a Sociological Theory of Religion.* New York: Anchor Books, Doubleday, 1967.

Berger, Peter L. and Thomas Luckmann. *The Social Construction of Reality: A Treatise in the Sociology of Knowledge.* New York: Irvington Publishers Inc., 1980.

Bit, Seanglim. *A Study of the Effects of Reward Structures on Academic Achievement and Sociometric Status of Cambodian Students.* Unpublished doctoral dissertation. University of San Francisco, 1981.

Blakely, Mary M.. *Refugees and American Schools: A Field Study of Southeast Asians in One Community.* Unpublished doctoral dissertation. University of Oregon, 1984.

————— "Southeast Asian Refugee Parents: An Inquiry Into Home-School Communication and Understanding". *Anthropology and Education* Quarterly. 14. 1. Spring, 1983.

Brown, L., and C. Gilligan. "The Interview Guide." *Meeting at the Crossroads,* 1992.

Caffrey, Margaret. *Ruth Benedict: Stranger in This Land.* Austin, TX: University of Texas Press, 1989.

Canniff, Julie G.. "Step by Step: A Field Study of Cambodian Religion and Culture in Portland, Maine" Part I and II. Unpublished research paper for the Pluralism Project. Harvard University, 1992, 1993.

Caplan, Nathan, John Whitmore, Marcella Choy. *The Boat People and Achievement in America: A Study of Family Life, Hard Work and Cultural Values.* Ann Arbor: The University of Michigan Press, 1989.

D'Andrade, Roy. "A Folk Model of the Mind". Dorothy Holland and Naomi Quinn eds. *Cultural Models in Language and Thought.* Cambridge: Cambridge University Press, 1987.

Denzin, N.K., Y. Lincoln eds. *Handbook of Qualitative Research.* Newbury Park: Sage Publications, 1994.

DeVos, George and Marcelo Suárez-Orozco. *Status Inequality: The Self in Culture.* Cross-Cultural Research and Methodology Series Vol. 15. Newbury Park and London: Sage Publications. 1990.

Durkheim, Emile. *The Elementary Forms of the Religious Life.* London: Allen and Unwin, 1915/1964.

Ebihara, May Mayko. *Svay: A Khmer Village in Cambodia.* Unpublished doctoral dissertation in Anthropology. Columbia University. 1966.

Ebihara, May Mayko, Carol A. Mortland, Judy Ledgerwood. *Cambodian Culture Since 1975: Homeland and Exile.* Ithaca & London: Cornell University Press, 1994.

Eisner, Elliot and Alan Peshkin, eds. *Qualitative Inquiry in Education: The Continuing Debate.* Teachers College Press, 1990.

Emerson, Ralph Waldo. *The Works of Ralph Waldo Emerson: Society and Solitude.* Boston and New York: Fireside Edition, 1870, 1898.

Erickson, Frederick. "Qualitative Methods in Research on Teaching". Wittrock, Merlin, ed. *Handbook of Research on Teaching.* New York: Macmillan, 1986.

——— "Transformation and School Success: The Politics and Culture of Educational Achievement". *Anthropology and Education Quarterly.* 18. 4. December, 1987.

Geertz, Clifford. *Local Knowledge: Further Essays in Interpretive Anthropology.* New York: Basic Books Inc., 1983.

Ghosananda, Maha. *Step by Step.* Berkeley, CA: Parallax Press, 1992.

Gibson, Margaret A.. *Accommodation Without Assimilation: Sikh Immigrants in an American High School.* Ithaca & London: Cornell University Press, 1988.

Grinberg, Leon, and Rebeca Grinberg. *Psychoanalytic Perspectives on Migration and Exile.* New Haven & London: Yale University Press, 1989.

Hinnells, John R. *A Handbook of Living Religions.* London: Penguin Books, 1984.

Holland, Dorothy, Naomi Quinn, eds. *Cultural Models in Language and Thought.* Cambridge: Cambridge University Press, 1987.

Holloway, Susan, Bruce Fuller, Marylee Rambaud, Constanza Eggers-Pierola, Bruce Johnson Beykont. *Through My Own Eyes: Mothers' Views of Child Rearing and Work Within Diverse Cultures of Poverty.* January, 1997.

Hopkins, Mary Carol. *Learning Culture: A Cambodian (Khmer) Community in an American City.* Unpublished doctoral dissertation. University of Cincinnati. 1991.

Huerta, Teresa. *A Humanizing Pedagogy: Effective Instructional Practices for Latino Students* Qualifying Paper. Harvard Graduate School of Education, 1998.

Ima, Kenji. "Testing the American Dream: Case Studies of At-Risk Southeast Asian Refugee Students in Secondary Schools." in Rumbaut, Ruben and Wayne Cornelius, eds. *California's Immigrant Children*. San Diego: Center for U.S.-Mexican Studies, University of California, 1995.

Inkeles, Alex, David H. Smith. *Becoming Modern: Individual Change in Six Developing Countries*. Cambridge & London: Harvard University Press. 1974.

Kiang, Peter Nien Chu. "New Roots and Voices: The Education of Southeast Asian Students at an Urban Public University." Unpublished doctoral dissertation, Harvard Graduate School of Education. 1991.

Kim, Young Yun."Personal, Social and Economic Adaptation: 1975-1979 Arrivals in Illinois". David Haines, ed. *Refugees as Immigrants: Cambodians, Laotians and Vietnamese in America*. New Jersey: Rowman and Littlefield Publishers, Inc., 1989.

LeVine, Robert A., Merry I. White. *Human Conditions: The Cultural Basis of Educational Development*. New York & London: Routledge and Kegan Paul, 1986.

LeVine, Robert. "Concepts of Socialization". *Culture, Behavior and Personality*. 1984

Mabbett, Ian and David Chandler. *The Khmers*. Cambridge, MA: Blackwell Publishers, 1995.

Maxwell, Joseph A. *Qualitative Research Design: An Interactive Approach*. Applied Social Research Methods Series. Thousand Oaks: Sage Publications, 1996.

Maxwell, Joseph A.. "Diversity, Solidarity and Community". Paper to appear in *Educational*. n.d.

———— "Diversity and Methodology in a Changing World". Paper to appear in *Pedagogia*. n.d.

Maxwell, Joseph A. and Barbara A. Miller. "Categorization and Contextualization as Components of Qualitative Data Analysis". Paper submitted to *Qualitative Sociology*. July 1993.

McGiffert, Michael ed. *The Character of Americans: A Book of Readings*. Homewood, IL: The Dorsey Press, 1970.

Mehan, Hugh. "Understanding Inequality in Schools: The Contribution of Interpretive Studies". *Sociology of Education*. 65. 1992.

Miles, Matthew, Michael Huberman. *Qualitative Data Analysis: A Sourcebook of New Methods*. Second Edition. Thousand Oaks: Sage Publications, 1994.

Mortland, Carol. "Khmer Buddhists in the United States: Ultimate Questions," in Ebihara, et al., eds. *Cambodian Culture Since 1975: Homeland and Exile*. Ithaca and London: Cornell University Press, 1994.

Nelan, Bruce. "Not Quite So Welcome Anymore," *Time*. Fall, 1993.

Nguyen-Hong-Nhiem, Lucy and Joel M. Halpern. *The Far East Comes Near: Autobiographical Accounts of Southeast Asian Students in America*. Amherst, MA: University of Massachusetts Press, 1989.

Noddings, Nel. *The Challenge to Care in Schools: An Alternative Approach to Education*. New York and London: Teachers College Press, 1992.

O'Carroll, Susan J.. *Bridging the Gap Between Culturally and Linguistically Diverse Parents and American Schools*. Unpublished masters thesis. University of Southern Maine. 1995.

Ogbu, John U.. "Cultural Discontinuities and Schooling". *Anthropology and Education Quarterly*. 13. 4. 1982.

——— "Origins of Human Competence: A Cultural-Ecological Perspective". *Child Development*. 52. The Society for Research in Child Development Inc., 1981.

Ogbu, John U., Maria Eugenia Matute-Bianchi. "Understanding Socio-cultural Factors: Knowledge, Identity and School Adjustment". *Beyond Language: Social and Cultural Factors in Schooling Language Minority Students*. Los Angeles: Bilingual Education Office, California State University, 1986.

Oliver, Donald W. and Kathleen Waldron. *Education, Modernity and Fractured meaning: Toward a Process Theory of Teaching and Learning*. Albany, NY: State University of New York, 1989.

Palacios, Jesus and Maria Carmen Moreno, "Parents' and Adolescents' Ideas on Children: Origins and Transmission of Intracultural Diversity." in *Parents' Cultural Belief Systems*, S. Harkness and C. Super eds. New York & London: The Guilford Press. 1996.

Peters, Heather. Study of Southeast Asian Refugee Youth in Philadelphia. Washington, DC: United States Government Printing Office. 1987.

Pho, Lan T. "Educational Background of Khmer Refugees," in Mory Ouk, Franklin Huffman and Judy Lewis. *Handbook for Teaching Khmer-Speaking Students.* Folsom, CA: Folsom Cordova Unified School District and Southeast Asia Community Resource Center, nd.

Portes, Alejandro. "Segmented Assimilation Among New Immigrant Youth: A Conceptual Framework," in Rubén Rumbaut and Wayne Cornelius, eds. *California's Immigrant Children: Theory, Research and Implications for Education Policy.* San Diego, CA: Center for U.S. Mexican Studies, University of California, 1995.

Portes, Alejandro and Rubén G. Rumbaut. *Immigrant America: A Portrait.* Berkeley & Oxford: University of California Press, 1990.

The Readers Digest Great Encyclopedic Dictionary and *Funk and Wagnalls Standard College Dictionary.* Pleasantville, NY: The Readers Digest Association, 1966.

Reinharz, Shulamit. *Feminist Methods in Social Research.* New York and Oxford: Oxford University Press, 1992.

Rogers, Annie. "Voice, Play and a Practice of Ordinary Courage in Girls' and Womens' Lives." in *Harvard Educational Review.* Vol. 63, No. 3. Fall, 1993.

Rumbaut, Rubén. "Portraits, Patterns, and Predictors of the Refugee Adaptation Process: Results and Reflections from the IHARP Panel Study". *Refugees as Immigrants: Cambodians, Laotians, and Vietnamese in America.* David Haines, ed. New Jersey: Rowman and Littlefield Publishers Inc., 1989.

Rumbaut, Rubén G., and Wayne A. Cornelius. *California's Immigrant Children: Theory, Research and Implications for Educational Policy.* San Diego: University of California, San Diego, Center for U.S. Mexican Studies, 1995.

Rumbaut, Rubén, Kenji Ima. *The Adaptation of Southeast Asian Refugee Youth: A Comparative Study.* Final Report to the Office of Refugee Resettlement. San Diego: Department of Sociology, 1988.

Seidman, I.E. *Interviewing as Qualitative Research.* New York: Teachers College, 1991.

Shore, Bradd. *Culture in Mind: Cognition, Culture and the Problem of Meaning.* New York and Oxford: Oxford University Press, 1996.

Sin, Bo Chum. *Socio-cultural, Psychological and Linguistic Effects on Cambodian Students' Progress Through Formal Schooling in the United States.* Unpublished doctoral dissertation. University of Oregon. 1991.

Smith-Hefner, Nancy J. "Education, Gender and Generational Conflict Among Khmer Refugees". *Anthropology and Education Quarterly.* 24. 2. 1993.

———— "Language and Identity in the Education of Boston-Area Khmer". *Anthropology and Education Quarterly.* 21 .3. September, 1990.

Spindler, George D., ed. *Education and Cultural Process: Anthropological Approaches.* Second Edition. Prospect Heights, IL.: Waveland Press Inc., 1987.

Spindler, George, and Louise Spindler. *The American Cultural Dialogue and Its Transmission.* London & New York: The Falmer Press, 1990.

Spindler, Louise. *Culture Change and Modernization: Mini-Models and Case Studies.* Prospect Heights, IL: Waveland Press Inc., 1977.

Spiro, Melford E. *Buddhism and Society: A Great Tradition and Its Burmese Vicissitudes.* Second Ed. Berkeley and London: University of California Press, 1970, 1982.

Stake, Robert. *The Art of Case Study Research.* Thousand Oaks: Sage Publications, 1995.

Strauss, Anselm, Juliet Corbin. *Basics of Qualitative Research: Grounded Theory, Procedures and Techniques.* Newbury Park: Sage Publications, 1990.

Suárez-Orozco, Carola. "Identities Under Siege: Immigration Stress and Social Mirroring Among the Children of Immigrants," in Anthony Robben and Marcelo Suárez-Orozco eds. *Cultures Under Siege: Violence and Trauma in Interdisciplinary Perspective.* Cambridge: Cambridge University Press, in press.

Suárez-Orozco, Marcelo, and Carola Suárez-Orozco. *Central American Refugees and U.S. High Schools: A Psychosocial Study of*

Motivation and Achievement. Stanford: Stanford University Press, 1989.

―――― "Some Conceptual Considerations in the Interdisciplinary Study of Immigrant Children," in H. Trueba and L. Bartolomé, eds. *Immigrant Voices: In Search of Pedagogical Reform*. Lanham, MD: Rowman and Littlefield.

―――― *Trans-Formations: Immigrants, Family Life and Achievement Motivation Among Latino Adolescents*. Stanford: Stanford University Press, 1995.

Trueba, Henry, Lilly Cheng, Kenji Ima. *Myth or Reality: Adaptive Strategies of Asian Americans in California*. Washington, DC: The Falmer Press, 1993.

Trueba, Henry T.. "Culturally Based Explanations of Minority Students Academic Achievement". *Anthropology and Education Quarterly*. 19. 1988.

Walker, Constance L.. "Learning English: The Southeast Asian Refugee Experience". *Language Disorders* .54. 1985.

Weber, Max. *The Protestant Ethic and the Spirit of Capitalism*. Translated by Talcott Parsons. New York: Charles Scribner's Sons, 1904/1958.

―――― *The Sociology of Religion*. Boston: Beacon Press, 1922/1991.

Wehlage, Gary. "The Purpose of Generalization in Field Study Research". *A Study of Schooling*. Tom Popkewitz ed. New York: Praeger, 1981.

Werkmeister, W.H. *A History of Philosophical Ideas in America*. New York: The Roland Press Company, 1949.

Welaratna, Usha. *Beyond the Killing Fields: Voices of Nine Cambodian Survivors in America*. Stanford, CA: Stanford University Press, 1993.

Wolcott, Harry F.. *Transforming Qualitative Data: Description, Analysis and Interpretation*. Thousand Oaks: Sage Publications, 1994.

Zhou, Min. "Growing Up American: The Challenge Confronting Immigrant Children and Children of Immigrants," in the *Annual Review of Sociology*, 23, 1997.

Index

A

Americanized, xxiii, 40, 105, 120, 122, 151, 211, 252, 258, 259, 262, 284, 290, 293

Angkor Thom, 50, 292. *See also* Angkor Wat

Angkor Wat, xii, xiii, 50, 67, 97, 100, 101, 176

animism, 33; folk religion, 62; *kru Khmer*, 56; *nak ta*, 49, 50, 58, 62

Asian: East Asian, 3, 15; Indochinese, 8, 14, 15; South Asian, 3; Southeast Asian, xvii, xviii, 1, 2, 3, 5, 7, 8, 9, 14, 16, 17, 24, 27, 28, 37, 38, 43, 53, 86, 268, 277

B

balance, xi, xiv, xvi, xx, 12, 15, 20, 22, 23, 41, 42, 61, 70, 71, 122, 136, 157, 188, 195, 199, 208, 210, 211, 242, 243, 246, 251, 253, 258, 265, 266, 270, 272, 275, 277, 290, 292, 294

Becker, Elizabeth, 51, 53, 60, 74

Berger, Peter, xviii, 31, 34, 42, 43

Buddha, xi, xxi, 51, 56, 63, 70, 100, 114, 141, 144, 153, 154, 170, 171, 174, 176, 178, 191, 197, 220, 241, 243, 294. *See also* Siddhartha Gotama

Buddhism: destiny, 6, 39, 68, 71, 102, 118, 179, 210, 221, 246; Eight-Fold Path, 115, 117, 249, 257; *karma*, 21, 34, 35, 64, 65, 66, 67, 68, 69, 102, 123, 124, 125, 153, 163, 167, 185, 242, 257, 270, 275, 288; karmic, xiii, 40, 65, 67, 71; merit, 21, 35, 39, 40, 45, 56, 59, 65, 66, 67, 117, 118, 120, 130, 131, 153, 157, 161, 198, 258, 275, 276, 277, 288; nirvana, 64; rebirth, xii, 34, 65, 130; reborn, 21, 113, 114; reincarnation, 33, 64, 68, 69, 163, 167, 169, 185, 221

Buddhist festivals, xi, xii, 51, 56, 64, 78, 96, 103, 160, 174, 220, 270; holidays, 103, 251, 257, 287

C

Caplan, Nathan, 2, 5, 6, 7, 24, 27, 43, 262, 266

Chandler, David, 49, 60, 62, 71

Choy, Marcella, 5, 24

coping strategies, 39, 40

cultural model, 23, 34, 36, 41, 69, 118, 119, 120, 124, 140, 159, 251, 253, 266, 270; cognitive models, 31;